THE

QUEST

THE

—[EXTERNALLY FOCUSED]—

QUEST

Becoming the Best Church
for the Community

Eric Swanson and Rick Rusaw

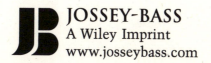

JOSSEY-BASS
A Wiley Imprint
www.josseybass.com

Published by Jossey-Bass
A Wiley Imprint
989 Market Street, San Francisco, CA 94103-1741—www.josseybass.com

Readers should be aware that Internet Web sites offered as citations and/or sources for further information may have changed or disappeared between the time this was written and when it is read.

Limit of Liability/Disclaimer of Warranty: While the publisher and author have used their best efforts in preparing this book, they make no representations or warranties with respect to the accuracy or completeness of the contents of this book and specifically disclaim any implied warranties of merchantability or fitness for a particular purpose. No warranty may be created or extended by sales representatives or written sales materials. The advice and strategies contained herein may not be suitable for your situation. You should consult with a professional where appropriate. Neither the publisher nor author shall be liable for any loss of profit or any other commercial damages, including but not limited to special, incidental, consequential, or other damages.

Jossey-Bass books and products are available through most bookstores. To contact Jossey-Bass directly call our Customer Care Department within the U.S. at 800-956-7739, outside the U.S. at 317-572-3986, or fax 317-572-4002.

Jossey-Bass also publishes its books in a variety of electronic formats. Some content that appears in print may not be available in electronic books.

Credit: Gin Lane, 1751 (engraving) (b/w photo) by William Hogarth (1697–1764) British Museum, London, UK/ The Bridgeman Art Library

Library of Congress Cataloging-in-Publication Data

Swanson, Eric, date.
    The externally focused quest : becoming the best church for the community/Eric Swanson and Rick Rusaw. — 1st ed.
      p. cm. — (Leadership network titles)
    Includes bibliographical references and index.
    ISBN 978-0-470-50078-1 (cloth)
      1. Communities—Religious aspects—Christianity. 2. Mission of the church.
    3. Church growth. I. Rusaw, Rick, date. II. Title.
  BV625.S85 2010
  261—dc22

                                           2009051931

Printed in the United States of America
FIRST EDITION
HB Printing   10 9 8 7 6 5 4 3 2 1

The Blogging Church: Sharing the Story of Your Church Through Blogs, Brian Bailey and Terry Storch

Church Turned Inside Out: A Guide for Designers, Refiners, and Re-Aligners, Linda Bergquist and Allan Karr

Leading from the Second Chair: Serving Your Church, Fulfilling Your Role, and Realizing Your Dreams, Mike Bonem and Roger Patterson

The Way of Jesus: A Journey of Freedom for Pilgrims and Wanderers, Jonathan S. Campbell with Jennifer Campbell

Leading the Team-Based Church: How Pastors and Church Staffs Can Grow Together into a Powerful Fellowship of Leaders, George Cladis

Organic Church: Growing Faith Where Life Happens, Neil Cole

Church 3.0: Upgrades for the Future of the Church, Neil Cole

Off-Road Disciplines: Spiritual Adventures of Missional Leaders, Earl Creps

Reverse Mentoring: How Young Leaders Can Transform the Church and Why We Should Let Them, Earl Creps

Building a Healthy Multi-Ethnic Church: Mandate, Commitments, and Practices of a Diverse Congregation, Mark DeYmaz

Leading Congregational Change Workbook, James H. Furr, Mike Bonem, and Jim Herrington

Baby Boomers and Beyond: Tapping the Ministry Talents and Passions of Adults over Fifty, Amy Hanson

The Tangible Kingdom: Creating Incarnational Community, Hugh Halter and Matt Smay

Leading Congregational Change: A Practical Guide for the Transformational Journey, Jim Herrington, Mike Bonem, and James H. Furr

The Leader's Journey: Accepting the Call to Personal and Congregational Transformation, Jim Herrington, Robert Creech, and Trisha Taylor

Whole Church: Leading from Fragmentation to Engagement, Mel Lawrenz

Culture Shift: Transforming Your Church from the Inside Out, Robert Lewis and Wayne Cordeiro, with Warren Bird

Church Unique: How Missional Leaders Cast Vision, Capture Culture, and Create Movement, Will Mancini

A New Kind of Christian: A Tale of Two Friends on a Spiritual Journey, Brian D. McLaren

The Story We Find Ourselves In: Further Adventures of a New Kind of Christian, Brian D. McLaren

Missional Renaissance: Changing the Scorecard for the Church, Reggie McNeal

Practicing Greatness: 7 Disciplines of Extraordinary Spiritual Leaders, Reggie McNeal

The Present Future: Six Tough Questions for the Church, Reggie McNeal

A Work of Heart: Understanding How God Shapes Spiritual Leaders, Reggie McNeal

The Millennium Matrix: Reclaiming the Past, Reframing the Future of the Church, M. Rex Miller

Shaped by God's Heart: The Passion and Practices of Missional Churches, Milfred Minatrea

The Missional Leader: Equipping Your Church to Reach a Changing World, Alan J. Roxburgh and Fred Romanuk

Missional Map-Making: Skills for Leading in Times of Transition, Alan J. Roxburgh

Relational Intelligence: How Leaders Can Expand Their Influence Through a New Way of Being Smart, Steve Saccone

Viral Churches: Helping Church Planters Become Movement Makers, Ed Stetzer and Warren Bird

The Externally Focused Quest: Becoming the Best Church for the Community, Eric Swanson and Rick Rusaw

The Ascent of a Leader: How Ordinary Relationships Develop Extraordinary Character and Influence, Bill Thrall, Bruce McNicol, and Ken McElrath

Beyond Megachurch Myths: What We Can Learn from America's Largest Churches, Scott Thumma and Dave Travis

The Elephant in the Boardroom: Speaking the Unspoken About Pastoral Transitions, Carolyn Weese and J. Russell Crabtree

CONTENTS

ABOUT LEADERSHIP NETWORK   IX

FOREWORD BY ALAN HIRSCH   XI

ACKNOWLEDGMENTS   XV

INTRODUCTION   I

Chapter 1   *What Kind of Day Is Today?*   4

Chapter 2   *Focus: They Choose the Window Seat, Not the Aisle Seat*   26

Chapter 3   *Purpose: They Practice Weight Training, Not Bodybuilding*   44

Chapter 4   *Story: They Live in the Kingdom Story, Not a Church Story*   70

Chapter 5   *Missions: The Few Send the Many, Not the Many Send the Few*   89

Chapter 6   *Partnering: They Build Wells, Not Walls*   111

Chapter 7   *Systems: They Create Paradigms, Not Programs*   133

Chapter 8   *Evangelism: They Deploy Kingdom Laborers, Not Just Community Volunteers*   155

Chapter 9   *Creativity: They Innovate, Not Replicate*   174

Chapter 10   *Outcomes: It's About the Game, Not the Pregame Talk*   200

NOTES   217

ABOUT THE AUTHORS   231

SCRIPTURE INDEX   233

INDEX   235

Leadership Network, an initiative of OneHundredX, exists to honor God and serve others by investing in innovative church leaders who impact the Kingdom immeasurably.

Since 1984, Leadership Network has brought together exceptional leaders, who are focused on similar ministry initiatives, to accelerate their impact. The ensuing collaboration—often across denominational lines—provides a strong base from which individual leaders can better analyze and refine their individual strategies. Creating an environment for collaborative discovery, dialogue, and sharing encourages leaders to extend their own innovations and ideas. Leadership Network further enhances this process through the development and distribution of highly targeted ministry tools and resources—including video, podcasts, concept papers, special research reports, e-publications, and books like this one.

With Leadership Network's assistance, today's Christian leaders are energized, equipped, inspired—and better able to multiply their own dynamic Kingdom-building initiatives.

In 1996 Leadership Network partnered with Jossey-Bass, a Wiley imprint, to develop a series of creative books that would provide thought leadership to innovators in church ministry. Leadership Network Publications present thoroughly researched and innovative concepts from leading thinkers, practitioners, and pioneering churches. The series collectively draws from a wide range of disciplines, with individual titles providing perspective on one or more of five primary areas:

- Enabling effective leadership
- Encouraging life-changing service
- Building authentic community

- Creating Kingdom-centered impact
- Engaging cultural and demographic realities

For additional information on the mission or activities of Leadership Network, please contact:

Leadership Network
2626 Cole Avenue, Suite 900
Dallas, Texas 75204
800-765-5323
www.leadnet.org
client.care@leadnet.org

As a writer and teacher on missional church, one of the axioms of leadership that we can assume is that *every organization is perfectly designed to achieve what it is currently achieving.* This comment usually raises a bit of pushback because it seems to put responsibility for any current situation back onto those who lead the organization. And this is in some ways true, but it's only half the truth. It also suggests that there is something in the inherited ecclesial templates handed down, and subsequently adopted without serious critical reflection, that tend to factor in the propensity for either growth, or decline. So, the issues do concentrate around leadership imagination and inherent design flaws in the way we conceive of, and do, church.

If your church is in decline, it is probably because you are organizationally designed for it. Don't complain . . . redesign! And you need to redesign along the lines that Jesus intended. You see, the Church that Jesus built is *designed* for growth—and massive, highly transformative, growth at that. It was Jesus who said "I will build my church, and the gates of Hades will not prevail against it" (Matthew 16:18). Hang on! It says that the gates of hell don't prevail against us! It is the Church that is on the advance here, not hell! Contrary to many of the images of church as some sort of defensive fortress under the terrible, relentless, onslaughts of hell, the Church that Jesus built is designed to be an advancing, untamed and untamable, revolutionary force created to transform the world. And make no mistake: there is in Jesus' words here a real sense of inevitability about the eventual triumph of the gospel. If we are not somehow part of this, then there is something wrong in the prevailing designs, and they must change.

The reality is that the Western church is in a precarious situation today. Missional observation in Australia indicates that between 12 to 15 percent of the population will likely be attracted to the prevailing contemporary church growth model. This is not actual attendance, which is way below this figure (around 2.8 percent), rather it indicates "market appeal" or cultural connectivity. The rest of the population, most of whom describe themselves as "spiritually open," will probably never find their place in a contemporary attractional church. It is simply out of their cultural orbit. If they are not repulsed by it, they are at least blasé and/or turned off to the cultural forms inherent in the model.

In the United States the situation is not much better. I estimate that in the United States the percentage of people who find their spiritual connection through an attractional church is probably up to 40 percent. Again this is not attendance, which is more around 18 percent.

In both Australia and the United States the demographics of the group likely to "come to church" are probably what we can call the inspirational middle class, family-values segment—good, solid, well-educated, hard working, middle-class, suburbanites with Republican leanings. Contemporary attractional churches are really effective in reaching non-Christian people fitting this demographic, but it is unlikely that it can reach far beyond that—leaving about 60 percent of the population out of the equation. So the question we must ask is, "How will the 60 percent of our population access the gospel if they reject the current expression of existing church?"

This is precisely the issue that the missional church seeks to address. My contention is that it is going to take an "externally focused," missional-incarnational, church approach to reach beyond the 40 percenters. It is only when the church decides to become the best church *for* the community that it at least has a fighting chance to reach the majority of the unchurched/dechurched population. The attractional church is about getting the community into the church. The missional, externally focused church is about getting the church into the community. Incarnational ministry, at its heart, is taking church to people by helping believers live out their calling among people who do not yet believe and follow Jesus.

The missional, externally focused church begins with the missionary questions: "What is good news for this people group?" "What would the church look and feel like among this people group?" Entering into a community through love, service, and blessing creates new proximate spaces as we become good news to the community. At the end of the day the impact of a church is not determined by who it wants to reach but by who it is willing to serve. Certainly missional living affects what happens outside the church, but it also greatly affects our own spiritual formation as disciples of Jesus. *The Externally Focused Quest* provides a significant part of the answer to the question of how we turn religious consumers into missional disciples that can impact the world around them for Jesus' cause.

Building on the already significant insights from their previous writings, Eric and Rick blend years of direct leadership experience with great theological insights and a real heart for missional impact, and so concoct a really good book for our time. Our appropriate compliment ought to be to follow their advice, move into our communities, and transform them in Jesus' name.

Los Angeles, California **Alan Hirsch**
January 2010 Missional author, dreamer, and strategist
(www.theforgottenways.org)

ACKNOWLEDGMENTS

WE WISH TO THANK KRISTA PETTY, who once again served as editor, welder, and jury-rigger for this, our third writing project. We are grateful to Sheryl Fullerton, executive editor at Jossey-Bass, for the opportunity to take this message to the world and to Joanne Clapp Fullagar, editorial production manager at Jossey-Bass, and Bruce Emmer, who through their meticulous attention to detail make us better than we are. We thank Brian Mavis, whose externally focused example helps keep us going in the right direction. Eric is most grateful to Scott and Theresa Beck and Leadership Network for the opportunity to work alongside so many passionate and gifted leaders whose example fuels the fires of his life. Rick is grateful to the staff and leaders of LifeBridge, who continually surprise him with ways to love and serve the community. Together we thank all the externally focused leaders who continue to lead, adapt, and innovate outside the walls of the church to advance the kingdom.

To Andy and Natalie, Jenda and Blaise—*kingdom workers in the Middle Kingdom, whose power of courage is surpassed only by the power of their love.*—E.S.

To the LifeBridge family. *Thanks for your friendship and encouragement. You have risked, loved, and seen beyond the walls of our church and are making a difference in our community. It has been a privilege to journey with you.*—R.R

THE

—[EXTERNALLY FOCUSED]—

QUEST

*As difficult as it is to learn to surf, it is far easier to catch a wave
than to cause a wave.*

EVERYWHERE WE GO, WE MEET PEOPLE WHO, after listening to either of us speak on externally focused church, will say something like, "What you said today was exactly what I've been thinking, but I didn't have the terminology or diagrams to explain it." There is a movement of God taking place, and as we often say, "As difficult as it is to learn to surf, it is far easier to catch a wave than to cause a wave." When God is causing such a wave, we can stand on the pier and let it break over us, or we can grab a surfboard, hit the surf, and have the ride of our lives. What will you do?

When we wrote *The Externally Focused Church* in 2004, we invited our readers to think differently about what church could and should be. We included nearly every church we were aware of that was loving and ministering outside its walls. In the past six years, the externally focused church movement has matured to the extent that projects and initiatives that were rare in 2004 are now quite common in 2010. Believers are longing to do something besides take notes in a worship service. Thousands of churches are rediscovering the DNA of the gospel and are living the gospel outside the walls of the church. Since 2004, we have been with scores of churches and thousands of people and listened to their stories and have tried to allow their experiences to deepen our own thinking about God's missional design in the world. We want to tell about all we've learned since 2004 through passionate practitioners of externally focused ministry. What we have discovered is contained in the nine missional paradigms that we write about here, and we believe they can determine what impact you will have on our changing world. For those of you who are new to the journey, we say, "Grab your board and get ready for the ride of your life."

One hundred years ago, if you were to take a survey of every one of the 1.65 billion people alive at the time and asked each person to check a box indicating religious preference, approximately 34 percent would check the box "Christian" in one of its forms—Protestant, Catholic, or Orthodox. Today, a century later, with all the technological advances, all the church planting, the phenomenal evangelistic success of the *Jesus* film, the expansion of the Gospel in Africa, Asia, and Latin America, and evangelistic efforts, the number of Christians has risen with the population, now estimated at 6.7 billion people, yet the percentage of Christians is still 34 percent. For all the investments of the past hundred years, we have just broken even. How can we change the trajectory of the church? Changing the trajectory will not come from doing harder, better, or more of what we've done in the past. Ministry effectiveness—changing the trajectory of the church—will come from understanding the times and hitching a ride on the wave where God is moving. We don't propose that we have all the answers, of course, but we are willing to follow the clues to see where God is moving among his people and among those who are searching for him.

Christian magazines love publishing lists of the best churches— "The 100 Largest Churches," "The 50 Most Innovative Churches," "The 50 Fastest-Growing Churches," and so on. Some pastors whose churches make these coveted lists often frame and hang these outcomes to display to the world that they are doing a good job. But what if "largest," "most innovative," and "fastest-growing" were the wrong measures? Is there something else we could be working toward?

One good question changes things. One great question has the power to change a life, a church, a community, and potentially the world. When we wrote *The Externally Focused Church,* our big provocative question was "If your church were to close its doors, would anyone in the community notice—would anyone in the community care?" It is no coincidence that this question set many church leaders on a journey, a quest. It is no coincidence that the word *question* comes from the same root as *quest*—a journey in search of something important. So let's think of questions as the beginning of a quest of discovery. Jesus was a master at asking great questions. "What will a man give in exchange for his soul?" "Who do you say I am?" "What good is salt if it's lost its savor?" "Do you believe I am able to do this?" "Do you want to be well?" "Why are you so fearful . . . you who have no faith?" How we answer such questions shapes our lives and our futures.

We've discovered that questions are malleable and that rearranging a word here or there can result in a totally different answer. "Pastor, may I smoke while I'm praying?" "No!" "Pastor, while I'm smoking, is it OK if I pray?" "Why that would be a wonderful idea!" Changing the beneficiary of a question is a powerful way to transform a question to a quest. As Martin Luther King Jr. noted, the question that the Good

Samaritan asked was not "If I stop to help this man, what will happen to me?" but "If I *do not* stop to help this man, what will happen to *him?*"[1] A powerful question has implications for life. John F. Kennedy adapted a phrase in a way that a half century later, the question we should be asking still resonates: "Ask not what your country can do for you—ask what you can do for your country."[2]

Most churches, blatantly or subtly, have an unspoken objective— "How can we be the 'best church in our community?'"—and they staff, budget, and plan accordingly. How a church answers that question determines its entire approach to its members, staff, prayers, finances, time, technology, and facilities. Becoming an externally focused church is not about becoming the best church in the community. The externally focused church asks, "How can we be the best church *for* our community?" That one little preposition changes everything. And this is the big question this book seeks to answer. This is your question; this is your quest.

We have written the book around nine big missional concepts that need to be addressed in your quest to become the best church for the community—focus, purpose, scope, missions, partnering, evangelism, systems, creativity, and outcomes. Understanding and applying the truths of each concept will provide many of the tools you will need for your externally focused quest. We can't guarantee that it will be easy to attain, but then again, things that we value and cherish rarely are. We're glad you've picked up this book. We're glad you've joined the journey. It's going to be a great ride.

CHAPTER 1

What Kind of Day Is Today?

The church must forever be asking, "What kind of day is it today?" for no two days are alike in her history.

David Smith, *Mission After Christendom*[1]

JESUS DIDN'T ASK, "Would you like to walk?" He asked the invalid at the pool of Bethesda, "Do you want to get well?" (John 5). Rick admits that when he first read that story in the Bible, he thought, "It didn't happen like that! What a rude question. Why did Jesus ask that? Of course the man wants to walk!"

Again, Jesus didn't ask if he wanted to walk. He asked, "Do you want to get well?" Maybe Jesus was alluding to something more than just walking. When he asks, "Do you want to get well?" Jesus is asking the man if he is ready for the change that is coming. The man's friends will most likely change. He won't be begging anymore; he won't be by the pool anymore. If he gets well, a lot of things would likely change.

"Do you want to get well?" That's the question Jesus asked the man at the pool, and it's the question we asked at the end of our first book, *The Externally Focused Church*. We thought that would be a good place to start this journey, asking some more tough questions about change—change that affects our churches and our communities.

We've come to discover that "Do you want to get well?" is one of many great questions Jesus asks. After thirty years in the "people" business—most of it with congregations and their leaders—we have found that we don't always want to get well. We want the pain or angst to stop, or we want good things to come, but the bottom line is that most of us don't really want change.

Have you ever noticed that the guy at the pool doesn't really answer this great question from Jesus? His response was something like, "Sir, every time I try to get in the water, someone always gets in ahead of me." In other words, he says, "I would if I could but I can't, so I am not. It's not my fault."

What is true for us as individuals is almost always magnified when we get in a group. We have been with thousands of church leaders, and we often talk about how we want to get better as people, as leaders, as congregations. We want to be more effective, reach more people, help people grow in their faith, serve more effectively. We want to get well! While a whole lot of us talk about what we ought to do, could do, might do, or should do, most of us end up sitting around the pool explaining to one another what's holding us back from change.

Change is hard but necessary. In *The Externally Focused Church*, we asked leaders to change their conversations by changing their questions. Instead of asking, "How big is your church?" ask, "What's your church's impact in the community?" We also asked, "If your church disappeared, would your community notice?" Asking those questions has sparked change—a lot of change—in our own churches and others.

That's what we want to do with this book. We want to see continued transformation in our churches and in our communities by asking better questions. Sometimes the questions are tough, but we have a responsibility to take the gospel that never changes to a world that will never be the same. In other words, Jesus is the same yesterday, today, and forever, but the world we are living in is changing every day. Are you ready to ask some more tough questions about your church and the community? Are you ready to change the conversation once again? Do you want to get well?

Waking Up to a New Day

A few years ago, Eric met a young pastor named Jeff Waldo from University Baptist Church, outside of Houston. Jeff had just finished a master's program in future studies from the University of Houston. After the disappointing discovery that he knew nothing of horoscopes, crystal balls, tarot cards, or fortune cookies, Jeff told Eric what future studies was about. Future studies is not about prediction but about imagining plausible and possible scenarios for the future so that we can plan accordingly. "If things continue along this trajectory, this is what we can expect." Of course, the future rarely has the decency to conform to our expectations, and prognosticators are notoriously bad at predicting future outcomes. Consider this prediction regarding the automobile from the *Literary Digest* in 1899: "The ordinary 'horseless carriage' is at present a luxury for the wealthy; and although its price will probably fall in the future, it will never, of course, come into as common use as the bicycle."[2]

Just how accurately can anyone predict the future? If anyone should know, it would be Phillip Tetlock. For twenty years, this psychology professor at the University of California, Berkeley, worked with 284 people who made their living as "experts" in prognostication about politics and economics. By the end of the study, the experts had made 82,361 forecasts, placing most of the forecasting questions into a three possible future outcomes: things would stay the same (status quo), get better (political freedom, economic growth), or get worse (repression, recession). What was the outcome? Statistically untrained chimps, with a dartboard, would have come up with more accurate predictions![3]

Predicting the future is not our goal here, but discovering today's trends and patterns is. Why? Those discoveries do help shape tomorrow and enlighten us. We must wake up and ask ourselves, "What kind of day is today?"

STEEPR: A Leadership Skill to Master

To understand the times and to be in step with what God is doing, all leaders need the ability to answer the question "What kind of day is today?" You probably remember the men of Issachar from 1 Chronicles 12:32 "who understood the times and [therefore] knew what Israel should do." In Luke 12:54–56, Jesus poses this question to the crowd: "When you see a cloud rising in the west, immediately you say, 'It's going to rain,' and it does. And when the south wind blows, you say, 'It's going to be hot,' and it is. Hypocrites! You know how to interpret the appearance of the earth and the sky. How is it that you *don't know how to interpret this present time?*"

So how do futurists think about the future? Jeff identified the constructs he and other futurists use. The broad bellwether categories futurists pay attention to are society, technology, economics, environment, and politics. To these five categories Jeff insightfully adds religion—now forming the acronym STEEPR. Using these six categories helps us think about what kind of day it is. It helps us become men and women who interpret the present and know what new questions to ask and what changes to make. Let's take a brief snapshot, from a 30,000-foot altitude, of what kind of day it is today using the STEEPR approach.

Society

What has happened in society in the past twenty years? How about the fall of the Berlin Wall, the collapse of Soviet communism, and end of the Cold War, just to name a few. For the past two decades, the United States, with a mere 4 to 5 percent of the world's population, has been the unilateral power in the world, producing a quarter of the world's economic output and militarily controlling land, air, space, and sea. People are on the move. Displaced by war, famine, or economic factors, the numbers of people migrating are greater than ever before. A friend recently told us that there were over 120 ethnicities in his Washington, D.C., ZIP code.

Society has its share of global problems. AIDS is a killer disease. Twenty years ago, HIV was barely making the radar screen. But this morning, we wake up to a different day. Thousands of children are orphaned every day by this deadly disease. And even curable diseases are taking their toll on the most vulnerable of our population: one child dies of malaria every twenty-nine seconds in Africa, and three people die every minute of tuberculosis.[4] "According to the World Water Council, 1.1 billion people live without clean drinking water, 2.6 billion lack adequate sanitation, 1.8 million die every year from diarrheal diseases, and 3,900 children die every day from waterborne diseases."[5] But could tragedy and opportunity for the church be two sides of the same coin?

As populations grow, we are becoming more familiar with how people around the world are living. Societies are no longer defined solely as nation-states but also can be defined by generations. Thanks to the Internet and the proliferation of American TV programming abroad, teens in New York City feel more akin to teens in Mexico City, São Paulo, or Tokyo than they do with an older generation in Des Moines.

Add to these global challenges our local challenges of divorce, fatherless children, broken-down family structures, the aging boomer population, and urban gang activity, and we have tremendous new potential growth opportunities for the church—if we see them as new avenues of ministry rather than hindrances to ministry. How will the church respond to the influx of migrants and immigrants? How will the church respond to the pervasiveness of AIDS and the need for clean water? How will the church respond to rapid social change? Do we know what day today is?

Technology

In *Bold New World,* the futurist William Knoke describes how he wrestled with describing what kind of day we live in today. Knoke puts forth the idea that human society was first organized as "dots"—small communities living in isolation from one another. Small bands of people living in isolation proved to be more efficient in terms of access to supplies of food and fuel. But isolation also meant that knowledge and ideas had little opportunity to spread and cross-pollinate. So if one tribe figured out a better way to attach the head of a spear to its shaft, that breakthrough never spread beyond that tribe, and progress as a whole was stunted.

In time, trade routes were established, carrying goods and ideas along the connections of overland paths and rivers. These dots were eventually connected by lines. These "first-dimension" people operated from point to point along the Amber Route of northern Europe, the Silk Road of Asia, the Roman Road of the Mediterranean, and the Inca Road of South America. As trade routes crisscrossed, the "second dimension" of the plane was formed, allowing people to explore the length and width of their world.

By the sixteenth century, thanks to technological maritime advancements, humans—especially Europeans—could circumnavigate the globe. By the end of the nineteenth century, 85 percent of the world's landmass was controlled by just a handful of European nations.[6] As odious as some aspects of colonization were, it was not without future beneficial ramifications. Niall Ferguson, a history professor at Harvard University, "argued that the British Empire is responsible for the worldwide spread of the English language, banking, the common law, Protestantism, team sports, the limited state, representative government, and the idea of liberty."[7]

The mid-twentieth century ushered in the "third dimension" with the advent and perfection of commercial air travel, satellites, and space travel. This third dimension—the "cube"—was controlled not by nation-states but by multinational corporations and airlines.

So what kind of day do we live in today? Knoke says that we live in the fourth dimension—a "placeless" society where "everything and everybody is at once everywhere."[8] Far and near are the same. The primacy of place is quickly being supplanted by the placeless society, where global communication is instantaneous and corporations run a "just in time" global assembly line.

Technology has played a tremendous role in this placeless society. Think about how it changes our habits and the way we live. For example, Eric carries one device, an iPhone, that serves as a phone, e-mail server, Web browser, camera, and video and music storage system—but then, you probably do also. This combination that allows him to stay connected to people all over the world. He talks to his brother in Australia and his grandchildren in Asia via a computer with a built-in camera through Skype. He keeps friends and family abreast of his activities (sometimes to the chagrin of his wife) via his blog (http://www.ericjswanson.com), Twitter, and Facebook pages and stores family pictures online with Shutterfly.

Consider how we access information. The Google search engine has become a verb—"to Google something" is understood to mean to track it down on the Internet. Google has the ambition "to organize all the world's information and make it universally accessible and useful."[9] But there is more. In 2000, Jimmy Wales launched a free online encyclopedia called Nupedia. There were seven arduous steps to get something published in Nupedia, from assignment to final approval. Ph.D.'s and other experts were recruited. Wales's editor in chief proposed a different solution: let the site users create and continually edit the content themselves! "Within five years, Wikipedia (*wiki* is a Hawaiian word meaning "quick") was available in two hundred languages and had . . . more than one million [articles] in the English-language section alone. . . . As for Nupedia, it managed to squeeze out twenty-four finalized articles and seventy-four articles still in progress before it shut down."[10] Wales's vision for sharing knowledge is compelling: "Imagine a world in which every single person on the planet is given free access to the sum of all human knowledge. That's what we're doing."[11]

Companies like Procter & Gamble, which alone has 7,500 researches, are using technology to solve their toughest problems. Rather than hiring more researchers, P&G is posting problems and challenges on the InnoCentive network, "where ninety thousand other scientists around the world can help solve tough R&D problems for a cash reward."[12]

Technology is changing how we access and customize our entertainment. Whereas the baby boomers (born between 1946 and 1964) of America grew up watching the same network television shows (*Bonanza, The Ed Sullivan Show, The Andy Griffith Show, M*A*S*H, Star Trek*), today's generation has literally hundreds of entertainment options through cable and satellite TV, XM and Sirius Radio, and the Internet. Audiences have the ever-increasing ability to piece together their own customized versions of digital music and video and access them through a variety of digital and screen-equipped devises. Singer Colbie Caillat's song "Bubbly" was downloaded 14 million times through her MySpace site before she even signed with a record label.[13] Singers and underground bands are taking a similar path by gaining a Web following and commanding a higher price before signing with a record company.

News stories, once the privy of reporters and telejournalists, are increasingly broken by common folk with a camera or cell phone. In May 2008, the earthquake that devastated Sichuan, China, was reported as it happened via camera cell phone and social media sites. The BBC reportedly heard of the quake via Twitter. The communication was powerful and instant. By contrast, in previous times, the government would have taken months to even disclose that an earthquake had occurred. In the summer of 2009, hundreds of Iranians used cell phone video cameras to capture the dissent of thousands of Iranians expressing their reaction to a flawed election. If you find yourself saying, "This is old news!"—and by the time you read this, it will be—you only help drive home the point of how quickly our world is changing.

On July 23, 2007, the first presidential debate was held in which questions from voters were asked via YouTube, bringing voters a little closer to the politicians.[14] The first question, from a voter named Zach, who introduced himself with "Wassup?" was a foretaste of things to come. Democratic candidates were asked questions about global warming by a snowman and about Second Amendment rights by a redneck brandishing an automatic weapon. Some questions came through guitar-wielding singers. What was clear was that Internet technology and politics would never be the same. This format has since become commonplace. The same can be true in reverse. Speakers and singers can instantly poll their audiences using an iPhone application. The Refuge Church in Concord, North Carolina, has been known to poll its audience of young adults in the middle of the message. Attentive twenty-somethings can text a response to the pastor's question, and his iPhone "app" instantly gives him the results of the poll. Nowadays, if you can imagine it, there's probably an app for it!

Churches and believers that understand the times are using digital communications beyond church walls to further kingdom causes. Walt Wilson, the founder and chairman of Global Media Outreach, reports that "each day, more than 5 million searches are done on the Internet for spiritual terms." On his own Web site, they "see a decision for Jesus Christ every 35 seconds."[15] Many churches use technology to start video congregations as part of their multisite expansion. They understand that once people are comfortable interacting with digital sound and digital images, it matters little if the speaker is on the stage, in the next room, five miles away, or home in bed, having delivered the message last night. Tech-savvy mission leaders are shrinking the world with technology.

There are now Internet churches with thousands of members who have never met in real life. To understand the times is to understand what is happening today with technology. Pastor Tom Mullins of Christ Fellowship Church in West Palm Beach, Florida, explains that his church has an online congregation of ten thousand people, each of whom stays online an average of forty-six minutes of a seventy-minute service. Because Christ Fellowship broadcasts church services in real time, it is not unusual to have people from other parts of the world respond to the message in real time. "Our objective is to connect people to a community and connect people to Christ," Internet church pastor Dave Helbig told Eric in early 2009. "The 'Is this real community?' question is asked only by those over thirty-five years of age. It's a beautiful thing. We had a quadriplegic baptized who was living locally but came to Christ online. Now he is doing follow-up for new believers all over the world as part of our Internet church. 'No one knows I'm a quadriplegic online,' he says." LifeChurch.tv, based in Tulsa, Oklahoma, has experienced more decisions for Christ at its Internet campus than it has at its eleven brick-and-mortar sites.[16]

Economics

There is no doubt that we in the United States, even in spite of our current economic crisis, are consumers, and many of us possess an abundance of stuff. We have "more cars than licensed drivers" and "spend more on trash bags than ninety other countries spend on everything."[17] To understand what is happening economically today, one has to consider what is happening with globalization. Globalization is the interconnectedness of people, goods, and services in the world. That your cell phone may have been designed in the United States and manufactured in China using components from Malaysia, Brazil, and Taiwan is symptomatic of globalization.

You've heard the word *outsourcing*. It refers to products and services that were once produced domestically by U.S. companies and workers that are now produced by the same companies in countries where labor is cheaper, environmental laws are looser, and people are desperate to better their lives. And no job seems to be safe from export. Call the service department of almost any company, and it is very likely that you will be connected to Bangalore, India, or another of the call centers scattered around India. Any job that can be outsourced either has already been outsourced or soon will be. Thomas Friedman, in a 2005 *New York Times* interview, noted, "When

I was growing up, my parents used to say to me, 'Tom, finish your dinner. People in China and India are starving.' Today I tell my girls, 'Finish your homework. People in China and India are starving for your jobs.'"[18] We are now competing with workers on a global scale. Fareed Zakaria, editor of *Newsweek International,* writes, "No worker from a rich country will ever be able to equal the energy and ambition of people making $5 a day and trying desperately to move out of poverty."[19]

To understand the economic forces of our world today, we need to understand what is happening with globalization and with China. China is booming—sustaining a torrid 9.5 percent annual economic growth rate for the past generation with no slowdown in sight.[20] "In two decades, China has experienced the same degree of industrialization, urbanization and social transformation as Europe did in two centuries."[21] Even amid the global recession of 2008–2009, China maintained a positive economic growth rate. The constant influx of rural migrant workers into the cities of China creates a stable and growing labor force that is paid, on average, around $70 a month to produce electronic parts, toys, socks, furniture, computers—you name it. Ted Fishman, author of *China, Inc.,* writes, "China is an ever increasing presence and influence in our lives, connected to us by the world's shipping lanes, financial markets, telecommunications, and above all, by the globalization of appetites. China sews more clothes and stitches more shoes and assembles more toys than any other nation."[22] Although China's gross domestic product is only seventh-largest economy in the world and only one-seventh the size of that of the United States, "in China one dollar buys about what $4.70 does in Indianapolis" making China's economy "closer to four-fifths the size of the U.S. economy than it is to one-sixth."[23] The Institute for International Economics in Washington calculates that "the average American household enjoys . . . savings that start at around $500"[24] because of China's low prices. If you have bought a color TV for under $90 or a DVD player for under $40, you have China to thank.

China is not alone as an economic juggernaut. "Over the past 15 years, India has been the second-fastest-growing country in the world—after China—averaging above 6% growth per year."[25] In a 2003 study by Goldman Sachs, researchers predicted that by 2040, India "will boast the world's third largest economy. By 2050, it will be five times the size of Japan's and its per capita income will have risen to 35 times its current level."[26] Daniel Pink notes that "each year, India's colleges and universities produce about 350,000 engineering graduates. That's one reason that more than half of *Fortune* 500 companies now outsource software work to India."[27]

The economic role of the United States is certainly impressive. "With 5 percent of the world's population, the United States has generated between 20 and 30 percent of world output for 125 years." After World War II, America's gross domestic product "made up almost 50 percent of the global economy." Today, thanks to the demise of economic communism (which left emerging nations with only one true economic alternative), the investment of Western capital around the world, and the free flow of goods and services, "between 1990 and 2007, the global economy grew from $22.8 trillion to $53.3 trillion," with emerging markets accounting for "over 40 percent of the world economy."[28]

While it can be mind-boggling to try to grasp economic trends, it is critical to gain an understanding of global economics. It often serves as the "X factor" for the future. Everything changes when the economy changes. We saw how true that is in 2008 when oil prices rocketed to nearly $150 a barrel in the summer before plummeting to under $40 a barrel in December. Gas prices surpassed $4.00 a gallon in July before returning to under $1.60 a gallon by the end of the year.

We could only wish that the other sectors of the economy—housing, industry, the credit and business markets—might rebound so well. Once mainstays of the American economy, these markets have now had to be bailed out by the government. The years 2008 and 2009 saw the financial markets plummet, with the best and brightest minds befuddled at finding ways to fix the ailing economy. And when the United States coughs, the whole world catches a cold. How does the church respond to people in need during a time of major recession? Do we know what kind of day it is?

Environment

The year 2005 was a wake-up call for Americans. The tsunami that washed over the coastlines of South Asia and East Africa in late December 2004, killing tens of thousands and leaving hundreds of thousands homeless, was just the beginning. Hurricanes Katrina and Rita hit our own shores with a fury, leaving in their wake devastation and loss on a scale largely unknown to this generation of Americans. Our sophistication and technology were no match against the unleashed forces of nature. Devastating droughts, floods, hurricanes, and earthquakes get nearly everyone's attention around the world. Environmental issues don't just affect the quality of life but threaten life itself. "Of China's 560 million urban residents, only one percent breathe air considered safe by European Union standards."[29] Over one billion people do not have daily access to clean drinking water.[30]

The environment is becoming more and more of an issue to politicians and public alike. Former vice president Al Gore garnered not only an Emmy Award for his documentary film *An Inconvenient Truth* but also shared in receiving the acme of all awards, the Nobel Peace Prize, for his lifelong environmental efforts. There are new economic opportunities associated with environmental issues. As energy prices climb, the quest for cleaner alternative energy sources is escalating, along with business opportunities and wealth awaiting the clever people who come up with solutions. Entrepreneurs like Richard Branson, founder of Virgin Group, committed $3 billion over the next ten years to combat global warming. It is a cause people are passionate about.

And now many Christians are getting on board. In early 2006, the *New York Times* published an article about eighty-six evangelical leaders who signed a document backing a major initiative to fight global warming, citing that "millions of people could die in this century because of climate change, most of them our poorest global neighbors."[31] Signers of the statement included presidents of thirty-nine evangelical colleges; parachurch leaders; and megachurch pastors, including Saddleback Pastor Rick Warren, Bishop Charles E. Blake Sr. of the West Angeles Church of God in Christ in Los Angeles, and the Rev. Floyd Flake of the Greater Allen A.M.E. Cathedral in New York City; as well as Hispanic leaders like the Rev. Jesse Miranda, president of AMEN in Costa Mesa, California.

In part, the statement read, "For most of us, until recently this has not been treated as a pressing issue or major priority. Indeed, many of us have required considerable convincing before becoming persuaded that climate change is a real problem and that it ought to matter to us as Christians. But now we have seen and heard enough."[32] In a television advertisement, Joel Hunter, pastor of a megachurch outside Orlando, Florida, stated, "As Christians, our faith in Jesus Christ compels us to love our neighbors and to be stewards of God's creation. The good news is that with God's help, we can stop global warming, for our kids, [for] our world and for the Lord."[33]

What is indisputable is that glaciers are melting and global temperatures are rising. Eleven of the twelve years from 1995 and 2006 were the hottest ever recorded."[34] In February 2007, the Intergovernmental Panel on Climate Change (IPCC), composed of more than two thousand scientists from 154 countries, released its summary report on global warming. By comparing different future scenario models, the consensus was that the world will warm 0.4 degrees Celsius (0.7 degrees Fahrenheit) in the next twenty years.

It seems that in spite of a growing scientific consensus that human activity and fossil fuels are at least partly responsible for disappearing ice caps and rising sea levels, many Christians take a stand *against* such findings simply because the findings are supported by scientists (or movie stars or Democrats or some other group). Whereas in the past, Christians were often at the forefront of science, believing they were discovering, through their research, the very manner, mind, and methods of God, scientific evidence, for some believers, is rejected simply because it comes from the field of science. Are we alienating the scientific community and the younger generation by clinging to stubborn provincial views? Are these people thinking, "How can I believe what this guy says about God and the unseen world when he rejects the evidence of the seen world?"

Maybe we need to get ahead of the culture on things God cares about—including stewardship of our planet. Peachtree Baptist Church in Atlanta has given legs to the stewardship of creation through its Faith and Environment Ministry. "We believe that we are called as Christians to care for and sustain God's creation," reads the church's environmental ministry mission statement.[35] The Faith and Environment ministry focuses on congregational and community activities that create awareness of earth stewardship. This is accomplished through educational programs, community events, and adopting green practices as a congregation. The ministry focuses on several Scriptures, including these:

> The land is mine and you are but aliens and my tenants. Throughout the country that you hold as a possession, you must provide for the redemption of the land [Leviticus 25:23–24].

> Is it not enough for you to feed on the good pasture? Must you also trample the rest of your pasture with your feet? Is it not enough for you to drink clear water? Must you also muddy the rest with your feet? [Ezekiel 34:17–18].

Would it be so radical for a church to have its own recycling center or administer a neighborhood car pool to get to church? Would it be that out of the ordinary? On a day like today, what should we be doing?

Politics

What are the political forces that are shaping our world today? Communism, as a political and social reality, no longer poses the political and military threat of yesterday. The largest country that still lives under the political banner of communism, China, has abandoned the economic principles of Marx and embraced a quasi-free-market economy.

And since the terrorist attacks of September 11, 2001, the United States has changed its tactics and position in world politics, not only going after terrorists but also engaging the countries that support them. In past generations, our battle was to stop the spread of communism. Today, American policy is to spread freedom and democracy around the globe. Nations that have declared themselves enemies of the United States and its policies are actively or covertly seeking the capacity to build nuclear weapons. Currently only seven countries have nuclear weapons, but that number is likely to change.

Closer to home, in some areas, the lines between the secular and the spiritual are becoming more clearly defined. Court battles are waged over the posting of the Ten Commandments in public places or the inclusion of "one nation under God" in the Pledge of Allegiance. The familiar commercial greeting "Merry Christmas" is slowly being replaced by "Happy Holidays." In Starbuck's in December, Eric picked up two different bags of coffee—a silver package labeled "Holiday Blend" and a red package labeled "Christmas Blend." When he asked about the difference between the two types of coffee, he was told that they were in fact identical! Apparently, Starbuck's felt caught in the middle this transition and learned to cater to both sides of the issue.

In the United States, politics and faith make unlikely bedfellows. The perception that evangelicals embrace a particular political party is not entirely inaccurate. "According to the National Election Pool exit poll, in 2004 Bush received 78% of the vote among white evangelicals, up 10% from 2000, according to Pew's final pre-election poll that year."[36] The potential danger of the link between faith and politics is alienation by affiliation. The 2008 election exit polls were not much different, with 74 percent of evangelicals casting votes for McCain and 25 percent voting for Obama.[37] Recently, a friend of Eric's was engaged in a conversation with a young Jewish woman who was investigating Christianity. Her main hesitation was expressed in her sincere question: "If I become a Christian, do I have to become a Republican?" How are we doing? The moral high ground is not a political platform. *Sojourners* editor Jim Wallace writes, "Endorsing political candidates is a fine thing, but ordaining them is not—the way that some leaders of the religious Right named George W. Bush as 'God's candidate' . . . and proclaimed that real Christians could vote only for him. . . . What do such tactics say about Republicans' respect for the black churches, when the African American vote was again almost 90 percent for the Democrats? Is something wrong with their faith?"[38] To reach a multicultural generation with the gospel is going to take some serious rethinking. The danger of affiliating too closely with any political party is that we can no longer judge that party's actions by the values of the kingdom—by which all political systems must be judged. Let's not forget that in Roman times, "to the populace all religions were equally true; to the philosophers all were equally false; and to the magistrates all were equally useful."[39]

No matter what your definition of the "right" candidate may be for a particular political position, we believe that we are never going to be able to legislate morality. Even we, the authors, don't agree 100 percent on matters of politics (which probably comes as no surprise!). We do agree that each of us as individuals and citizens has a responsibility to participate in the political process and that the church needs to rise above politics and look to engage our communities at the point of need. The political landscape is changing. Are you willing to understand what kind of day it is?

Religion

For a long time in the history of the world, the only channel you could get was the God channel. It did not matter where you set the tuner, you received the God channel. He was the reason the sun came up, the rain fell, and the harvest would come. Then in the fifteenth and sixteenth centuries, through the influence of men like René Descartes and Francis Bacon, we began to understand more about how the world functions. We grew in our understanding of the mechanics of life on earth and the earth itself, and the more we understood, the less God was needed.[40] Of course, there were still plenty of places for God; theologians called this "God in the gaps." We needed God when we couldn't explain things. However, once we understood the science of how things functioned, we had less need for some imaginative way to explain it.

This led naturally to the science or modern channel, and for a long time, it was the dominant channel. You could still get the God channel, but you had to lean out the window and put aluminum foil around your ears. For those of you over the age of forty, the Modern channel was the primary channel for the culture we grew up in; that is why books like *Evidence That Demands a Verdict* were so important to Christians.[41] There was evidence we could get our hands around and help others do the same so they could know God.

We are living during a seismic shift in culture. With all of our scientific and technological advances, we have become a channel-surfing culture. Today, there are fifteen hundred channels vying for reality, each claiming it has the truth. Today, only three out of ten adults believe that there is any absolute moral truth; under the age of thirty, that number drops to less than two out of ten.

For the church today, there is good news and bad news in this. The good news is that the God channel is again up and running; the bad news is that there is a lot of noise out there. The result is that we live in a world where evidence isn't the key but experience is.

Spirituality is up and church is down (a deeper look at that is just a few pages away). According to the Gallup Organization, 66 percent of Americans would make or agree with this statement: "The church has little or no value in helping me find meaning or purpose in life." We keep playing the game as it has been played for years, and many of us aren't even aware that someone has changed the rules. We don't want to get well. We don't want to know what day it is. Spiritual conversations are more likely to be sought out at Starbucks than in our churches today.

So let's look at a few religious trends today to which we must pay attention:

THE DIVISION OF THE WORLD ALONG RELIGIOUS LINES

In *The Next Christendom*, Phillip Jenkins predicts that in the future, religion will be the most defining characteristic of people, taking precedence even over national identity. In a world of shifting political boundaries, people will identity with a religious faith more strongly than with the country they live in. He writes, "At the turn of the third millennium, religious loyalties are at the root of many of the world's ongoing civil wars and political violence, and in most cases, the critical division is the age-old battle between Christianity and Islam. . . . The critical political frontiers around the world are not decided by attitudes toward class or dialectical materialism but by rival concepts of God."[42] Because the religions of both the crescent and the cross are highly evangelistic and have the world as their goal, is a collision course inevitable? Civil conflicts in sub-Saharan Africa, the Middle East, Indonesia, Bosnia, and elsewhere are basically religious wars disguised as civil wars. What kind of day is today?

THE RISE OF THE MEGACHURCH

"At latest count, there are 1,210 Protestant churches in the United States with weekly attendance over 2,000, nearly double the number that existed five years ago."[43] A 2002 study by the Lilly Foundation discovered that half of the people who go to church attended churches in the top 10 percent of church size.[44] Clearly, more than half of all churchgoers prefer large churches. Megachurches tend to be full-service churches with programming geared toward everyone from children to senior adults. The size of megachurches also gives them an increased capacity for service.

"Nearly half of [megachurches] say they partnered with other churches in the past five years on a local community service project (54%) or on an international missions project (46%)."[45] The influence of megachurch leaders is still taken seriously. According to *Megachurches Today, 2005,* an extensive study conducted by the Hartford Institute for Religion Research and Leadership Network, found that "during 2005, four mega-church pastors were on the *New York Times* bestseller lists—one of the books, with 26 million sales to date, has become the best-selling hard-cover nonfiction book in U.S. history . . . (and has been translated into 309 languages). Another megachurch pastor has sold 45 million copies of all his books. The third, a first-time author, crossed the 3 million mark in a year."[46]

But what of those who don't attend a megachurch—or any church, for that matter?

THE SHIFT FROM INTERNAL TO EXTERNAL

Sometimes movements begin from a central location and spread like the ripples when a rock is thrown into a pond. The movement from internal to external is different. All over the world, we meet pastors and Christian leaders who almost simultaneously have come to the conclusion that unless their church is engaged in the conversation, rhythms, needs, and dreams of their communities, it's not the church that Jesus wants them to be. We'll tell you about some of these leaders in the course of this book. So far, we've found that working with leaders from Oslo, Berlin, Mumbai, Mexico City, San Salvador, Kuala Lumpur, Beijing, Alberta, and dozens of other cities, a story is unfolding about what the church could be and should be. Church is more than just a worship center or a mini-seminary. Rather church is the visible and visceral expression of Jesus living among a people.

CHANGES IN WHAT IT MEANS TO BE "EVANGELICAL"

Young evangelical Christians are giving a new face to Christianity. They are arguably more socially aware, more connected, and more globally oriented than evangelicals of previous generations. They are more apt to rally around bringing help to hurting people, ending human trafficking, pursuing issues of justice, fighting AIDS, stopping genocide in Africa, and putting an end to global warming than they are to march against gay marriage or for prayer in school or in favor of the posting of the Ten Commandments. Michael Gerson, a senior fellow at the Council on Foreign Relations, makes an interesting observation: "I've asked young evangelicals on campuses from Wheaton to Harvard who they view as their model of Christian activism. Their answer is nearly unanimous: Bono."[47] Evangelicals are no longer (if they ever were) a unified political bloc. Thirty-five percent of evangelicals now say that the religious right does not reflect their views; 40 percent oppose a constitutional ban on same-sex marriage.[48] In the fall of 2007, the *Los Angeles Times* reported, "A decade ago, an overwhelming majority of non-Christians, including people between the ages 16 to 29, were 'favorably' disposed toward Christianity's role in society. But today, just 16% of non-Christians in that age group had a 'good impression' of the religion . . . with just 3% of the 16- to 29-year-old non-Christians indicating favorable views toward [evangelicals]."[49]

Rick McKinley, pastor of Imago Dei in Portland, Oregon, was interviewed in late 2007 by *USA Today* reporter Tom Krattenmaker. Krattenmaker writes, "Ask McKinley whether he and his community are evangelical Christians, and he'll tell you yes—and no. 'We'd say 'yes' in terms of what we think about the authority of Scripture and those things,' says McKinley, who is finishing his theology doctorate this year. 'What you have is evangelicalism define doctrinally, which we'd agree with, and defined culturally, where we would disagree. Culturally, it has been hijacked by a right wing political movement.'"[50]

RISING INTEREST IN SPIRITUALITY BUT MOVEMENT
AWAY FROM THE ORGANIZED CHURCH

In the summer of 2007, Eric and his wife went to Ireland and Scotland with several other couples to learn more about Celtic Christianity. The most thought-provoking lesson was given by Peter Neilson—a missional church planter from the Church of Scotland. He said, "When Moses met God on the mountain—that was spirituality. When he came down and told the people what God said—that was the beginning of religion." Have we lost spirituality in our construction of religion?

Let's take a look at spiritual interest. In a 2005 *Newsweek* poll, 79 percent of people described themselves as "spiritual" (while only 64 percent describe themselves as "religious"). Fully 84 percent indicated that spirituality is "very important" or "somewhat important" in their daily lives.[51] Interest in spiritual things is acceptable and on the rise. The decline of a purely rationalistic approach to life has given people permission to express their spiritual side. The singer Bonnie Raitt summed up the attraction of spirituality at a recent concert in New York City this way: "Religion is for people who are afraid to go to hell. And spirituality is for those of us who have been there and back."[52] People have plenty of room in their lives and space in their minds for the ethereal and nonmaterial aspects that spirituality provides. Jesus is as popular as ever. It's not unusual to have pictures of Jesus on the covers of *Time* and *Newsweek* at least once or twice a year.

Although spiritual interest is high, people are looking for new places to find spiritual vitality and authenticity. According to a recent study that actually tracked the attendance of two hundred thousand orthodox (Catholic, mainline, and evangelical) churches in the United States revealed that "in 2004, 17.7% of the population attended a Christian church on any given weekend."[53] Reggie McNeal writes, "A growing number of people are leaving the institutional church for a new reason. They are not leaving because they have lost faith. They are leaving the church to preserve their faith. They contend that the church no longer contributes to their spiritual development."[54] George Barna calls these folks "revolutionaries—confidently returning to a first-century lifestyle based on faith, goodness, love, generosity, kindness, simplicity and other values deemed quaint by today's frenetic and morally untethered standards."[55] Barna estimates there are twenty million such revolutionaries in the United States today.

The missiologist and researcher Ed Stetzer reports in a recent study on alternative faith communities "that a growing number of people are finding Christian discipleship and community in places other than their local churches. The study found that 24.5% of Americans now say their primary form of spiritual nourishment is meeting with a small group of 20 or less people every week."[56] Stetzer continues, "About 6 million people meet weekly with a small group and never or rarely go to church. . . . There is a significant movement happening." Is today a day of postcongregational Christianity?

Neil Cole, author of *Organic Church,* defines church as "the presence of Jesus among his people, called out as a spiritual family to pursue his mission on this planet." Cole goes on to say, "The church could meet in a traditional building, a living room, under the trees, or in a parking lot. What's important is Christ among us and being a family on a mission. If those elements are present, it doesn't matter how many you have or where you meet."[57] As one Boulder County resident pointed out to us, "The [institutional] church is like a set of training wheels. Training wheels help you learn to ride a bike, but after you learn to ride, you don't need them anymore."

The missiologist Darrel Guder writes, "We ring our bells, conduct our services, . . . and wait for this very different world to come to us. Pastors continue to preach sermons and carry on internal polemics over doctrines as though nothing outside has changed, but the reality is that everything has changed and the people are not coming back to the churches"[58] David Smith observes that the real problem of Christian mission in the modern West is not the absence of spiritual hunger in the postmodern generation but rather the church's failure to recognize the existence and significance of this quest on the part of thousands of people beyond its doors. Even where such recognition does occur, there is often a refusal to respond on the terms set by the searchers rather than on those dictated by existing ecclesiastical traditions and structures.[59]

In former times, if one wanted to be part of a spiritual community and wanted biblical content, one had to show up at a central location at a given time. Such a world no longer exists. Through technology, people have figured out new ways to stay connected to people they care about. The world's best content can be downloaded from the Internet at any time, day or night. The largest university in the world, Phoenix University, figured out long ago the value of rented buildings and digital content. A collapse in the church culture certainly does not mean the collapse of the church. Church is also taking new expressions in the form of "simple church" or "organic church" whose goal, much like Starbuck's and McDonald's, is not size but ubiquity—the church in every space and every place. This idea is expressed in a large ad by Embassy Suites Hotels in *USA Today*. It was headlined, "Because One Giant Hotel in One Location Would Have Been a Dumb Idea," followed by a listing of all the hotel properties around the world.[60] Part of our task is to help shape what church needs to be for the twenty-first century and how to reach and grow people that may never be part of what we currently call "church." It's that kind of day.

Liminality

A couple of years ago, Eric read *Mission After Christendom* by David Smith. (A quote from this book opened this chapter.) In this book, Smith suggests that we are currently in a time of transition, limbo, or "liminality," which he defines as a state between two cultural paradigms, on the cusp between the modern era and the postmodern era. A liminal state describes young boys in tribal societies who are pulled from their mothers and live together for a season before their initiation into manhood: no longer children but not yet men. Liminality describes the people of Israel when they were carried off into captivity by the Babylonians. Everything they trusted in that had worked in the past no longer worked. In a liminal state, what used to seem true is true no longer, and what will be true in the future has not yet been fully revealed. This is liminality. Because major cultural shifts, such as from modernity to postmodernity, occur over decades rather than months (Smith suggests that the modern era ended with World War I), we might want to learn to be comfortable with liminality. In liminal times, there is confusion because the path is unclear. As Eric has the opportunity to speak to groups of Christian leaders and pastors, he often asks, "If you know, with confidence, what you are doing in ministry, please raise your hand." There is much more laughter than hand-raising. We live in a liminal time.

What If We Don't Understand the Times?

Just think of all the major changes in society, economics, environment, politics, and religion that we have experienced since the turn of this century. The world we live and work in is radically different than the world we lived in just a decade ago. And it is safe to say that the world will be very different ten years from now than it is today. The implications are staggering. Programs and tactics that worked in the past won't necessarily be the ones that will be effective in the future.

If the church is God's enterprise in the world, then we who are stewards, managers, and entrepreneurs in the enterprise need to be as discerning and as savvy as in any other organization; indeed, given the stakes, we would argue even more so than in any other enterprise. The future will not be shaped by doing more or better or harder what we have done in the past. The key is not skating where the world was but where the world will be.

Admittedly, when you look at the church landscape, statistics show that many of us have been content to do what we have always done. We have not always understood how to act or react to this liminal state in which we find ourselves. We have confused method with message and have often been more concerned with maintaining what we are doing than with innovating new solutions to meet current and future needs and sharing the timeless message of Christ. Are we driving on 2010 highways in vehicles that are decades old? No wonder we aren't keeping up with traffic.

If we don't take time to understand and embrace today, we are left with only looking back; which often leads to self-preservation and maintenance. Even if we happen to be a church that has a lot of people, so much of our energy can be spent on simply attracting people and keeping them coming back. We have to ask ourselves not "What kind of day was yesterday?" but "What kind of day is today?"

Here's the Good News

Smith writes, "Despite the feeling that we are in a dark tunnel, the present liminality offers the potential for a fresh missionary engagement in a radically changing social context." And quoting Alan Roxburgh, he invites us to be part of the solution: "We too face a point at which God appears to be terminating our known world and inviting us to a new world in which the true nature of the church and its mission can be recovered."[61] This means that this is a time to experiment and discover. There is a lot of white space on the map! Can you think of anything more exciting to be a part of?

After the army of Israel faced significant defeat and was reduced to a handful of stragglers, David regrouped his assets. One of those assets was the men of Issachar mentioned at the start of this chapter. They are described quite simply as men who knew how to understand the times. These men provided David with insight, vision, and a timely understanding. Who are the men (and women) of Issachar in your life?

There is a lot of conversation, both positive and negative, about the church today. With all of its warts, wounds, and wobbles, we both love the church. We love the church because God loves the church. While there is plenty to be frustrated by and certainly much that needs to change, the church is God's answer for the world and our communities. The church that looks to be the best church for its community looks beyond itself. Today is actually a great day for the church when we understand the times.

It's Sunday Morning!

At a Sunday evening worship service at the Mayan Theater in Los Angeles, Mosaic's Erwin McManus told about going to the U2 concert at the Staples Center in early November 2005. Bono is not only U2's lead singer but also, oddly enough, serves in a prophetic capacity to the secular world and the church around the world as an advocate for the poor and downtrodden. To a packed house, Bono took the stage, grabbed the microphone, and yelled, "Do you know what today is?" When the crowd responded that it was Wednesday night, Bono responded, "It's not Wednesday night. It's Sunday morning!" Sunday morning is the earliest part of the first day of the week. It's a time for fresh beginnings, fresh thoughts, and new ways for God to be part of our lives and for us to be part of his wonderful kingdom mission here on earth. What kind of day is today? Today is Sunday morning!

The Leadership Challenge

We feel that this book will be of benefit to every Christ follower, but it is usually leaders who have the ability to bring about the changes needed to bring the future into the present. The Leadership Challenge presented at the end of each chapter broadens the scope of application of the chapter from the individual to the church or organization. It is our hope that this feature will bring forth insights and questions to help you lead the externally focused journey.

- What deep changes have you experienced in society, technology, economics, environment, politics, religion, and your own organization in the past five to ten years?
- What do you expect the future will be like in the next five to ten years in these same areas?
- How should these changes influence missional living?
- Where is most of your energy currently going?
- Who gives you insight and provides glimpses of future vision and timely understanding?

CHAPTER 2

Focus: They Choose the Window Seat, Not the Aisle Seat

Calls command that you attach yourself to something infinite and lasting so you can escape the life you thought you deserved and replace it with the life you were meant for.

John P. Schuster, *Answering Your Call*[1]

GOLD MEDALLION. THAT'S RICK'S STATUS with Delta Air Lines. It began in the mid-1980s when his work at a small college and seminary in Cincinnati, Ohio, required a great deal of traveling. Cincinnati is one of Delta's hubs and one of just a handful of airlines flying in and out. It made sense to sign up for the frequent-flier program. It didn't take long for him to learn a couple of things. First, frequent fliers rarely see anything but airports, rental car buses, and hotel rooms; don't actually get to travel; are just in a lot of different places seeing the same things. Second, there are some tricks to maximizing the amount of frequent traveler awards earned, including always fly the same airline, rent from the same car company, and stay in the same chain of hotels. Some frequent travelers even do odd things to accumulate miles; one friend took a round-trip flight to Paris at the end of the year just to maintain his elite status. Seriously, he left Houston, flew to Paris, got off the plane, went down a few gates, boarded another plane, and returned to Houston. (There are therapists for this kind of thing!)

Gold Medallion isn't Delta's highest status, but it does get a special reservation number, shorter security lines, an occasional upgrade, and nice luggage tags. Eric, who is a part of the million-mile club of United Airlines, also knows what it's like to spend a lot of time on planes. We admit to you that for a long time, both of us preferred to be seated in aisle seats near the front. When the plane had landed, the taxiing stopped, and that little bell sounded, indicating that passengers were now free to move about the cabin, we could spring out of our seats, grab our carry-on bags, and be the first off the plane to catch a rental car bus to head to an identical-looking hotel room anywhere in the world!

The aisle seat afforded more options, greater freedom, and faster exits. We could get to life faster. But recently, there have been some changes. First, Rick doesn't travel nearly as much as he did and now requests a window seat. Eric too. Neither of us is exactly sure why we changed seats. It's probably because we aren't in nearly as big a hurry as we were before and also because the window seat offers a little more privacy. We've also learned that once in a while, there are actually things that you can see only from the window seat.

To draw a parallel, it can be very easy for us do ministry from the aisle seat. We are busy, and there are a lot of things to get done. The needs and issues that arise in the congregation are demanding. There is plenty to do, and we are busy doing it. There isn't anything wrong with this. In fact, there are times we have no choice. It isn't that the aisle seat isn't necessary or important. Someone needs to be in the aisle seat. The danger comes when we see life *only* from the aisle seat—to the exclusion of every other perspective.

It never occurred to Rick that when his Gold Medallion profile specified "aisle seat," there might be more going on than he was aware of. "There were times," he recalls, "when the pilot would say, 'If you will look out to your left you can see . . . ,'" and I would lean over the guy in the middle trying to catch a glimpse of whatever it was. Most times, though, I didn't care what was going on outside. I was interested only in getting to where I was going—usually onto another plane and into another aisle seat!"

You will often find the frequent fliers in the aisle seats. They are easy to spot: they have an entire language of their own, and they understand the needs and behaviors of frequent travelers. Unfortunately, many of them seem to have little patience for anyone outside their circle. They have a way of seeing things and system for maneuvering all the travel that makes perfect sense to them.

How many times are church leaders like the aisle-seat frequent fliers? We have our own language and use strange words like *fellowship, sanctification,* and *righteousness.* We have our own way of doing things and a way of seeing the world that makes perfect sense—to other people inside the circle.

We can think of churches also as either "aisle-seat" or "window-seat." Aisle-seat churches are almost exclusively preoccupied with what is happening inside the four walls of the church; window-seat churches, by contrast, have a focus that is external to the church, and their vision extends far beyond the four walls. If you want to be the best church in the community, choose the aisle seat (in first class, if you can), but if you want to be the best church *for* the community, slide over to the window seat.

Attractional and Missional Churches

In Matthew 22:2–5, Jesus gives a kingdom parable to describe the external focus of window-seat churches that also describes the process of building the kingdom. Jesus chooses his words carefully and deliberately. This is about a king who invites friends and neighbors to his own son's wedding reception.

> The kingdom of heaven is like a king who prepared a wedding banquet for his son. He sent his servants to those who had been invited to the banquet to come, but they refused to come. Then he sent out more servants and said, "Tell those who have been invited that I have prepared my dinner: My oxen and fattened cattle have been butchered, and everything is ready. Come to the wedding banquet." But they paid no attention and went off—one to his field, another to his field.

Luke's account adds:

> But they all alike began to make excuses. The first said, "I have just bought a field, and I must go and see it. Please excuse me." Another said, "I have just bought five yoke of oxen, and I'm on my way to try them out. Please excuse me." Still another said, "I just got married, so I can't come" [Luke 14:18–20].

This parable describes the conundrum of what some refer to as an "attractional church." The attractional church is one that through its presence, programming, and marketing—everything from cool Web sites to four-color brochures to word-of-mouth—seeks to attract people to its services. But like the busy people in the parable, many, many people "pay no attention" or "make excuses" as to why they cannot come to the banquet. Even a second attempt at describing the sumptuous meal did little to attract these busy people. It is like saying, "Look what we have on the menu. We've brought in Emeril Lagasse, Bobby Flay, Paula Deen, and Rachael Ray, and they are preparing their finest dishes. Won't you come?" If the finest food and a hand-delivered invitation can't fill the banquet hall, what chance do pastors have trying to persuade the community with their menu of relevant teaching, inspiring worship, a great youth ministry, fabulous facilities, and so on?

The operative words in the attractional model are *come to*. In the attractional mode, we are asking people to substitute something they think is valuable and important for something we think is valuable and important. We don't know what happens on Sunday mornings in your community, but in our Colorado community, Sunday mornings are prime time for youth sports. Families are off skiing or snowboarding or taking a summer drive in the Rockies. Eric even says only half-jokingly that perhaps we should advertise like this: "Church: for people with nothing better to do on a Sunday morning." In essence, what Jesus is saying is that even if the king himself invites people to his own son's wedding reception where the finest of foods are served, a great many people will still not come. If people just don't show up because of the host or the quality of the cuisine, what chance do we have? The inadequacy of being an attractional church is that the banquet hall is far from full. If you are an attractional church, most likely you are already approaching the limit of all you are able to attract to your church. Yet your banquet hall is far from full. Fortunately, for the king, his criterion of success was not "Has everyone been invited?" or "Does everyone know what time the banquet is?" or "Does everyone know what we have on the menu?" but rather "Is my banquet hall full?"

Because the banquet hall was not full, the parable has a second component that reveals a second strategy. The king augments his "come to" strategy with a "go to" or "go out" strategy: "Go to the street corners" (Matthew 22:9), "Go out . . . into the streets and alleys of the town. . . . Go out to the roads and country lanes . . . so that my house will be full" (Luke 14:21, 23). The attractional church is a "come to" church. Externally focused churches can best be described as "go to" churches or sometimes as "missional" churches. These churches think of incarnation as much as they think of invitation. The good news is that you don't have to sacrifice one strategy to employ the other. You should want your church to become the best attractional church it can be. When people come to your church, there should be a full fare of what they can partake in. They should leave mumbling the words of the queen of Sheba and singing the church's praises: "'Everything you said this would be is true . . . and way more besides all you told me' (1 Kings 10:7). The teaching is very practical, my teens love the youth group, and I can hardly pull my kids away from Sunday school." People should be surprised by the excellence and authenticity of what your church offers, but simply recognize this: you are not reaching all you could be reaching by a "come to" strategy alone. You can also extend your reach into the community as far as you can through your "go to" model—employing those in your church to go into the highways and hedges of your community. This is what window-seat churches do. We find ourselves telling pastors wherever we go, "The only thing more difficult than getting the church to go into the community is getting the community into the church." It is actually far easier, through regular influence, to get the church into the community than through sporadic contact try to get the community into the church.

The Early Church: A Window-Seat Church

The life and teachings of Jesus Christ were profound, holistic, and transformational. His threefold ministry encompassed teaching, preaching, and healing (Matthew 4:23, 9:35). To walk as his disciple, one was to "be merciful just as [God] is merciful" (Luke 6:36), love as Jesus loved (John 13:34, 35), and be a neighbor to all in need (Luke 10:29–37). In the early centuries of the church, the Christ followers, through their compassion and kindness, served the people around them, resulting in an estimated 40 percent growth per decade of the early church.[2] David Bosch's research on the expansion of the early church pieces together "a remarkable picture of the early Christians' involvement with the poor, orphans, widows, the sick, mineworkers, prisoners, slaves, and travelers. 'The new language on the lips of Christians . . . was the language of love.' But it was more than a language; it was a thing of power and action: This was a 'social gospel' in the very best sense of the word and was practiced not as a stratagem to lure outsiders to the church but simply as a natural expression of faith in Christ."[3]

Throughout the following centuries, the church played a major role in meeting social needs and curing social ills. Christians were at the forefront in the abolition of slavery, the enactment of child labor laws, and the establishment of public schools, universities, orphanages, and hospitals. Christian leaders like William Booth and Jane Addams led the way in restoring the bodies and minds, as well as the souls, of those who were converted. The Catholic scholar Thomas Massaro writes of the social impact the church has had throughout the centuries:

Many of the laudable social institutions and practices that we take for granted today have their roots in teachings and activities of the Christian community, including the Catholic Church. For example, the complex system of hospitals and modern health care from which we all benefit sprang from charitable works that were sponsored by churches, both Protestant and Catholic, in previous centuries. Modern labor unions and group insurance policies are an outgrowth of various activities of guilds and sodalities, agencies through which members of the medieval church practiced mutual support, often under direct religious auspices. Churches organized the first schools in our nation and in other lands, and much of our educational system at all levels is still religiously affiliated. It was the church that cared for poor families before there were public social service agencies. The contemporary social work and nursing professions grew out of the efforts of church personnel, largely nuns, and laywomen, Catholic and Protestant alike, to assist families in need of resources, expertise and healing. For good reason, then, the church has been called the "godmother of the nonprofit sector."[4]

Reasons the Church Is Not Engaged

Is this the kind of impact the church is experiencing today? For most churches, this transformational role has all but disappeared. One pastor is said to have noted, "The normal Christian life has become so sub-normal that the normal Christian looks abnormal."[5] Monte Schmidt, pastor at Rolling Hills Community Church in Tualatin, Oregon, commented in a phone conversation, "Service has always been the DNA of Christianity, but for most people, it is a recessive gene in the gene pool." Why has much of the church withdrawn, either physically or psychologically, from the community that God has placed it in? We believe there are four factors that have influenced the withdrawal of the church from the community. These factors are missional, theological, secular, and personal.

Missional Factors

First there is a missional factor. Dr. Ram Cnaan, director of the Program for Religion and Social Policy Research at the University of Pennsylvania, writes:

> While religious organizations—the Church with a capital C—
> [have] sponsored many social programs throughout the world,

congregations have historically been reluctant to become involved in social programs. After all, the primary mission of a congregation is to provide a religious framework and communal site for worshiping. Its second mission is to sustain the congregation and to guarantee resources sufficient to carry out its primary mission. Social services delivery can come only after these two missions are achieved.[6]

Cnaan defines the practical pressure that keeps churches buckled in their aisle seats. Congregational leaders ask, as leaders from our own churches have asked from time to time, "How can we meet all the needs 'out there' when we have so many needs right here in our church? First, let's meet the needs within the church, and then we will have greater capacity to meet the needs 'out there.'" In early 2006, the researcher Thom S. Rainer wrote, "In a recent survey of churches across America, we found that nearly 95% of the churches' ministries were for members alone. Indeed, many churches had no ministries for those outside the congregation."[7]

In early 2007, the findings from a study conducted for *Facts & Trends* were released to the public. The study was the result of an extensive survey conducted in all fifty states among a representative sample of 811 Protestant church senior ministers. The survey revealed that

> 39 percent essentially are not highly interested in offering more programs for the community, saying they would rather focus on their own congregation than on the community, they would rather focus on spiritual needs than on physical needs, it's not a major priority for their church, their community has no major needs, other organizations do these things better than they do, or their congregation or community really [isn't] interested in community outreach. This is consistent across all major denominational groups, as well as between evangelical and mainline churches.[8]

The "mission" of the church cannot merely be to maintain itself. Jesus never commanded the church to merely survive.

In 2008, Eric received the following e-mail from an associate pastor that explains the difficulty of moving from the aisle seat to the window seat.

June 3, 2008

Eric,

So here I sit at Starbucks . . . yeah, I think I hate this place today. Listening to Wayne Newton so stop trying to push that on me. But that's not why I am writing. I have been involved in this whole externally focused church idea and thoughts for a while. Your article about paradigm shifts[9] put on paper some thoughts that have been stirring in me for about three years or so. As I drove around my community, I was saddened by two very crazy thoughts: how come there are so many needs, and why are there so many churches being built, yet the community is unchanged?

So all these thoughts led me to get fired from my position as an associate pastor—probably for the best anyway. I approached the church with applicable ways to integrate more into our community instead of trying to invite everyone to the church (which doesn't make sense to me anyway). So I suggested little ways to make a Sunday church more passionate and directed to community transformation. That truly is my passion—to see community changed regardless of what happens to the church growth numerically. I proposed simple suggestions: What if we asked the each small group to own a neighborhood in the small community and twice a year serve them somehow? They could throw a block party, provide a day out through free child care, a physical service project, invite a person to talk on safety issues . . . whatever, just something small to get their feet wet . . . just trying to get them to think differently.

I suggested that when we do events, we think them through differently. For example, why don't we invite children to the church for a movie night? What if we worked with the mothers' group in the community and plan a movie night at the park and then give the mothers group the credit for pulling it off? What if we did a capital campaign to pay the homeowners' association fees for the single parents?

These were just little ideas, but they led to a huge problem. It was not about the church then! So I kept gently trying to be a visionary and lead by example. I gathered a small group of people, and we began. After fourteen years of ministry, you would have thought I would have learned how to be institutionalized. Nope . . . haven't learned that yet. So after fourteen years, I got the boot and was shown the door. Exact quote: "We are about the Sunday service and growing in worship." So I just wanted to say thanks for getting me fired. No, just kidding. It's cool and I trust God for what is next. I know my passion to see community changed and for churches to get it. I am totally in love with Jesus and I know he gets it.

Thanks man,

A Once and Future Associate Pastor

It's heartbreaking to read a story like that, but the pushback is often all too real.

Theological Factors

A second issue is theological. Beginning with the Reformation, many believers wanted to separate themselves from the corrupt practices of the established church and state. There could be no cooperation, capitulation, or collaboration with Christians who were less dedicated and set apart than they themselves hoped for. The Swiss Brethren Anabaptists, for example, came up with seven areas of common agreement, among which was Article IV, titled "Separation from the Abomination," in the Schleitheim Confession of 1527:

> We are agreed on separation: A separation shall be made from the evil and from the wickedness which the devil planted in the world; in this manner, simply that we shall not have fellowship with them and not run with them in the multitude of their abominations. This is the way it is: since all who do not walk in the obedience of faith, and have not united themselves with God so that they wish to do his will, are a great abomination to God, it is not possible for anything to grow or issue from them except abominable things. For truly all creatures are in but two classes, good and bad, believing and unbelieving, darkness and light, the world and those who [have come] out of the world, God's temple and idols, Christ and Belial [the devil] and one can have part with the other. . . . He further admonishes us to withdraw from Babylon and the earthly Egypt that we may not be partakers of the pain and suffering which the Lord will bring upon them.[10]

Often Christians of this same ilk will quote verses like 1 Corinthians 6:17: "Wherefore come out from among them, and be ye separate, saith the Lord" (almost always quoted in the King James Version). But we firmly believe that this separation is a separation of values and life choices and not a separation of geography, since one cannot be salt, light, and leaven at a distance. These transformational agents work only when they actively mix with what needs to be changed.

Sometimes theological trends shape behavior. Toward the end of the nineteenth century, the eschatological teaching of premillennialism became a prominent popular theology of the day. A tenet of premillennialism is the imminent return of Jesus Christ, followed by a thousand-year reign of Christ on earth. A prerequisite to Christ's return was the preaching of the gospel to the entire world "as a testimony to all nations, and then the end will come" (Matthew 24:14). It was this conviction that helped fuel the great missionary efforts of the late nineteenth and early twentieth centuries. An aberration of this teaching, however, was that any effort Christians expended trying to make this world a better, more livable place, as opposed to getting people into heaven, was to hinder and delay the return of Jesus Christ. It was this attitude that exempted the church from engaging in the ills and hurts of the community. This theological stance, which set itself against amillennialists, who don't accept a literal thousand-year reign of Jesus, was the beginning of what the church historian David Bosch refers to as the "great reversal,"[11] when most of the evangelical church, as it came to be called, exempted itself from societal ills.

Secular Factors

The third reason churches have refrained from social ministry is because of the secularization of social services. Although it can be argued that the fount of human services is the church, little by little the church has both relinquished this role and been eased out of it by government and human service agencies—the "professionals." Diana Garland, writing in *Christianity and Social Work,* notes that secularization is not without effect: "'The spontaneous will to serve,' so evident in earlier church volunteers, was subverted by the drive for professionalization. Previous values that had stressed compassion, emotional involvement, and vigorous love of humanity . . . were 'educated out' in preference for a 'scientific trained intelligence and skillful application of technique.'"[12] Average congregants often feel underqualified to engage the homeless, immigrants, orphans, widows, and others in need when so much expertise seems to be required.

The church is often absent from the conversation regarding societal ills and social needs. A few years ago, both of us were sitting in a meeting with some city officials looking over a publication titled *Quality of Life in Boulder County, 2005: A Community Indicators Report.*[13] In this report, there was not a single reference to churches being part of the solution in addressing the top community needs such as at-risk youth, health care, and homelessness, although "public agencies," "businesses," and "nonprofit agencies" were frequently cited. Addressing the absence of religion-based literature in social services, Ram Cnaan reports that in a review of more than thirty-five thousand abstracts of articles for social workers published between 1977 and 1997, only 220 mentioned the term *religion.* Further analysis failed to identify a single source that dealt with a religion-based social service organization as a service provider or partner for social work. Nor was there any mention of religion-based social services that complement the services provided by the state, foundations, residents' associations, and academic disciplines.[14]

Cnaan further notes that similar patterns were found in papers presented at academic conferences, in textbooks, in course outlines, and in encyclopedias of social work. Surely an aisle-seat church that focuses primarily on itself is not the church that Jesus came to build. Believers are called to be salt (Matthew 5:13) and light (Matthew 5:14), not for and to themselves but for and to the world around them.

In August 2007, an editorial appeared in Canada's *Vancouver Sun* newspaper regarding Tenth Avenue Alliance Church's ministry to the homeless. The church "runs a daily drop-in service for people, some of whom are homeless, as well as an Out of the Cold program that provides overnight accommodation for homeless people."[15] The city demanded that the church obtain a social services permit because its ministry to the homeless didn't qualify as "church use." We can hardly blame the city for such a misconception when we as the church have been content to sing, pray, and take notes within the confines of the four walls.

Personal Factors

Sometimes we just want to stay in the aisle seat because venturing to the window seat and engaging in what we find is just too hard even when we are in ministry. A while back, Eric received this e-mail from a good friend, Ian Vickers, who is committed to serving people on the margins. He's far from tossing in the towel, but the conflicted emotions are all too real.

> Hello Eric,
>
> I thought about you today as I was reviewing some of my week. Monday was a day filled with interesting emotional highs and lows. At 8:30 a.m. I tried to help a homeless guy out, but it did not go so well. He ended up calling me a "#@%&* pastor" for not helping more. After he was done, I realized that a wristband on his arm was from one of the local hospitals. Well, I offered to take him to a place where he could get some help and then to pray for him. He said, "I don't need any #@%&* prayer. I am going to sue this #@%&* church." Yeah, he was one frustrated guy. I still prayed for him but struggled to see Jesus in disguise through this event.

A Timely Look at the Scriptures

In April 2008, Eric asked Rich Nathan, lead pastor of Vineyard Church in Columbus, Ohio, to lead a devotional for the sixty cross-domain missional leaders assembled at the Facilitation Space of Leadership Network in Dallas, Texas. Rich's insights on why churches don't engage with broken people outside the church were cogent and powerful. Rich began by reminding us of the two grandest parables in the gospel of Luke—the Prodigal Son (Luke 15) and the Good Samaritan (Luke 10). In the case of the Prodigal, this younger son was a victim of his own personal rebellious sin. No one duped or coerced him into his circumstances. He willingly, consciously, and deliberately walked away from his family to pursue a lifestyle of partying, drunkenness, and licentiousness. He is today's drug addict or alcoholic or teenage single mom. Rich points out that in cases like that of the Prodigal Son, God rescues people through forgiveness, and we often do not realize just how far his forgiveness extends. So we stand in the background with our arms folded like the older brother, wanting nothing to do with helping this poor-choosing individual. After all, we wouldn't want to enable a person to the point of codependency. Our problem is that we don't understand grace. God rescues through forgiveness. The good news of the gospel is that "no matter what you've done, you can turn to God and be forgiven," and it sounds too good to be true.

In the parable of the Good Samaritan, the injured man was not a victim of his own personal sin but rather the victim of being sinned against—social sin. There was the victim, beaten and robbed of everything he had and left for dead on the side of the road. But look! Hope is on the way in the form of God's people—the priest and the Levite. But no, they pass by on the other side of the road. Most likely they were on their way to Jerusalem and had sacred or spiritual duties to perform, and must not the spiritual take precedence over the physical? Others can mend the physical body, but only God's people can carry out God's work. Right? What good is it to send well-fed people to hell? We've got to care for the souls of people. Most often we don't engage in healing the hurts because at the end of the days, we are twenty-first-century Gnostics. We value the immaterial and eternal to the exclusion of the physical and temporal. We are resistant to a gospel that has social implications. We'll leave that to others. So as both parables point out, we cleverly devise an apologetic for disengagement. The first parable calls us to evangelism—to extend grace and forgiveness to the most unworthy. The second parable calls us to engagement in social action—charity, mercy, and justice.

And this two-fisted gospel must be big enough that we can wrap both arms around a hurting world.

Writing with tongue in cheek, Atlanta's Robert Lupton, in his wonderful little book *Theirs Is the Kingdom*, expounds:

> People with a heart to serve others want to know that their gifts are invested wisely. At least I do. I don't want my alms squandered by the irresponsible and the ungrateful. And since I'm often in a position to determine who will or will not receive assistance, I've attempted to establish criteria to judge the worthiness of potential recipients. (The following is truncated and bulleted for convenience.)
>
> - A truly worthy poor woman—is a widow over sixty-five living alone without family
> - A truly worthy poor young man—out of school, unemployed but not living off his mother
> - A truly worthy poor young woman—has illegitimate children conceived prior to Christian conversion and is now celibate
> - A truly worthy poor family—is devout, close-knit. Has a responsible father working long hours at minimum wage wherever he can find work.
>
> I want to serve truly worthy poor people. The problem is they are hard to find. Someone on our staff thought he remembered seeing one back in '76 but can't remember for sure.[16]

Focus

"Where is the focus of our church?" Is it inside or outside the church? Aisle churches think a lot about internal programs—activities that meet the needs of those inside the church. At the end of the day, the church has been reduced to a warehouse of religious goods and services. Aisle churches "count nickels and noses" as a measure of their effectiveness. Churches that choose the window seat think that church should be something more. Church is not merely caring for those you have but going after those you don't have. In his book *The Present Future*, Reggie McNeal writes:

> The target of most church ministry efforts has been on the church itself and church members. Just look at how the money is spent and what the church leadership spends time doing. We have already rehearsed the poor return on investment we are seeing for this focus.

The church that wants to partner with God on his redemptive mission in the world has a very different target: the community. In the past, if a church had any resources left over after staffing Sunday school, and so on, then it went to the community. In the future, the church that "gets it" will staff to and spend its resources on strategies for community transformation.[17]

We like what Reggie says. When you look at the resources (time, finances, and staffing), how much of those resources are expended outside the church?

One Hundred Sheep, Ten Coins, and Two Sons

In Luke 15, Jesus tells three stories that all convey a similar message. They are stories of focusing on going after what we don't have rather than focusing on what we do have. This is a three-part parable of people who have chosen the window seat. The first story is of a man who had one hundred sheep and loses one of them. It would be easy enough to say, "Oh, well, I still have ninety-nine sheep." Instead the shepherd leaves the ninety-nine sheep and goes after the lost sheep until he finds it. And when he finds the lost sheep, he throws a party in celebration. The focus is not on what he had but on going after the one he didn't have.

Jesus then tells the second part of this trilogy, about a woman who had ten silver coins and loses one. She is not content with having the nine coins but searches the entire house, looking in every nook and cranny until she finds it. And when she finds it, she also calls her friends and neighbors together in celebration.

The third part of this trilogy is much more personal. We've already looked at this parable once, but let's look again at the prodigal son. It's the tale of a father who had two sons, the younger of whom, taking his share of the family estate, left home and spent everything he had on "wild living" in a foreign country. The Scriptures say that one day he came to his senses and headed back home, all the while rehearsing his apology speech. But Jesus adds an interesting twist: "But while he was still a long way off, his father saw him (probably positioned from the window seat) and was filled with compassion for him; he ran to his son, threw his arms around him and kissed him" (Luke 15:20). And like the shepherd and the coin-endowed woman, he also threw a party in celebration in finding what was lost. Externally focused churches certainly appreciate and value what they have as much as the shepherd valued his ninety-nine sheep, the woman valued her nine coins, and the father valued his elder son. But the focus was not on what they had but on what they did not have. Energy was put toward going after what was lost.

Blindness and the Nearsighted

Sometimes we just don't get it . . . until God intervenes. Do you remember when Peter was hanging out at Simon's beach house in Joppa (Acts 9:43)? Through a vision, God showed Peter that he needed to go to Caesarea and preach the gospel to a non-Jewish centurion and his family. Although the writings of Moses clearly foretold that Jesus was to be a blessing to all peoples (Genesis 12:3; Ephesians 3:4–10), Peter and his Jewish brothers were "blind" to this truth. The author of the book of Acts takes two full chapters to tell Peter's story of converting the Gentiles and how the Jewish believers finally "got it" (Acts 11:18).

As human beings, we always suffer from some type of blindness. Look at the life of John Newton.

On business trips, he would spend several hours praying and reading the Bible each morning, with another round of prayers at midday. As a ship captain, he enjoyed long spells of solitude on deck, keeping a diary and recording that he knew no "calling that . . . affords greater advantages to an awakened mind, for promoting the life of God in the soul."[18] His expensive cargo required extra officers and crew, reducing his onboard responsibilities. "I never knew sweeter or more frequent hours of divine communion, than in my last two voyages to Guinea, when I was either almost secluded from society on shipboard, or when on shore. . . . I have wandered through the woods reflecting on the singular goodness of the Lord to me."[19] John Newton recorded those words while transporting African slaves and having his savings invested in the slave ship business. "For more than thirty years after he left the slave trade, during which time Newton preached thousands of sermons, published half a dozen books, and wrote *Amazing Grace* and 279 other hymns, he said not a word in public against slavery."[20]

Newton was blind to what is now so obvious. Even though he penned the words "I once was blind, but now I see," apparently he only had the ability see things up close. He was nearsighted. When he truly became "sighted," he devoted the remainder of his life to speaking out and attempting to end the slave trade.

Blindness and nearsightedness are still prevalent today. At the 2005 HIV/AIDS Summit, Saddleback pastor Rick Warren narrated his own story of blindness. "I have two advanced theological degrees and have read the Bible cover to cover dozens of times. I don't know how I missed over twelve hundred verses on the poor and disenfranchised. How did I miss the biggest health crisis in history?"[21]

At the same event, Bill and Lynne Hybels told of God opening their eyes to the economic, political, and health crisis in Africa. Lynne tells of meeting U2 lead singer Bono in a coffee shop and saying to herself as she walked out, "I think God just used a rock star to change my life." We all need these types of second conversions.

Sometimes when we speak, we ask everyone in the audience to stand up. Then we project a picture of a cow on the screen and ask the people in the audience to sit down when they recognize the object. About half the people sit down immediately and find it hard to believe that people all around them are still standing. During the next minute, a few more utter, "Oh, I see it," and sit down. About 30 percent just stand there wondering what it is that they don't see. But once the object is pointed out, it is so obvious that you cannot *not* see it. From that point on, it is obvious. We think it's the same with the orientation of a church. Once a church gets engaged outside the walls, it discovers that's really where the action is. Did you ever notice that every pilot that is flying the plane always has the window seat? If one is going to lead, one must do it from the window seat. You've got to look out the window.

Turning Their Chairs Around

Hope Presbyterian Church is a large suburban church in Cordova, Tennessee (population 40,000), within earshot of Memphis. Hope began in 1988 with a core group of twenty-five people and today has a weekly worship attendance of over six thousand. Looking out the window has almost always been a part of Hope's DNA. Though the setting is suburban, the focus is urban. Each week, Hope sends over one hundred people to seven different sites around the city to help children increase their reading proficiency. Hope sponsors year-round food and clothing drives and provides coaches, equipment, and uniforms for inner-city youth baseball and softball programs as part of its RBI (Return Baseball to the Inner City) initiative. The church has adopted a ten-block area, known as the Caldwell community, in Memphis for community transformation. It pushes the boundaries of conventional church by paying half the wages for dozens of boys and girls (fourteen to sixteen years of age) in the inner city to work as interns with local businesses, where they learn work ethics, skills, and accountability. The church's "Scrubs Team"—a volunteer janitorial crew—saves $135,000 annually to put into missions. The director of urban ministries, Pastor Eli Morris, began attending Hope two months after it opened its doors and was the first staff member hired at Hope. The first week he was on the job, he was working side by side with members of Hope and members of the community building a house for a working-poor family in the inner city—something they have done twenty-five times in the past fifteen years. Twice a year Eli, leads a four-day "urban plunge" into inner-city Memphis. Over the years, every leader at Hope has been a part of one of these missional forays into the city.

How does a church get such focus? Eli's heart was touched when he was student teaching at the toughest, poorest junior high school in Memphis while a student at Memphis State. "That's where my heart flipped. The teacher I was working under was a pastor who made his living as a history teacher. His influence on me radically transformed me."

Eli speaks to every class of new members that come through the doors of Hope. As the group sits in a large circle, facing one another, Eli asks, "How much space is between us in this circle?" The answer is usually three hundred to four hundred square feet. Then Eli has everyone turn his or her chair outward and asks, "How much space is outside the circle? What you see is the focus of Hope." Then Eli adds, "If you're coming to Hope to get all your needs met, you are in the wrong place. The 'story' is *out there*, not in the church." Eli is finding that the work the church performs is not only transforming the community but also transforming the people of Hope. "Our people have found that to spend oneself on the work of the gospel is the most refreshing experience in their faith walk. To come home tired and sore with blistered hands has proved to be their new definition of the gospel. The gospel has historically been a set of doctrines and theology, which of course it is, but the new definition for our people is the gospel in sweat and blood and relationship and tears—pouring out their lives into the lives of others."

Churches that transform communities are those that are inwardly strong but outwardly focused. An increasing number of churches are rediscovering their focus and thinking differently about what church should be. These are externally focused churches—window-seat churches that measure their effectiveness not by how many congregants are sitting in the pews but rather by how many congregants are engaged in the community. These are churches that firmly believe that if they are not engaged in meeting the needs of their communities, they are not the church that Jesus called them to be. Does your church take the window seat or the aisle seat?

The Leadership Challenge

Changing seats is always difficult—especially if you've been buckled in the aisle seat for decades. Is it hard to become a window-seat church? Absolutely! But as we have opportunities to speak to pastors and Christian leaders around the world, we find ourselves saying, "As difficult as it is to get the church to go to the community, there is one thing even more difficult—getting the community to go to the church. As difficult as it is for the church to engage the community with words and works of love and grace, it is exponentially more difficult to try to entice the community into the church." Pastors and Christian leaders have the chance every week to influence the behavior and actions of the people who do come to church but have very little influence on those who do not come to church. Where are you focusing your influence?

CHAPTER 3

Purpose: They Practice Weight Training, Not Bodybuilding

I'm not looking for an audience to fill up the church; I'm looking for an army to change the world.

Pastor Danny Carroll, Water of Life Community Church,
Fontana, California

FROM THE OUTSIDE LOOKING IN, weight training and bodybuilding look nearly indistinguishable—presses, squats, thrusts, flies, pullovers, and curls. The ambient sound of weight training and bodybuilding likewise are similar—the grunts and groans, the distinctive clang of the weights hitting the floor. But as much as these activities look and sound alike, there is a huge difference in *purpose*. Athletic records are continually being shattered largely because the strength and capacity of athletes is increasing thanks to weight training. Before the 1970s, training with weights was thought to make athletes "muscle-bound," so swimmers, golfers, and baseball players rarely, if ever, touched a barbell. To be competitive today, athletes must be training with weights. For athletes, weight training is a means to a greater end—to build strength, balance, and flexibility to go "faster, higher, stronger" in a given sport. Athletic records have fallen as swimmers, runners, baseball players, football players, and even golfers spend time in the weight room. Tiger Woods changed golf forever through his commitment to weight training, but he is hardly a bodybuilder. Athletes train for their event. Their training is not the event.

Bodybuilding is different. Bodybuilders train with weights for the sole purpose of making the body as muscular, beautiful, symmetrical, and physically imposing as possible. Quarts of oil, six-pack abs, a good tan, and a smile bigger than a swimsuit are all that are required to enter a bodybuilding contest. Churches that transform communities are those that build the body of Christ not to show off the size and strength of the body but to expand the capacity for ministry and service. They are internally strong but externally focused. The church is more like a training facility than a performance stage. Kirbyjon Caldwell, pastor of Windsor Village United Methodist Church in Houston, says, "The point of church growth is not to collect new people and cage them with church programs. The goal of church health is not to fatten church members up for show. . . . The church exists to equip people, according to their calling and gifts, to be salt and light in their churches, communities, family, workplace, media, and government—in the whole society."[1]

Bodybuilding churches that focus on themselves may very well be the most impressive and best churches in their communities, but it is the weight-training church that has the chance of being the best church *for* the community.

Understanding Purpose

Understanding Ephesians 2:8–10 is pivotal in the theology of externally focused churches. We wrote extensively on this subject in our earlier books, *The Externally Focused Church* and *The Externally Focused Life*,[2] so we'll be brief. Ephesians 2:8–9 tells us *how* we are saved—by grace through faith in Christ. Ephesians 2:10 tell us *why* God saved us—to do the good works that he prepared in advance for us to do. Every person who has experienced Ephesians 2:8–9 (that is, who has been saved by grace through faith) should, *by definition,* also be experiencing Ephesians 2:10—the good works God has prepared for him or her to do! We not only have a God-shaped vacuum in our lives but also a *purpose-shaped vacuum* in our lives. That God has prepared these good works beforehand implies that these good works are ours to discover, not invent.

Understanding this has dynamic implications for leaders. The leader's job then becomes nothing less than giving every person continued opportunities to discover his or her Ephesians 2:10 calling. A worthy goal would be for everyone who is a Christ follower to be living out the good works God has created us to do. God has designed us to be his hands, feet, and voice in our world, and every major resource he gives us is given not just for personal experience but to make a difference in the world. Evangelistically, we believe that the more people who are living out their Ephesians 2:10 calling, the more people will discover grace in their Ephesians 2:8–9 calling. Let's look at a few Scriptures that help unpack this concept.

> It was he [God] who gave some to be apostles, some to be prophets, some to be evangelists, and some to be pastors and teachers, to prepare God's people for works of service.
> *Ephesians 5:11–12*

God has not sent oil boys to grease us up for competition but gifted leaders to prepare us for service. When the Word of God is preached or taught, it is not just to help us feel better about ourselves but to equip us *"for every good work."* Missional thought leader Alan Roxburgh says, "The role of the pastor is shifting from one who tends to the hurts and needs of the congregation to one who teaches and trains the congregation to tend to the hurts and needs of the community."[3]

> "All Scripture is inspired by God and profitable for teaching, for reproof, for correction, for training in righteousness; so that the man of God may be adequate, equipped for every good work." (NAS)
> *2 Timothy 3:17*

God's Word is not a protein shake to add muscle mass; it is more of an energy bar that is useful today in enabling us to do what we need to do today.

> And let us consider how we may spur one another on toward love and good deeds.
> *Hebrews 10:24*

God gives us like-minded friends to encourage us and spur us on toward making a difference. Spiritual friendships are a precious gift. Augustine, writing in the year 397, describes what we love in friends:

> To make conversation, to share a joke, to perform mutual acts of kind-
> ness, to read together well-written books, to share in the trifling and
> in serious matters, to disagree though without animosity—just as a
> person debates with himself—and in the very rarity of disagreement to
> find the salt of normal harmony, to teach each other something or
> to learn from one another, to long with impatience for those absent, to
> welcome them with gladness on their arrival. These and other
> signs come from the heart of those who love and are loved and are

expressed through the mouth, through the tongue, through the eyes, and a thousand gestures of delight, acting as fuel to set our minds on fire and out of many to forge unity. This is what we love in friends.[4]

> Each one should use whatever gift he has received to serve
> others, faithfully administering God's grace in its various forms.
> *1 Peter 4:10*

God gives us spiritual gifts not to edify ourselves but rather to "serve others." The focus is outside ourselves, for the good of others, not ourselves.

> Command those who are rich in this present world not to be
> arrogant nor to put their hope in wealth, which is so uncertain,
> but to put their hope in God, who richly provides us with
> everything for our enjoyment. Command them to do good, to be
> rich in good deeds, and to be generous and willing to share.
> *1 Timothy 6:17–18*

Wealth is entrusted to us so that we have a greater capacity "to do good, to be rich in good deeds."

Here's the point: Every major resource God has given us—leaders to prepare us, the Word to equip us, the body to encourage us, spiritual gifts to enable us, and wealth to pay for things—all points us toward *doing something* in this world. Once we really grasp this concept, ministry can be seen for what the Scriptures present it to be—an integral part of every Christ follower's life. This is not bodybuilding. It is weight training.

The Tipping Point of Growth

Each one of us instinctively seeks our own well-being in at least three areas. Using a truncated version of Abraham Maslow's "hierarchy of needs" to illustrate our point,[5] we contend that we seek first to have our basic physical needs met (see Figure 3.1).

Physical needs are basic things like food, clothing, shelter, and security. We also structure our lives in such a way that our relationships with others are working. And last of all, we seek to be connected to God. To act purposefully to see that our physical, relational, and spiritual needs are met is the practical expression of what it means to love oneself. That makes sense. We say that one can learn through good teaching, personal Bible study, preaching, reading Christian books, and so on, but we don't grow until we begin loving, serving, and giving ourselves to someone outside of friends and family. Loving those who love us comes as a natural

Figure 3.1

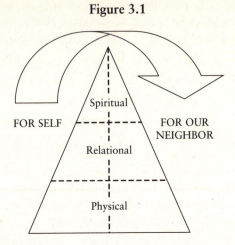

expression of being part of the human family. Jesus pointed out that everybody, including "sinners," does that (Luke 6:31–35). Real spiritual growth occurs when the physical, relational, and spiritual well-being of our neighbor is as important as our own. This is what it means to "love our neighbor as ourselves," a crucial part of the Great Commandment (Matthew 22:37–39). The theology that values the spiritual but not the physical comes from those who always have food in their stomach and slept in a warm bed last night.

People who cross the tracks or cross the ocean often find themselves thinking, "God doesn't care less for these people (or children or AIDS victims) than he cares for me. I've got to do something."

Weight Training in Boulder

In the summer of 2008, three young women, aged nineteen to twenty-two, embarked on the adventure of their lives—to Africa. They had forged a friendship over the year. Sally was a regular customer at Buchanan's Coffee Pub, across from the University of Colorado, where Leah and Andrea served as baristas. They also connected in a small Bible study group at a nearby church. Leah and Andrea were going to Africa, and they invited Sally to go along. In Sally's words, "We had absolutely no idea what we were getting ourselves into; we only knew that we were ready![6] The three young women applied to go to Uganda through a nonsectarian service placement organization called Service Learning International (ELI; http://www.eliabroad.org), and after obtaining passports and getting the requisite immunizations, they were on their way to Africa. After landing in their city and taking a leisurely tour, they came across a decrepit underresourced orphanage that was being closed by the government because of its awful condition. The women explain:

> It was a place that made your heart break. There were over 150 children living in a cramped four rooms with dirt floors and only a few doors, overflowing latrines, and absolutely no room for the kids to play. [The orphanage] was also a boarding school, but unfortunately there was an absence of electricity or windows and therefore some of the children had class in dark rooms while the others were taught outside in the blazing sun. The conditions were horrifying, and I feel that in order to fully understand, one has to go and witness it firsthand. . . . I fought back tears during my entire visit to the 150 vulnerable children. It is unthinkable to realize that these children are tucked away in an alley living lives in horrible conditions but all the while with huge smiles on their faces. We realized that something had to be done and that we were, no matter how unprepared we felt, the ones to do it.[7]

They would start a new orphanage that would be called Musana ("sunshine" in the local language) Children's Home. Sally, Andrea, and Leah understood that God cared just as much for these little ones as he cared for them, and they wanted to be the hands, feet, and voice of Jesus to each of these children. Sally and Leah have returned to Colorado to raise money for their new enterprise, while Andrea has stayed behind in Uganda to care for the children. On the plane ride home, Sally penned these words in her journal, copied from the book *Night,* written by Nobel laureate and Holocaust survivor Elie Wiesel:

> There is so much to be done, there is so much that can be done. One person . . . of integrity can make a difference, a difference of life and death. As long as one dissident is in prison, our freedom will not be true. As long as one child is hungry, our life will be filled with anguish and shame. What all these victims need above all is to know that they are not alone; that we are not forgetting them, that when their voices are stifled we shall lend them ours, that while their freedom depends on ours, the quality of our freedom depends on theirs.[8]

Because the lives of these three young women will never be the same, there will be 150 children in Uganda whose lives will never be the same.

Weight Training in Dallas

Bob Roberts of Northwood Church in Keller, Texas, ties spiritual growth and health to ministry and service. He puts it this way:

> I once believed that engaging the world and the poor was about helping them, but I've learned that serving humanity in the name of Jesus brings us far more than we give—it's the number one tool of discipleship in the world. If you truly want your church to be missional, put down your books, logs, and conferences, and touch the neediest people closest to you; then pick one spot in the world and engage however you can. You'll learn far more by doing than by reading.[9]

Weight Training in Cincinnati

Maybe learning by doing is what Chef David Falk is experiencing in Cincinnati. In May 2009, he recruited eight of Cincinnati's best chefs to prepare a dinner to celebrate the culmination of GO Cincinnati, a daylong service event involving twenty-five churches and 6,500 volunteers. David called his venture GO Grub. David has discovered the intersection of passion and purpose. He says, "I'm so glad God picked me to be a conduit for GO Grub." David is now talking about starting a social enterprise restaurant that would not only employ many people who are looking for a way out of poverty but also give all profits to charity: half to fight forced prostitution around the world and the other half to fight poverty in Cincinnati. He's learned (and grown) far more by doing than by reading.

Research

In 2006, the School of Social Work at Baylor University released the findings of its study of over 6,400 congregants from thirty-six congregations regarding the connection between service and faith. The study revealed at least two significant things:

> (1) Those who were personally involved in community ministry were not only more likely to volunteer time to help others, provide hospitality to strangers, and participate in activities promoting social justice, but also more likely to pray, attend worship service, and give financially to the church, and (2) although participating in community ministry once a week or more tended to be associated with higher scores on measures of faith, participating in worship [or] activities more frequently is *not* associated with higher scores on measures of faith.[10]

Clearly, growth and service go together.

Healthy churches and service also go together. Kevin Ford, president of TAG Consulting, administered the company's Transforming Church Index, a 110-question survey, tabulated from over 25,000 respondents. Here's what he concluded: "Nothing could have prepared me for the biggest surprise from our data. I had expected a slight gap between the two sets in 'members involved in ministry,' but what we found more closely resembled a canyon: Among healthy churches, 93 percent of members considered themselves to be involved in some form of ministry (though not necessarily at their church), compared to only 11 percent of members in the less healthy churches."[11]

No doubt about it: a healthy church is a serving church, and a serving church is a healthy church. Without service, we become like the would-be marathoner who is always carbo-loading but never racing.

Building Capacity in Young People

Another 2006 study by Baylor University's School of Social Work indicates that the best way to build and strengthen the faith of young people is not through the church service but through community service. The study of more than six hundred adolescents from thirty-five Protestant congregations also revealed a few keys to effective service. First, it must be "authentic service that meets real human needs." Second, this service must be coupled with the opportunity to process the experience with adults. They want to serve alongside adults. Third, "young people need to be partners in ministry, not solely the object of ministry." This is an important and empowering distinction for developing new generations of spiritual leaders for today as well as tomorrow." Coinvestigator Diana Garland concludes the report by writing, "This should be a compelling argument for congregational leaders to be intentional about involving parents and youth together in community ministry programs. The opportunities to help our youth grow in their faith literally are as close as the neighborhoods outside the church's door."[12]

When teens serve alongside their parents as partners in ministry, they are living out a vital experience of what it means to be authentically Christian. Researchers Thom and Sam Rainer have come to similar conclusions:

> Many of our churches are producing a lot of soft and self-centered Christians. And the young people in our churches are getting the message. . . . Churches that are outwardly focused are sending a different

message. . . . That is the irony . . . the outwardly focused church creates better inwardly focused assimilation. As our young people meet the needs of others, they see that they are important to the life of the church, and thus they are prone not to enter the ranks of the dechurched.[13]

A Different Kind of Senior Year

At LifeBridge Christian Church, Rick continually sees students and young adults take risks in service. They have time, energy, and innovation to make even more happen than young people are usually given credit for. Recently, Rick and his wife celebrated with their daughter Chelsea as she graduated from Longmont High. This year's graduation broke with tradition by having several student speakers instead of an address by an outside speaker or a favorite teacher. One of the consistent themes among those student speakers was getting involved, serving others, and staying connected by helping. This is definitely a change in direction, a very positive one. Their talks were inspirational, even to Rick, who has participated in many such ceremonies himself. He recognizes in his daughter and her peers a growing movement toward finding a way to serve and not simply a desire to "be served."

Senior year is supposed to be full of fun and final memories, yet Chelsea and three of her friends faithfully volunteered for The Closet, an "almost new" clothing center for single moms and their children. They assisted in collecting clothes and sorting and placing them on racks. They also helped at the counter during the open hours; as a result, they were invited to provide child care for many of the women they met and often did so free of charge.

Often seniors have most of their graduation credits earned and don't have to take a full schedule. Many have a "free block" during the school day. A group of students in one of Chelsea's classes spent this free time tutoring at a nearby middle school. Through a connection with the local police department, many of these students also provided mentoring opportunities for families in need. On Halloween, students went trick-or-treating for coats that were then provided to the community homeless center. More than two hundred coats were collected that Halloween night.

Through the student ministry at LifeBridge, twenty-five students planned, organized, and held a prom for students with special needs. They helped get prom gowns and tuxedos and created a special night. With tears in his eyes, one dad stood and watched his daughter get her picture taken in her gown. He said, "I have to be honest: I thought that I would never see this happen. These kids are to be commended for their compassion."

Unfortunately, when people think of Colorado and high school, they think of the Columbine tragedy. Luckily, many young people are seeing beyond fear or an apathetic attitude toward life. They are life-giving! Although Chelsea's senior year didn't make headlines, she and others made an impact on the world.

What the Willow Creek Study Revealed

In 2004, Willow Creek Community Church began a daunting research project to better determine how they could help Christians grow. Church leaders had been operating on what they termed the "church activity model," whereby "a person far from God participates in church activities" and is magically transformed into "a person who loves God and loves others."[14] Armed with this hypothetical model, they began their research. Here is one of their conclusions: "We found that church involvement drives Christian behavior somewhat, which means that the more people participate in church activities, the more likely they are to serve, tithe, etc. But higher levels of activity do not seem to drive spiritual growth, when defined as 'increasing love for God and others.' Church activity alone made no direct impact on growing the heart . . . a stunning discovery for us."[15] Church activity might be useful for bodybuilding, but it was not found to be the critical ingredient of weight training.

From Stairstep to Journey

A few years ago, Eric was leading a group of pastors in a Leadership Community for Externally Focused Churches. On the final morning of their time together, he asked a Lutheran pastor, Peter Morin, to lead the devotional. Peter is a strong communicator, and he ended his devotional by saying this: "I don't remember much from seminary, but I do remember one professor who drew this diagram on the last day of class." Peter then proceeded to draw the symbol for "infinity" (see Figure 3.2). As he continued retracing the figure eight, he quoted from his professor. "He told us that the Christian life was the journey in and the journey out. . . . We go in for renewal and out to give ourselves away to a broken world. What takes us in brings us out, and what takes us out brings us back in again. It is the rhythm of life, of balance—in and out, out and in. It's a journey, not a destination." And for Eric, the nickel dropped. That made so much sense.

Figure 3.2

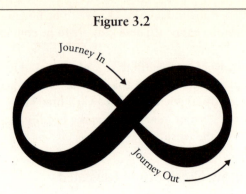

Most of us have probably been raised with a stairstep approach to Christianity. We have our 101, 201, 301, 401 classes. We run on a mantra of "Bring them in, build them up, and send them out" (see Figure 3.3). We have "discovery group," a "training group," an "action group"—and from Eric's ministry training, "Win, Build, Send." All of these formats are very linear and very modern. After all, we can't send people until they've been won and built. One can't get to third base without touching first and second bases. Folks can't attend 301 until they've first been to 101 and 201. But this view of spiritual formation that Peter explored that morning was different. The Christian life was a continuous and fresh journey of expenditure and renewal.

Eric explains:

> This was more akin to my own experience. Sure, I have skills, experience, and knowledge that I did not have thirty years ago, but I—and, I suspect, those who know me best—wouldn't necessarily say I'm a better person. The Christian life is not so much about getting better and better (after all, who could really stand us then!) but rather a journey inward to renew and the journey out to expend ourselves on a world in need.
>
> A journey in fellowship with the living God is much more descriptive of my walk and ministry.

Eric shared this diagram with one pastor, who immediately said, "That's it! That's the logo we'll use for our church!" As Eric probed deeper, the pastor explained that his leadership team had just simplified their church into just two areas, internal—all the stuff that happens inside the church—and external—everything the church does outside the four walls. "Going inward is loving God, and going outward is loving our neighbor as ourselves."

Figure 3.3

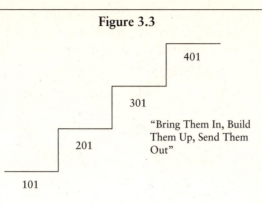

401

301

201

"Bring Them In, Build
Them Up, Send Them
Out"

101

An Even Better Discovery

In August 2007, Eric and Liz traveled with friends to Ireland and Scotland for a class called "The Celtic Trail." It was a great time of learning, discovery, and surprise. Celtic Christianity was introduced to the people of Ireland by Patrick in the early 400s. It thrived, almost as an entity unto itself, until the leaders were reined in by the Roman church leaders at the Synod of Whitby in the mid-600s. But being island communities, the Celtic Christians adapted to the new ways but never lost their unique flavor of the faith. For the Celts, Christianity did not have the pomp of the Roman Empire or the Roman church. Christ was personal. Jesus met them in the smallest and most routine tasks of life—in preparing the morning fire or milking a cow or in the sunshine of summer. They were very much Trinitarian in their beliefs, and there is strong evidence that Patrick did indeed use the shamrock to help explain the mystery of the Trinity to early converts. As Ian Bradley explains in *The Celtic Way*:

> The Celts saw the Trinity as a family. . . . For them it showed the love that lay at the very heart of the Godhead and the sanctity of family and community ties. Each social unit, be it family, clan or tribe, was seen as an icon of the Trinity, just as the hearthstone in each home was seen as an altar. The intertwining ribbons of the Celtic knot represented in simple and graphic terms the doctrine of perichoresis—the mutual interpenetration of Father, Son, and Holy Spirit.[16]

So the Celtic knot (see Figure 3.4) became a symbol of the Trinity. The knot has no beginning and no end. The Father flows into the Son and the Son into the Spirit and the Spirit into the Father.

We think Peter's diagram of the journey inward and outward (Figure 3.2) could be well augmented with the help of the Celtic knot—simply because our journey also includes people! The Celtic Christians had a flow to their lives that included three elements:

- A contemplative devotional life that strengthened their belief in God
- A desire to live and belong in community with like-minded souls on their journey
- A sense of mission that drove them to show compassion and bless the world

So they journeyed between believing, belonging, and blessing (see Figure 3.5)—renewing themselves in Christ, refreshing themselves in community, and expending themselves on the world. Unlike other monastic communities, who were big on contemplation and community but lacking in mission, the Celtic church sent out missionaries to spread the gospel from their monastic communities at Iona and Lindisfarne and elsewhere. But the blessing as they went forth implied that they would return—"May he bring you home rejoicing at the wonders he has shown you." Christ would always be on their left and on their right, above and below them, in the heart of all they spoke to.

Figure 3.4

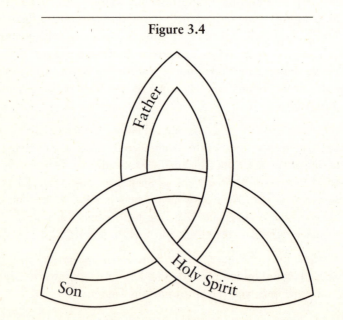

Each of us was created to *believe,* to *belong,* and to *bless.*[17] Believing is our connection to Christ, belonging is our connection to like-minded believers, and blessing is our ministry to a broken world. Now we'd like to share a couple of observations about the diagram in Figure 3.5. First, all three elements are essential for healthy Christian living. If we believe and belong without blessing, we are like a monastic community that keeps its members accountable to one another but is separate from the world. If we believe and bless without belonging, we become the type of Christian George Barna describes in is book *Revolution*—one of the 20 million Americans that have left the church because the church is not their connection point to ministry.

"These are people who are less interested in attending church than in *being* the church," he explained. "We found that there is a significant distinction in the minds of many people between the local church—with a small 'c'—and the universal Church—with a capital 'C.' Revolutionaries tend to be more focused on being the Church, capital C, whether they participate in a congregational church or not."[18]

As good as this may sound, it is important to remember the words of Ronald Rolheiser:

> A century ago, a prominent Protestant theologian, Frederick Schleiermacher, tried to point this [wanting God but not wanting the

Figure 3.5

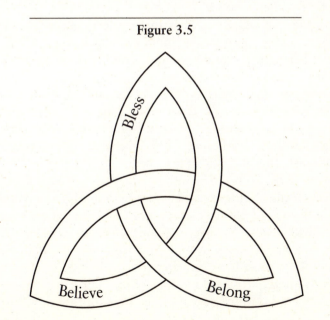

church] out in a book with a curious title: *Speeches on Religion for Those Among the Cultured Who Despise It.* Schleiermacher pointed out that, separate from historical religion, namely, the churches with all their faults, the individual in quest of God, however sincere that search, lives the unconfronted life. Without church, we have more private fantasy than real faith. . . . He submits that real conversion demands that eventually its recipient be involved in both the muck and the grace of actual church life.[19]

If we belong and bless without believing, we are akin to any other service organization, such as the Rotary Club or Meals on Wheels (as good and substantive as these organizations are). We need all three. We need to believe, belong, and bless.

The second observation we want to make is how flexible the sequencing of these three components is. Those who came of age in the late 1960s and 1970s were taught that one first had to believe before one could belong. Look at the words contained in the last page of the *Four Spiritual Laws* booklet, giving guidance to one who has just received Christ as Savior and Lord: "Several logs burn brightly together, but put one aside on the cold hearth and the fire goes out. So it is with your relationship with other Christians. If you do not belong to a church, do not wait to be invited. Take the initiative; call the pastor of a nearby church where Christ is honored and His Word is preached. Start this week, and make plans to attend regularly."[20]

Do you see the message? "Now that you believe, you can belong." Those in a younger generation would push back and say, "We invite people to belong first—to do life with us, to participate with us, and then many of these folks end up believing. For us, a person can belong way before the person believes." The Celtic knot gives us a third entry point for conversion—to be involved in blessing. We can invite nonbelievers to serve and bless with us as their first exposure to Christianity. Blessing might lead to believing and then belonging or to belonging and then believing. This is just the way it works.

A few months ago, our friend Ian Vickers from Christ Community Church in Omaha, Nebraska, told us that he invited his neighbor to come with him to an evangelistic crusade in his city. His neighbor's response? "I have absolutely no interest in going to hear an evangelist." A few months later, Ian dropped by and extended another invitation: "Hey, you want to come with me to help package 200,000 food packets for Mali, West Africa?" His neighbor responded, "Sure. Can I bring my wife and kids?" Ian says that several of his neighbors are now part of his church, and they all entered through doors of service. Blessing can also be the entry point to the faith journey, as all people are invited to serve in our world.

One final observation: notice that our variation of the Celtic knot has a space in the middle that is unnamed. What goes in this white space? We would contend that it is missional leadership, the type of leadership that acts as a dynamo, helping every person, every family, every small group go through this cycle of *believe, belong,* and *bless* on a regular basis. How could every teen be engaged? How could every senior adult be engaged? How could a single mom with three adolescent boys be engaged in *believing, belonging,* and *blessing* every three to six months? How can you, as a leader, structure the church so that every person has the opportunity—no, the experience—of *believing, belonging,* and *blessing*?

If You Want to Live Longer

Could there actually be health and longevity benefits of believing, belonging, and blessing? Research from Duke University and the University of Texas show that an "underlying belief system . . . provides comfort and improves health and that regular engagement in worship can extend one's life from seven to 14 years.[21] Want to live long? Believe.

The MacArthur Study of Successful Aging "established that people with strong social connections enjoy better health. Other studies have since shown that this translates into longer life."[22] In 2005, we heard John Ortberg speak at the National Outreach Convention in San Diego. He spoke on what kind of person God uses to change communities. In the Harvard University study he described, seven thousand people were tracked for nine years. Those who were not in community were three times as more likely to die prematurely as those who were in community. In fact, people who smoked and drank and over-ate but were in community had a better life expectancy than those with better health habits who were out of community. "Better to eat Twinkies with friends than broccoli alone." It is belonging to a group of supportive friends that leads to health and longevity. Want to live longer? Belong.

Research by the Buck Institute for Age Research found that "people who volunteer at two or more organizations have a 44 percent lower death rate than those who don't do any charitable work . . . , comparable to exercising four times a week."[23] Want to live longer? Bless. Longevity comes from a life of believing, belonging, and blessing.

For the Sake of the 98 Percent

Saint Paul's Church in Shadwell, East London, is one of the historical churches of London. Founded in 1656 and originally known as the
Church of the Sea Captains, Saint Paul's was home to explorer Captain
James Cook. It is where Thomas Jefferson's mother had been baptized—
and it had dwindled to a mere ten weekly attendees by December 2004.
The bishop of London considered closing the church and turning the
buildings into an educational facility. But this was not to be the fate of
Saint Paul's Shadwell. Holy Trinity Brompton, the birthplace of the Alpha
movement, sent a hundred of its best people in January 2005 to replant
Saint Paul's. Ric Thorpe was appointed vicar. Over a seafood dinner one
night outside of Faro, Portugal, Ric explained to Eric the mission of the
church. In his parish in Shadwell, he noted, 98 percent of the people had
no church affiliation. He then sketched out, on a napkin, the structure
of his church—a large equilateral triangle with several smaller triangles,
representing midsized communities, called "pastorates," contained within
the larger triangle (see Figure 3.6). Each corner of the triangle represented
a focus of the church's mission. Pastorates are the smaller missional communities within the church. "Up" represents worship and connection to

Figure 3.6

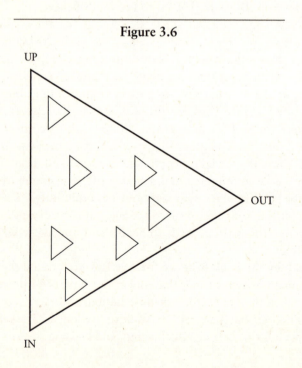

God. "In" represents community and the congregants' relationship with one another as believers. "Out" represents ministry to the city.

Ric said that each pastorate ministers to the community of Shadwell. Then he redrew the triangles as isosceles triangles and said, "Some groups are stronger on worship, while others are stronger on community, but *all* groups have a ministry to the city for the sake of the 98 percent who don't know Christ."

The Purpose of Strength

Why has God given your church a large capacity or allowed you to grow to the size you are and have the influence you have? Both of us have two sons and a daughter and count ourselves blessed for having such good kids. Eric's kids are grown and married, but when the boys were in high school and getting to be as strong as baby oxen, their parents would tell them, "Do you know why God made you strong? God made you strong to help the weak." When Andy went off to college at Arizona State University, one of his classmates, a petite girl of nineteen, put her car up for sale and soon had an interested buyer. The man asked to take her car for a drive and then, under the pretense of having to spend some money on it to get it fixed, would not return the car to her unless she paid him $250— money Megan didn't have. Talk about a scam! Megan repeatedly called the man, but he refused to return the car until the evening Megan showed up at his door. When the man demanded money from her, Megan said, "Well, I've brought some friends who might help you change your mind." Andy and his buddy Nick stepped onto the porch. Andy stands six-foot-two and wrestled for ASU. Nick was a menacing six-foot-five. The perpetrator swallowed hard and said, "I suppose you're going to kick my [butt]." "We're seriously thinking about it." He handed over the keys. God gives strength to help the weak. Power is given not to dominate but to serve.

King David's prayer in Psalm 72 for his son Solomon reflects the heart of a father that understood the place of power. As Solomon assumed the throne of Israel, David prayed that Solomon would use his power for the benefit of others and not just to aggrandize himself. He prayed that his son would use his power to care for the poor, help orphans, speak up for immigrants, and defend the defenseless. What is the purpose of influence? To speak up for those without influence. What is the purpose of power? To speak up for those without power. Why did God make you strong? To defend the weak.

If your church is strong and has influence, these assets were not given just to make your church bigger and stronger. Rather the strength and capacity are to be used to help others. So what do you have that you can use to help those outside the church? In the spring of 2009, in the midst of the global recession, leaders from Calvary Community Church in Westlake Village, California, took a special offering to help the hurting in their community. The congregation stepped forward with $60,000 to help those outside the church who were facing financial setbacks.

Depth and Frequency of Engagement

If you want to build strength, increase your capacity, and have a sustained influence and impact in your community, there are two measurements to think about—externally focused *depth of engagement* and externally focused *frequency of engagement*. A few years ago, Eric was talking with Eli Morris from Hope Presbyterian Church outside of Memphis. Over a plate of ribs at Neely's Bar-B-Que, Eli sketched three concentric circles depicting how he gauges the spiritual progress of folks at his church. "There are people who give money and things, there are people who engage in projects, and there are people who engage with people. Life change happens when people engage with people, so we want to move people from the outer circle (those who give money and things) to the inner circle (those who engage in ministering to people)." Wow! That was very insightful. Let's look at each of these levels of engagement.

Money and Things

If you are honest, you would probably admit that giving money and things is pretty painless and doesn't stretch you much. Giving money and things to those outside of family and friends is a good thing but at the end of the day may not change us much. Martha Manning once said, "My idea of perfect charity was to help people without actually having anything to do with them."[24] Throwing a ten-spot in the plate or giving a toy for tots, a shoebox of love, or a winter coat is a good thing. Money and things is a good starting point but not a good ending point.

Projects

As you engage in projects, you give more of yourself—your time and talents—to causes that God cares about in your community. Projects might include building a Habitat for Humanity home or refurbishing rooms at the local safe house. In June 2004, Eric's home church, Calvary Bible Evangelical Free Church of Boulder, deployed more than seven hundred people to clean, paint, landscape, and refurbish an elementary school, middle school, and high school in the community. In 2005, the church joined with people from two other churches in town to paint, landscape, and clean five more local public schools. Sixteen hundred people engaged in this incredible project, dubbed "SHAREFEST 2005." Apart from the labor, people from churches wrote notes of appreciation to the faculty and staff of these five schools. On Sunday morning, these three churches canceled their own services and held a joint service on the University of Colorado campus at which they honored school board officials and school faculty and administrators. The school board estimated that the churches' actions saved the district an estimated $300,000. Afterward, some sixteen hundred people gathered on the lawns of the campus to enjoy Memphis barbecue (a pattern to his life seems to be emerging). Calvary Bible senior pastor Tom Shirk wrote of this experience to those who served:

> Did not our hearts overflow with joy as we celebrated the incredible service at Mackey Auditorium? What a historic gathering! 1,600 people from three churches worshiping the living Christ with triumphant joy on CU's campus! It was the culmination of a weekend of outstanding service which reinforced for us the unexpected lesson: it's more fun to WORK together than to PLAY together! Please, please, please, appreciate the spiritual reality of this past weekend. . . . Serving together in SHAREFEST 2005 was the richest experience of joy we have ever known.

Serving in projects together brings joy and growth and helps make the invisible kingdom visible to those around us. By the summer of 2009, more than thirty churches had come together for six different days in the "Summer of Service" to work in schools and nonprofit organizations. Rick's LifeBridge Christian Church was named "St. Vrain Valley School District's Volunteer of the Year for 2009" for its continued engagement with schools in the community.

People

As helpful as money and projects can be, lives are most likely to be changed when people engage with people. People feel their worth only when affirmed by other people. Good deeds can be done from afar, but good news can only be shared up close. Love is a shared experience. Engaging with people might include helping third graders read, youth mentoring, job skills training, or working with orphans on a mission trip. Part of the path of spiritual formations is to move from giving money and things to engaging in projects and sharing your life and love with people. Omar Reyes of Northwood Church in Keller, Texas, sees people working with people as crucial to service. "When people serve, something happens. When they make contact with people, something happens to the heart; there's a joy that they sense that only comes from God. And if I can get them to feel that, they'll only want more. And so we create these opportunities to connect them with people. My job is to create all these avenues to really move our people out into the community."[25]

Frequency of Engagement

The other measurement of engagement is *frequency*. If giving of your resources, talents, and love is beneficial to you and those you serve, it could also be argued that greater frequency would increase the benefits to those serving and those being served. In other words, if engaging in giving, serving, and loving once a year is beneficial, wouldn't five times a year be even more beneficial? For illustration's sake, we could keep track of our serving on a yearly, quarterly, monthly, and weekly basis. We've devised the grid in Figure 3.7 on which to do just that.

Figure 3.7

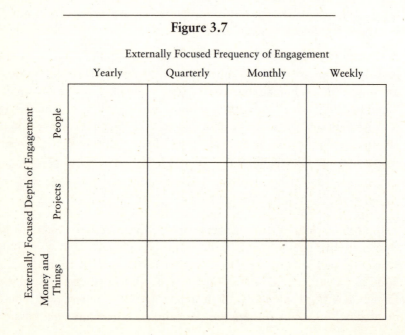

Externally Focused Frequency of Engagement

On a grid like this, you can plot your own current level and frequency of engagement as well as that of others in your congregation. Most likely, if you were to use dots to represent congregational engagement, the chart would be weighted toward the left and toward the bottom—perhaps as shown in Figure 3.8.

Part of the leadership challenge is to help people move in greater depth and with greater frequency this year than they did last year. "If you gave money and things last year, let's engage in a project or two this year. If you've been involved in projects for a while, let's see if you can try your hand at working with people." So if people are engaging in greater depth and with greater frequency, we should expect the church "scatter plot" to look more like Figure 3.9.

Here's one more thing to think about: what we are really addressing here is spiritual formation. Spiritual formation is about growing the size of our heart. Our friend Jack Jezreel of JustFaith Ministries reminds us that all spiritual formation is about growing the size of our heart— moving from the (*phileo*) love of the preferential (friends and family; ours and mine) to the wide, boundless (*agape*) love of the unconditional. What prevents us from engaging in greater depth and frequency is the size of our heart. It is our limited heart size that limits our capacity to selflessly serve others. We need to remember that our hearts do not grow stronger

---

Figure 3.8

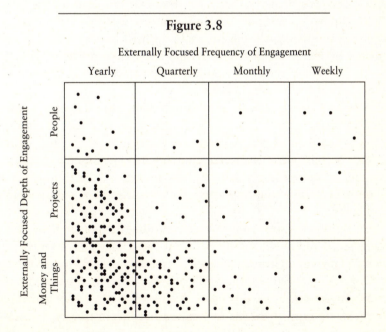

Figure 3.9

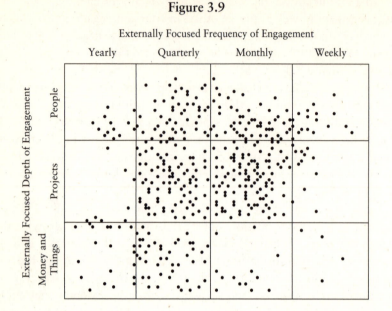

Externally Focused Frequency of Engagement

before we exercise but only after we exercise. Spiritual formation has a simple and practical measurement: "Who do you have room in your heart for this year that you didn't have room in your heart for last year?" "Whom are you serving, loving, and ministering to that can do nothing for you in return?" Jack suggests that all Christ followers need to have someone in their lives, apart from friends and family, that they are loving and giving themselves to that can do nothing in return. As simple as it sounds, this is really very challenging.

Recently, Eric was talking to a church planter friend about requirements for membership. With Jack's thought at the forefront of his mind, he suggested that all people can participate in the life of the church, but they become members of that church when they bring to the pastor the name of one person whom they are loving, serving, and ministering to that can do nothing for them in return. That'd be quite a church, wouldn't it?

One thing we know about weight training is that the heart is not strengthened and muscles don't grow until after they are exercised. This helps explain why, in increasing depth or frequency, we feel overchallenged most of the time. But what if God's plan for his church was to build a community of big-hearted people? With increased engagement comes increased discomfort but also increased fulfillment (see Figure 3.10).

Figure 3.10

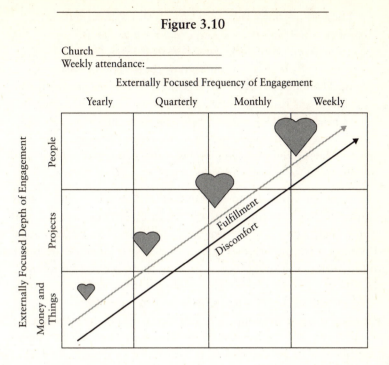

Church _____
Weekly attendance: _____

If you think of the people you know who are most fulfilled, most likely they are big-hearted people who are loving and serving others.

Without belaboring the point, we think you can see how helpful a tool this chart can be.

"I Need a Prayer!"

This is where the rubber hits the road, so to speak. It is in serving people that most of us have had our faith stretched or challenged. Every once in a while, we are blessed to see this combination of service and spiritual growth come alive. One of Rick's favorite moments happened in the LifeBridge church lobby one weekend. John (not his real name) came up to Rick between services and said he needed a prayer. Rick explains:

> I figured he needed me to pray for him about something. People often stop me after our worship services, and he had probably seen me praying with folks in the lobby. But to my surprise, he really wanted "a prayer." He said to me, "I don't need you to pray for me. I need

you to write one down and give it to me." This was one of those curious moments in ministry that keeps leadership interesting!

"Why do you need me to write a prayer for you, John?" I asked.

He said, "I volunteer sometimes down at the Inn Between [a transitional housing unit] as a trim carpenter. I was getting an apartment cleaned up and ready for a new resident. While I was in the lobby taking a break, one of the residents heard I went to church here. He told me he had a lot of trouble and asked me to pray for him. I told him, 'Dude, I don't know how to pray, but I will get one and be back.' So Rick, I need you to write me a prayer!"

Rick took a few minutes to explain that he didn't need anyone to write out a prayer for him, that he already had the words inside, but Rick offered to help him get the words out. John also went to the bookstore and bought a couple of books on prayer. "Next time we are teaching about prayer at LifeBridge, guess who is probably paying attention?" notes Rick. Service encounters almost always provide an opportunity for growth, no matter where a person is in spiritual maturity.

Rick sees people show up to LifeBridge worship services week after week who are looking for something. Some are looking for hope and grace and peace. Some come looking for God or to grow in their relationship with him. Pretty much everyone comes looking for a way to make their lives count.

At LifeBridge, Rick speaks in terms of three things he wants to see happen. He often tells his congregation to "Discover Grace, Grow in Grace, and Live Gracefully." He explains:

> *Discover Grace.* Our hope is that when people discover grace—Christ and God's gift of grace through the cross—that they will have an eternity change.
> *Grow in Grace.* We also hope that we can help them grow in understanding that grace. As a result of knowing Christ, we want them to have a life change.
> *Live Gracefully.* We also want them to get engaged in living out grace—to find ways to serve and allow grace to show up in how they live. We want to help them change their part of the world.

Eric and Rick have both heard a number of different ways to say these same things. What language do you use or need to develop to clarify your mission and vision for the local church? Whatever language you use, we believe it imperative that it includes always *moving* people toward finding greater significance and purpose in serving God. Jesus invites us to get engaged deeper and with greater frequency. Yes, that means it gets messier. But like a child who sees a mud puddle for the first time, let's touch it with grace and see what God does as a result!

The Leadership Challenge

Lately, when Eric has the opportunity to address an audience, he'll ask this question: "How many here want to change the world? If you want to change the world, raise your hand." With the exception of those who are writing down the question, every hand goes up. And then while the hands are still raised, he often adds this caveat: "Isn't it sad how few people are regularly given the opportunity to do so?" What if the church became the place where people could regularly be given the opportunity to engage the world in such a way that it would somehow be different, that something or someone would be better because of them? At the end of the year, what if your one evaluative question to every person under your watch was expressed in the question "How has God used you to change the world this past year?" Could you imagine what it would be like to have a congregation of fifty, five hundred, or five thousand, each with an answer to that question and a story to tell? The job of a leader is to provide the theology, motivation, and opportunity for every Christ follower to have a positive answer to that question.

Building on a conversation about changing the world, Eric's son Andy added his insight: "What if church were a place where you could say, 'Come to my church. We'll help you change the world.' What if that became the best reason for inviting someone to church? The invitation is not 'We have the best preaching, teaching, worship, or youth program,' but rather 'We'll help you change the world.'" If everyone wants to change the world, then why not structure church so that people are given regular opportunities to do so?

CHAPTER 4

Story: They Live in the Kingdom Story, Not a Church Story

When our works supersede our words, God's kingdom shows up.

Murray Robertson, senior pastor, Spreydon Baptist Church,
Christchurch, New Zealand

In November 2007, Eric and a friend attended a three-day seminar called "Story" led by the screenwriter Robert McKee. McKee's former students have garnered 27 Academy Awards and 141 Emmy Awards for their screenwriting. Many of the movies and TV shows you enjoy, such as *Forrest Gump, The Da Vinci Code, CSI,* and *Law and Order,* are products of McKee's students. (If you want to see the impact of McKee's teaching, rent the movie *Adaptation* starring Nicolas Cage, in which Cage actually attends a McKee seminar.) McKee starts promptly at 9:00 A.M. on Friday morning and does not accept people being tardy. Anyone with a pager or cell phone that goes off is immediately fined $10. A second offense means expulsion from the class. Absolutely no talking is allowed in class. These are the kinds of rules one can make if one is so successful and prominent that people compromise their personal freedoms to get what they really want: to become a master of the good story well told.

McKee begins by telling us that the world has an insatiable appetite for stories. We just can't get enough of them. He says, "Writing a great story is why God put you on this earth." The seminar was an incredible experience. McKee, who is in his late sixties, lectured from 9:00 A.M. to 8:30 P.M. for three consecutive days, allowing only three fifteen-minute breaks and one hour for lunch. There was no interaction, just straight lecture—and all eighty people in attendance loved every moment. All of us were amazed at his skill and coveted his passion for communication. He is a student of humanity. The things he said about story writing were very insightful. "A great story does two things: first, it transports you to a world you've never been to, and second, once you are there, you find yourself in the story." Wow! Think about your favorite movies or stories. Isn't that what they did?

Jesus was this kind of storyteller. The story of the Good Samaritan transports us to a place we've never been to (on the road leading from Jerusalem to Jericho), and once we are there, we find ourselves in the story—as priest, Levite, bystander, victim, Samaritan, innkeeper, or donkey. In the parable of the Prodigal Son, where are we? Who are we? McKee, quoting Aristotle, says that the ending of a story should give listeners what they want—but not what they expect. This is probably why parables are so memorable. They give us surprise endings. It is the unlikely Samaritan who is the hero. It is the father putting his best robe on the shoulders of his rebellious son. It is all the laborers receiving the same wage even though they worked for differing lengths of time.

What Kind of Story Have We Been Telling?

Tim Keller, pastor of Redeemer Presbyterian Church, tells us that "every 'world-view' has to answer the question: 'what is wrong with life and how can it be fixed?' Every world-view singles out some part of the good creation as being the main source of the problem (thus 'demonizing' something) and singles out some other part of the fallen creation as being the main solution."[1] So a Marxist worldview would have one diagnosis and one cure, as would the moralist, a free-market economist, a right-wing conservative, a left-wing liberal, and an evangelical Christian. The story or worldview Eric adopted, believed, and shared with others, using Keller's construct, went something like this: What is wrong with the world is sin—humanity's rebellion against God. People were created to have a relationship with God, but they sinned against God and that relationship with God was broken. What was the solution? Jesus came to earth, lived a sinless life, and so was able to die in our place. Jesus' death and resurrection make it possible for people who put their faith in him to be restored to a relationship with God and go to heaven when they die. As more people are transformed through a right relationship with God, societies are transformed and our world is changed. This is all true—but it's not complete.

It is personal but not comprehensive. The facts are correct, but that's not the story. In the paraphrased words of the English novelist E. M. Forster, "A fact is that the queen died and the king died. A story is that the queen died and the king died of a broken heart."[2] Is there a fuller story to tell?

The Rest of the Story

A fuller or thicker story might go something like this: In the beginning, when God created the world, everything was good. Man's relationship with God was good, man's relationship with fellow man (or at least Eve) was good, and man's relationship with the world was good. In Eden there was wholeness. Man and woman lived in harmony with their environment and talked freely and openly with God. They were knowing recipients of God's good gifts. There was physical work to be done in the garden, tending plants and nurturing fruit-bearing trees. They were told they could eat and enjoy the fruits of their labor. There was also work to be done that would summon the best of their creativity in naming the animals, with the finality that "whatever the man called each living creature, that was its name" (Genesis 2:19).

Man and woman were not only in fellowship with God; they were in partnership with God—perhaps not full partners, but junior partners. God created the living plants in the garden, but man was given the responsibility to "work it and take care of" the garden (Genesis 2:15). God "created the beasts of the field and all the birds of the air" (Genesis 2:19), but he entrusted to man the responsibility of naming each animal. Man was also created for leadership in God's dominion. There were no creatures formed that were higher in God's creative hierarchy than man himself. It was humankind who was created to "rule over the fish of the sea and the birds of the air, over the livestock . . . and over all the earth" (Genesis 1:26). The climate was such that man had no need of clothing and there was seemingly no need, or at least mention, of permanent shelter.

In this idyllic setting, God was clearly in charge. It was his domain, and he set boundaries defining what was and was not permissible. Man lived in harmony with woman—a partner taken from his own flesh. Her well-being was attached to and could not be separated from his well-being and his good. They would be united as one and be called husband and wife—terms that have meaning only in the context of the corresponding opposite. Man was a steward and trustee of the earth. But then there was a great interruption.

The Inciting Incident

The Fall is what McKee would call the "inciting incident." The inciting incident is the scene in the story that throws life out of balance and begs for resolution. This great God story's interruption was called "sin," and everything changed. Man's relationship with God was broken. I imagine that when Adam and Eve were walking out of Eden after being expelled, Adam may have turned to Eve and said something like, "OK, we really blew it, and I do feel a bit of spiritual emptiness, but this is still a great place to live." But sin's reach affected personal relationships. Imagine the pain and grief when Adam and Eve discovered that one of their boys was dead and the other was a murderer! Adam probably turned to Eve and most likely uttered the first curse word, something like "#@&*! This sin thing is way bigger than I imagined." Sin affected humanity's relationship not only with God and one another but also with the environment—the world God placed them in. No longer would the earth bring forth its fruit. Adam and Eve would have to labor to make the earth productive. Moreover, the earth was now broken, and there would be earthquakes, tornados, hurricanes, erupting volcanoes, and tsunamis that would ripple down through millennia, destroying both property and innocent lives (Luke 13:4). Romans 8:22 reminds us that because of sin, the "whole creation has been groaning as in the pains of childbirth right up to the present time."

Brokenness was not the way that God intended things to be. It was the aberration of a broken world filled with violence or indifference toward and hatred of neighbor, exploitation of the weak, tribal factions, pride, covetousness, drunkenness, marital strife, conniving, and chicanery.[3] Once the people in the audience see the inciting incident, they know a scene is coming that resolves and restores a new balance. There must be another scene—the "mandatory scene."

The "Mandatory Scene"

This "mandatory scene," as McKee calls it, is necessary for all stories. Our mandatory scene is the redemptive plan that God would bring forth through his son, in his timing. In the fullness of time, Jesus came to earth and lived his life doing exactly what God the Father wanted him to do, culminating with his death on the cross to pay for the sin of the whole world. He didn't die only to restore humanity's relationship with God (if that were not enough); his death is the basis of reconciliation between people and also with creation itself. The apostle Paul tells us in Colossians 1:19–20, "For God was pleased to have all his fullness dwell in him, and through him to reconcile to himself all things, whether things on earth or things in heaven, by making peace through his blood, shed on the cross."

Everything that was lost in the Fall was redeemed through the cross and will one day be fully restored. After Jesus' conversation and interaction with Zacchaeus, he says, "For the Son of Man came to seek and to save what was lost" (Luke 19:10). Certainly he came to seek and save the lost, but even more important, he came to seek and save *what* was lost. Everything that sin and the Fall took away, Jesus came to restore and make new. That's what makes the gospel such incredibly good news!

In response to the observable brokenness of the world, we often hear people today say, "It is what it is." But we believe there is more. As Christ followers, we should find ourselves saying, "It is what it is, but it's not as it's supposed to be, can be, and some day will be." How would that look on a T-shirt?

An Unexpected Ending

McKee said that the ending of a story should give hearers what they want but not what they expect. The Austrian philosopher and priest Ivan Illich "was once asked what is the most revolutionary way to change society. Is it violent revolution or is it gradual reform? He gave a careful answer. Neither. If you want to change society, then you must tell an alternative story."[4] Where's the unexpected in our stories? We've been telling the church story and are currently living out the consequences of that story. But what if we understood and told the kingdom story?

McKee informs us that there is no story without conflict. "These men who have caused trouble all over the world have now come here. . . . They are all defying Caesar's decrees, saying that there is another king, one called Jesus" (Acts 17:6–7). The kingship of Jesus was an affront to the kingdom of Caesar, and that was enough conflict to warrant the death of Jesus and persecution of the disciples. McKee also tells us that there is no love story without a rival. The love story is between Jesus and his Bride (the church), and Satan is rivaling for our affection and allegiance. This creates what is recognized as a love triangle. Every scene in the movie ends with a choice that defines the character of the central characters. The harder the choice, the better defined the character becomes. Isn't it satisfying to know that the conclusion of every scene of history is God choosing us? It defines who he is. Now, will we choose him?

The Importance of the Kingdom

How important is the kingdom? The word *kingdom* is mentioned 152 times in the (NIV) New Testament and 116 times in the Gospels (NIV). (By contrast, the word *church* is mentioned just three times in the Gospels—all in the book of Matthew.) The first public words of John the Baptist and Jesus in the gospel of Matthew were to announce the kingdom (Matthew 3:2, 4:17). The first prayer request that Jesus taught his disciples was "Thy kingdom come . . ." (Matthew 6:10). The first priority of the believer was to seek God's kingdom (Matthew 6:33). The kingdom was to be the central message of the apostle's teaching (Matthew 10:7), and the "bookend" passages of the book of Acts (Acts 1:3, 28:31) are all about the kingdom. The apostle Paul mentioned the kingdom no less than sixteen times in his writing and in his speeches. So how did we lose the kingdom? Why has the kingdom been relegated to a future residence? How was "kingdom" co-opted and replaced by "church?"

In his book *The Unshakable Kingdom and the Unchanging Person,* the great missionary statesman E. Stanley Jones writes:

> The three historic creeds, summing up Christian thought and doctrine among them, mention once what Jesus mentioned a hundred times. The greatest loss that has ever come to the Christian movement in its long course in history was this loss of the Kingdom. For the thing that Jesus called the Good News, the Gospel, has been lost. Not silenced, but lost as the directive of the movement. The Christian movement went riding off in all directions without goal and without power to move on to that goal. The substitutes became the goal. . . . A crippled Christianity went across the Western world, leaving a crippled result. A vacuum was created in the soul of Christendom; the Kingdom of God became an individual experience now and a collective experience in heaven. . . . Vast areas of life were left out, unredeemed—the economic, the social, and the political.[5]

All this talk of the kingdom begs the question "What is the kingdom?" The answer we've come up with is that "the kingdom of God is any place over which God has operative dominion." Although God is the creator of everything and everyone (Psalm 24:1), the kingdom of God extends to those social structures, geographical areas, or regions of the human heart where God's reign is effective. The kingdom is where the king is reigning. So if Jesus is reigning as king in your own life, "the kingdom of God is within you" (Luke 17:21). The kingdom is often referred to as being both "present and not yet," meaning that the reign of God is currently active but will one day culminate in the full expression of his reign. That will be the day that the "kingdom of the world has become the kingdom of our Lord and of his Christ, and he will reign for ever and ever" (Revelation 11:15). That's a great ending.

Comparing the Church and the Kingdom

What happened to the kingdom? Perhaps it is helpful to distinguish between kingdom and church. In doing so, we admire the words of Howard Snyder: "Kingdom people seek first the Kingdom of God and its justice; church people often put church work above concerns of justice, mercy and truth. Church people think about how to get people into the church; Kingdom people think about how to get the church into the world. Church people worry that the world might change the church; Kingdom people work to see the church change the world."[6] We sometimes forget that God designed the church to be a venue where God's kingdom is realized and made visible in our communities. The church does not exist for itself. The church exists to proclaim and demonstrate that the kingdom is near.

What's the biggest difference between "church" thinking and "kingdom" thinking? Here's a list we've come up with; you can probably make your own additions to it.

CHURCH	KINGDOM
Local	Global
Internal focus	External focus
Great Commission	Missio Dei
Propositional truth	God's narrative story
Monologue	Dialogue
Exclusive	Inclusive
At center of society	Central to society
Evangelism is the goal	Evangelism is starting point
Stairstep growth	Journey
Programs	Organic
Gospel of salvation	Gospel of the kingdom
Proclamation evangelism	Proclamation and demonstration
The gospel explained	The gospel lived out
Sunday	Every day
Addresses only the soul	Affects all aspects of society
Rapture—escape mentality	Material, social, earthly, secular
Sacred versus secular	Integration of sacred in the secular
Growing *my* church	Growing *the* church
Focus on transaction	Focus on transformation
You go to church	Wherever the church is, you encounter the kingdom

What Is Kingdom Work?

In the broadest sense, anytime we are involved in making this world more reflective of the place that God will ultimately make it in the coming kingdom, we are involved in kingdom work. A bigger, thicker story creates a space for those who are not yet members of God's kingdom to be engaged in kingdom work through medicine, teaching, peace making, orphan adoption, drought relief, AIDS/HIV ministry, clean drinking water, and other causes.

Here's something to think about: millions of people around the world are aware of the fact that "things aren't the way they are supposed to be"—that something is broken. N. T. Wright, in his book *Simply Christian*, refers to this awareness as echoes of the voice of God that remind every person that something is broken and flawed, that things are not the way God created them to be. The four echoes are the longing for justice, the quest for spirituality, the hunger for relationships, and the delight in beauty.[7] Those compassionate souls who are working to end sex trafficking or to dig wells in Africa are listening to the echoes and recognize that they are fixing something that is broken. Those who are concerned about global climate change, water pollution, and the number of CO_2 particles circulating in the air may be passionate about fixing those things because they sense that things aren't what they are supposed to be. They may not know the theology, but they do know that all of creation is groaning as it awaits redemption, and they want to be part of that redemption. Rather than writing this very large segment of society off as secularists, liberals, environmentalists, or the like, why not use this common awareness of brokenness to connect them to the larger story?

Daniel Pink, in *A Whole New Mind*, writes, "Humans are not ideally set up to understand logic; they are ideally set up to understand stories."[8] More important, we believe they long to be part of a meaningful story. After all, there are no bit players in the story God is writing. Some people sense that people are disconnected from God; others sense a certain solidarity with those who hurt; still others sense the brokenness of the world. Some want to save lives, others want to save the planet, and others want to save souls. The point is that all of these can play a part in God's redemptive story.

Isn't This Work for the Church?

Yes! And God would love to use the church first, but when the church isn't paying attention, he will raise up others who will do the work. He raised up Artaxerses, Cyrus, and Nebuchadnezzar (Isaiah 10:12–19, 45:1–6), whom he describes as his tools to accomplish his work. With this in mind, we see that there is plenty of room for the likes of Bill and Melinda Gates, Warren Buffett, Bono, Richard Branson, and Angelina Jolie to carry out God's bigger story. God's kingdom work is accomplished by believers and unbelievers—often working side by side. Who fetched the water for Jesus' first miracle in John 2? Not the believing disciples; it was the servants who fetched the water and brought the wine to the wine steward. It was the Asiarchs, the secular officials of Ephesus, who were identified as "friends" of Paul who gave Paul friendly counsel (Acts 19:30–32 NAS). The best advice and counsel Moses received was from his Midian father-in-law, Jethro (Exodus 18; Deuteronomy 1). God's work often involves people of good faith working alongside people of goodwill. We'll talk more of these unlikely partnerships in Chapter Six.

Becoming Part of the Kingdom

At this point, it is important to affirm that kingdom work does not in any way merit our entrance into the God's kingdom (Matthew 7:21–23). Jesus gave the crystal-clear requisite for entering the kingdom of heaven in John 3. In his discourse with Nicodemus, Jesus told him, "I tell you the truth, no one can enter the kingdom of God unless he is born of water and the Spirit. . . . I tell you the truth, no one can enter the kingdom of God unless he is born again" (John 3:3–5). Anyone and everyone who enters the kingdom will come through the same door as Nicodemus—by faith.

Creating Something Better

We are usually very quick to point out the shortcomings of the culture and society we live in. We are art critics, but are we willing to be artists? James Boyce gives these pointed comments:

> Until we produce our own quality art, our hysterical denunciations of what is admittedly "artistic trash" will fall on deaf ears. Until we show how Christians in government can and should function, being concerned not just for our rights and privileges but for the good of all and with justice for all, we will rightly be ignored. . . . [Quoting an associate,] "If we have not paid our dues by years of making positive contributions to culture, we simply do not have the cultural clout to pontificate about cultural crises." Only by participating in such cultural endeavors and thus by modeling what we believe can and should be done will we gain a hearing and actually begin to effective.[9]

We tell a better story by modeling a better story and inviting others to be a part of that story. The acts of mercy depicted in Matthew 25:31–46 (feeding the hungry, giving water to the thirsty, welcoming the stranger, clothing the naked, comforting the sick, and visiting the prisoner) would be a good starting point for any church or individual that desires to be more kingdom-minded. These are not church growth strategies but rather an extension of what Jesus wants his church to be doing in the world and something for which we will need to give an account. It seems that we do these acts of mercy not to convert others but because we ourselves have been converted. Are you doing anything to feed, provide clean water, clothe, welcome, comfort, or visit those who need to experience God's touch on their lives?

A very popular question in recent years has been "What Would Jesus Do?" It's a good question, but to determine what Jesus would do, we must look and see what he did. We see him looking at the community (people) with compassion. We see him disrupt the tired, worn-out ways in which things had always been done. We see him meeting physical needs while engaging spiritual needs. Jesus clearly viewed the world through kingdom lenses.

A Kingdom Experiment

About a year ago, Rick's church began an experiment with several of its small groups of four to six couples. It involved some basic teaching on money and stewardship. With each group's permission, church leaders tracked the giving that the individuals in each group gave to the church and at the end of each month gave back to the group half of what its members gave. For example, if the group gave collectively $1,000, it got $500 back, with the promise that the group look for kingdom opportunities in which to invest those returned dollars.

One of the guidelines was that people could not channel the funds to a relative or friend. They were instructed to look and pray for opportunities to use those dollars to meet real needs. Here are a few examples of how that money was used:

- One group adopted a nearby low-income elementary school and provided resources that the principal used for various students. Those dollars went toward school supplies, coats and clothing, after-school program costs, or special needs that the principal noticed among the students.
- Another group helped a family whose home had burned down and also gave money to a family in which both parents had lost their jobs.
- One group helped a single mom with car repairs.

We have learned a few things from this experiment in kingdom giving. The groups were both blessed and challenged by looking for ways to use the resources. Lots of discussion, prayer, and vetting out real needs occurred. Many people who had previously felt that they had no real control over how their giving was being used liked that they had an opportunity to direct the resources and see the results. Interestingly, all groups except one saw an increase in giving—the same group that struggled with what to do with the dollars. It wasn't long before the half the church was keeping for the general fund was greater than what the whole had been previously. As people got more engaged in kingdom thinking and seeing where their investment went, their giving and hearts grew.

One real blessing was watching how a group got engaged not only financially but often in much more physical ways. Rick explains:

> My son David and his wife, Brittany, were in one of the experimental giving groups with other young couples. Their group gave money to help a family who had three children, and one of the three has special needs. The dad lost his job, and this group helped meet some of the family's financial needs during the transition. David and Brittany even started turning down my dinner invitations because they were babysitting. I assumed it was for another family member, but David said, "No, the family our group is helping has been taking turns watching the special-needs child so that the parents could do some shopping and other things." The group engaged relationally as a result of getting engaged financially. Jesus did have something to say about treasure and heart, didn't he?

The church did have to make some adjustments in the experiment along the way. One group had an individual whose giving was significant. This person agreed that only a small percentage of his giving would be counted in the small group's overall total so as not to dilute the gifts of all the others in the group. The church also had to establish some basic guidelines for who would be eligible to receive church funds and for complying with IRS donation and record-keeping requirements.

This experience has taught Rick's congregation that the fifty-fifty approach is an excellent way to achieve kingdom giving, The small financial risk to the church is well worth the risks taken for the kingdom.

The More Compelling Story

How compelling is it when we tell a kingdom story rather than simple a church story? Just ask staff at Whittier Area Church in Whittier, California.[10]

While most churches would see the Christmas Eve offering as a good year-end giving opportunity for the church, Whittier put on kingdom glasses and saw potential for supporting more than the church. Leaders were challenged to get involved in the AIDS crisis in Africa and set a goal to collect $150,000 on Christmas Eve in 2006. It was a stretch, as the congregation's largest Christmas Eve offering to that point had been $27,000.

The news that the Christmas Eve offering would be given exclusively to the AIDS crisis spread like wildfire. The entire community was invited to view an AIDS video featuring Bono that had been shown at the Willow Creek Leadership Summit, and the community was also invited to join the service and participate in giving.

Scores of people came to Whittier's Christmas Eve service. The moment of giving to the Malawi Children's Hospital was a highlight of the service. "Women and men wept as they gave because many people really gave sacrificially. Children had lemonade stands to raise money, and one couple gave up fertility treatments so they could give to this cause," says Colleen Marks, community pastor for Whittier. When the offering was counted the next day, the senior pastor, William Ankerberg, was like a father in a waiting room. "It was finally announced that our church of 2,400 people had raised $518,000 for the children's hospital in Malawi! To raise $150,000 was a stretch for us, but to go so much beyond taught me that God is so much bigger than us. He is a God of abundance," she says.

The next weekend, people gave $300,000 to the general fund at Whittier Area Church in addition to the Malawi offering—another record-breaking moment for the church. "In the aftermath of this, many have sponsored children from Malawi, and others have a strong desire to visit there and be a part of the mission there. People are hungering to reach out and look beyond themselves. I'm grateful I am at a church where giving and serving is the heartbeat of who we are," says Colleen.

If Jesus Were Mayor

In 2004, Bob Moffitt of Harvest Foundation released a book titled *If Jesus Were Mayor*. What a fascinating thought as it relates to the kingdom of God! How would things be different if Jesus was in charge? What kind of story would unfold? Moffitt poses these profound questions:

- What would He do about street children and the homeless?
- What would He do about alcoholism, drug abuse, and other addictions?
- How would He strengthen families?

- How would He promote safe drinking water, adequate housing and food, health services, garbage and sewer systems, and decent roads?
- What would He do about fair wages and adequate employment?
- What would He do about unwanted children and care for the sick and elderly?
- What would He do to bring beauty—clean streets, trees, flowers, and public parks?
- What would He do in the education of children and adults?[11]

This is a challenging thought, isn't it? But when we are praying, "Thy kingdom come, thy will be done on earth as it is in heaven," isn't this what we are asking for, the practical expression of Jesus' reign? What would it look like to pray, "Thy kingdom come, thy will be done in [your city] as it is in heaven"? What would your city look like?

Vintage Vineyard

What happens when a church engages outside the walls? Could a kingdom-minded, externally focused church really help bring about some of the transformation that Bob Moffit posits is possible? In 2007, Reggie McNeal and Eric, through Leadership Network, started something called the Missional Renaissance Leadership Community. This community met four times for two days in an eighteen-month period and was made up of ten senior pastors, who were asked to bring with them an associate pastor, a city official, a CEO of a business, and an executive director of a major nonprofit organization. This first community was great! It had mayors and executive directors of United Way and art museums. It had CEOs of nationally known businesses. By gathering together with cross-domain leaders, Eric and Reggie hoped to accomplish things church leaders alone could not accomplish—and they were not disappointed. Because Leadership Network is adamant about measurement, they got back some very positive results before the third gathering. Summing up the accomplishments of the previous six months, Executive Pastor Will Shearer from Vineyard Church in Columbus, Ohio, reported on some of the progress that was made:

- Recruited over two hundred new volunteers to serve in community justice–oriented ministries—prison ministry, free health clinic, free legal clinic, after-school programs, and the like.
- Held a three-day "justice revival" with more than forty churches and denominations; total attendance for the three evenings exceeded ten thousand people called to action in response to Jesus and his concern for the poor and marginalized in the community.

Each night, an invitation to receive Christ was issued, with hundreds of people responding.

- Legislative initiatives: Dan Franz, Vineyard's pastor for urban and mercy ministries, has been taking a lead role among central Ohio pastors speaking out in the "public square" about the payday lending and gambling industries. Legislation limiting the rate of interest charged by the payday lending industry (reducing the APR from 391 percent to 28 percent) was passed by the Ohio General Assembly.
- Vineyard Columbus sent out forty-one teams to pass out grocery bags, clean up houses and yards, and do a variety of similar service projects.
- Mentor training: Vineyard partnered with Columbus public schools and Big Brothers Big Sisters of Central Ohio to recruit and train more than fifty new mentors (most of them from Vineyard) to serve one hour per week in Columbus schools as one-on-one mentors with middle school and high school students. This is part of Project Mentor (sponsored by Nationwide Insurance to the tune of $600,000), the goal of which is to line up ten thousand mentors by 2012 to serve in Columbus public schools.
- In collaboration with the office of the mayor, Vineyard held a "dropout prevention summit" in October 2009.
- In collaboration with the nonprofit sector, Vineyard Community Center's free legal clinic has initiated with the other prominent free legal clinics in Columbus the hosting of a series of "debtors' rights" workshops to help individuals facing home foreclosure or personal bankruptcy.
- In collaboration with the private sector, Vineyard Community Center has developed a volunteer-led career development program (including career coaches and job search workshops) and is now partnering with a privately owned human resource firm to launch job training and job placement activities as well. The center has also partnered with local banks to host personal finance workshops focusing on budgeting, credit card debt, and the like.

Furthermore, Lead Pastor Rich Nathan drafted a working document titled "Toward the Common Good" that he presented to state legislators as an outline for social reform that included promotion of marriage, welfare reform, divorce reform, adoption reform, livable wage legislation, the importance of fatherhood, helping children of prisoners, and the reintegration of prisoners into society. This document is helping define how the faith community and government can work together to solve problems people care about.

Becoming a Pretty Good Church

Doug Roé and Scott Sliver loaded up their families and headed thirty miles north of home. They moved to Dayton, Ohio, from Vineyard Community Church in Cincinnati with a dream to plant a new church. They knew they would have to take risks and experiment to get this endeavor off the ground, so they developed a catchy slogan: "Dayton Vineyard—A Pretty Good Church." That gave them the needed freedom and space to stretch and to grow.

Having grown up in the area, both Doug and Scott were anticipating success. However, their start-up wasn't as successful as they'd planned. After one failed attempt and comments like "The Vineyard we like; you we don't," they felt somewhat dejected. But the duo did not give up. Doug went back to Scripture and noted twenty-one things Jesus did during his earthly ministry and began putting prayer and kindness into action.

They began with what they could afford: seven bags of groceries. They loaded them into a beat-up Toyota and drove to low-income apartments around the city. Knocking on doors, they would ask, "Are you in need of groceries, or do you know someone who is?" Many times people would point to a neighbor's home and say, "They are having a hard time; you could help them."

Doug and Scott would always seek to pray for people they met. Interestingly, as they went out serving, people began to show up at the weekend meetings. Some came out of interest, wanting to know what a "pretty good church" looked like. Others came to enjoy the safe atmosphere and to join in serving others: belonging before believing.

Soon this pretty good church outgrew the smoky airport hotel and moved to a storefront. In the lobby were always bags of groceries for the needy and items for upcoming block parties for the less served neighborhoods. They also began what they called the Back Door Ministry. Each Thursday, they'd hand groceries out the back door of the building. During this time, they also began a ministry for the poor in a storefront. Each Thursday morning, Doug and others would have a small Bible study and give away any supplies they had gathered.

Miracle Thursday

Doug showed up disappointed one Thursday. He didn't have the resources to purchase supplies for the day. He gathered the people together, taught about Jesus feeding the five thousand, and then admitted that he didn't have any supplies for the day. The only thing he knew to do next was pray—because there was nothing else to do without supplies. A few minutes later, a truck driver knocked on the door. "Someone told me you could use some food. I've a tractor-trailer full. Can you use it?" Ever since that day, God has granted favor and kept this pretty good church well supplied.

Where is Vineyard Dayton now? It has multiple church campuses and a huge kingdom impact, including a life enrichment center, which offers life-sustaining services to the community. The budget for the center is over $2.5 million dollars a year, and there are only two paid staff members. More than thirty other businesses, churches, and organizations support the center through serving and giving.

Here's what the "pretty good" Dayton campus includes:

- Food Pantry Thursdays—still serving, praying for miracles, and caring for the homeless
- Biltmore Hotel Tuesdays—serving the elderly, establishing family groups, and meeting needs
- The Joseph Project Computer Lab—operating in partnership with Montgomery Job Services to provide basic computer skills training, food stamp applications, and other services five days a week
- Block Party on Main Street—a party in the heart of the city held every other month in spring and summer, attended by more than four hundred people seeking fun and prayer
- A Pretty Good BBQ—a smoky barbecue celebration each May on Main Street in downtown Dayton

Here's what's available at the "pretty good" Beavercreek campus:

- The Joseph Project—where neighbors help neighbors with food pantry items Monday through Friday
- Second Saturday Outreach—a monthly event
- Community FunFest Carnival Games and Community BBQ— serving, playing, and praying for residents of low-income apartments monthly in spring and summer
- Kiss Dayton Valentines Week—servant evangelism in the city
- Fourth of July Water Giveaway
- Stuff the Bus!—a school supply drive that recently won a community award from the school system
- FunFest: A Safe Place for Families on Halloween—a party for five thousand people in costumes!

- Turkeys Giving Away Turkeys—unannounced delivery of Thanksgiving dinners to low-income residents by 350 church families and friends
- Making Christmas Dreams Come True—a full sit-down Christmas dinner for fourteen hundred people (eight hundred of them kids). (Each child makes a craft and a gift for Mom and Dad and receives a present from the church, and each family is prayed for and given a bag of groceries.)

What about Jobs?

The way we see it, the folks at this "pretty good" church are building the kingdom and got a church along the way—with seven bags of groceries as their start.

A Story That Changes the World

What is the story we've been telling? Often our story presents the gospel as a rescuing force as opposed to an empowering force in our lives. The gospel is a call to safety and refuge rather than a call to adventure. Jesus did nothing less than call people to follow him in his kingdom ventures. And he's still doing the same thing today. Pastor Bob Roberts, says:

> I once believed that if I could just get a person "saved" and coming to church, that would change the world. I was wrong. The gospel of the kingdom and the gospel of salvation both get conversions. The difference is that the gospel of salvation is finished at conversion. The gospel of the kingdom begins at conversion and engages comprehensively and holistically the entire person and community. It takes Matthew 25 seriously. You aren't fighting culture; you're creating a new culture by letting the gospel engage every domain of humanity, health, education, economics, communication, art, agriculture, and so on.[12]

Externally focused ministry focuses on the kingdom rather than the church for the simple reason that there are many things externally focused churches engage in that do not directly benefit the church itself. People may come to faith in Christ and join another's fellowship. Kids at the elementary school may all learn how to read, but the fruit of a commitment to a local school may not be realized for twenty years. If churches only have a local church perspective, eventually the business manager or executive pastor will say something like "We've been doing this externally focused ministry for a couple years now; what has been the result in our attendance and giving?" If the direction has not been "up and to the right," most likely the conclusion will be "Let's try something else." We'd like to report that all externally focused, kingdom-minded churches grow dramatically and some pastors do swear by the growth they have seen, but the truth is that some churches grow and some don't.

We can say that many of the things you do will bear fruit in people's lives, in other churches, or in the community. A few years ago, Eric was in Dallas speaking at a conference on becoming an externally focused church. During one of the first breaks in the session, a man introduced himself as David Valentine, pastor of the First Baptist Church in Huntsville, Texas. He introduced his church by saying it "ran around five hundred in church and three hundred in Sunday school every week." Then he told the most amazing story:

> One thing you may not know is that Huntsville Prison is the release point for prisoners in the criminal justice system in the state of Texas. Five days a week, up to 150 prisoners are released into society. They are given $75 and a bus ticket. Not surprisingly, most of them find their way back to prison within a year or two. About five years ago, we began sending around a hundred of our folks over to the prison to begin working with soon-to-be released prisoners—helping them with jobs, clothing, connecting with family, and the like. It made such a difference in the lives of these prisoners that the prison officials asked us if we knew of any other churches in Texas that might have a similar interest in working with prisoners. So we started working on that. Last year, of the seventy-five thousand prisoners who were released back into the state of Texas, we were able to connect forty thousand of them with caring believers and churches in the communities they were returning to.

David, his staff, and his church have a kingdom mind-set. When Eric asked him if his church had grown much in the last five years, he responded that the church was around five hundred then and five hundred now. But if you are a pastor, what would you rather have, a church of five hundred and a kingdom impact on forty thousand or a church of forty thousand and an impact on five hundred? Every week, David's church members also send volunteer teams to minister to nearly twelve hundred correctional officers and Texas Department of Criminal Justice staff, bringing snacks, soft drinks, bottled water, and an occasional lunch. When asked why they are doing this, they answer, "Because we love people and want to make a difference in their lives." They are on call to minister to staff and families of prisoners as those occasions arise. Their love and service have not gone unnoticed. In 2003, they received the the governor's award for Volunteer of the Year from the Texas Department of Criminal Justice. In 2002, within their denominational family, they received the "Salt and Light" Award for community ministries sponsored by the Center for Community Ministries of the Baptist General Convention of Texas. We imagine that when David goes to bed at night, he falls asleep quickly. We imagine that when he wakes up, he has a bounce in his step because he has ceased trying to create the best church in the community but may very well have created the best church for the community.

The Leadership Challenge

Robert McKee says the test of a good movie is that you walk out saying to yourself, "That was a great story." As a leader, what story are you telling? What story are you inviting people into? McKee says a good movie has you asking throughout the movie, "What happens next?" as opposed to "Where is this thing going?" People that are sitting in church are asking the same types of questions. They are either asking, "Where is this thing going?" or "What happens next?" As leaders, we need to create a compelling story that every person longs to be a part of.

CHAPTER 5

Missions: The Few Send the Many, Not the Many Send the Few

In crossing cultures, the missionary teacher becomes a learner, the one who is in possession of divine revelation discovers new truth, and he who seeks the salvation of others finds himself converted all over again.

David Smith, *Mission After Christendom*[1]

WHEN ERIC FIRST BEGAN IDENTIFYING AND CONVENING externally focused churches in 2003, the folks at Leadership Network were adamant about distinguishing between local and global ministry—between community ministry and "foreign missions." It just made sense. Externally focused ministry was limited to a congregation's community engagement. Four years later, as Eric was convening his fifth externally focused leadership community with Leadership Network, he began getting pushback from the participants who were not separating local from global. In our flattened world, they wanted to take what they were learning overseas and bring it back home and take what they were learning at home and bring it overseas. Many ministry leaders had assumed the position over all local and global ministries. Leaders like Bob Roberts were increasingly using the hybrid term *glocal* to convey the thought that externally focused ministry had to include the world. Eric also began to get a number of requests that made him aware that something new was happening in global missions. The calls and e-mails went something like this: "I know you know a lot of people that are doing cool things around the world. Do you know of any good global outreach people? But don't send me any 'missions pastors' who just want to divide the missions budget pie and hold a missions fair every couple of years."

We began to sense that God was doing something new in the area of global missions because our world was changing. In times past, an effective missions program was measured by how many missionaries had been sent from the church. Missions was a specialty ministry for the dedicated few who were sent and supported by the congregation. The quality and effectiveness of missions was manifested through pictures, yarn, and maps. The more yarn, the better the missions program. But as pastors rediscovered their equipping role (Ephesians 4:11–13) and opened their missional eyes, they discovered that everyone can play and everyone can go.

Most externally focused churches want to be the best church for the community and for the world. More and more Christ followers are engaging locally *and* globally, and the numbers bear this out. Since 2000, "12 percent of active churchgoers reported having gone overseas on a short-term mission project while in their teens . . . up from 5 percent in the 1990s, 4 percent in the 1980s, and only 2 percent before that."[2] More churches are engaging globally—above and beyond financial support of missionaries. Approximately one-third of U.S. congregations send mission teams overseas, averaging eighteen members every year.[3] But strategies and tactics that served the church for decades were no longer working or at least not working as effectively as they had worked in the past. New global wine was calling for new global wineskins, and we felt that a book on the externally focused church would not be complete unless we addressed what we are seeing happening with churches that are effectively engaging not just across the street or across the tracks but across the world. We'll explain what we mean.

When Jesus left his marching orders to the early church, part of his commission included the scope of its mission. It was to make disciples in Jerusalem (the place where it was), Judaea (the country that contained Jerusalem), Samaria (the country to the north, populated by people the Jews historically despised), and to the ends of the earth. These four domains—Jerusalem, Judaea, Samaria, and the world—represent different combinations of culture and geography, as depicted in Figure 5.1:

- *Across the street:* This is your Jerusalem—reaching people who are like you and live, work, and play within geographical proximity.
- *Across the country:* This is your Judaea—reaching people who are culturally similar to you but geographically distant.

Figure 5.1

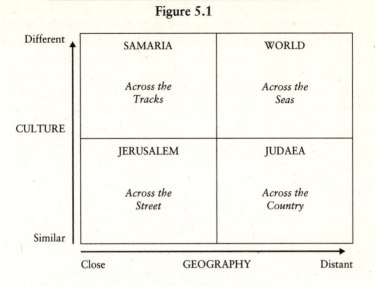

- *Across the tracks:* This is your Samaria—reaching people who are geographically close but culturally different.
- *Across the seas:* This is your "ends of the earth" ministry—reaching people who are both culturally different and geographically distant.

Figure 5.1 Even though geography and culture are the variables, the mission is the same—making disciples, passionate followers of Jesus. Rob Wegner, pastor of Life Mission at Granger Community Church, is praying and working to facilitate the change from missional activity to missional lifestyle: "We were given one mission—the Great Commission—and every follower is called to embrace it. The question we ask ourselves is not 'Does our church have Jesus' mission?' but 'Does Jesus' mission have our church?' In the past, it's been 'getting people into church'; then, as we became more externally focused, it was 'getting people out of church.' Now it is 'helping people be the church wherever they are.'"[4]

The Changing Centers of Christianity

The big news for us in America is this: the center of Christianity has made a seismic shift from the western to eastern hemisphere and from the northern to southern hemisphere. That is big news. On a beautiful July afternoon, Eric strolled down the Pearl Street Mall in Boulder, Colorado, and stopped in at Art Source International, one of the largest purveyors of antique maps in the world. Browsing through documents under the title "Rare Maps," he stumbled on a document taken from an 1886 atlas titled *The Distribution of Christian Religions Throughout the World* that visually depicted the number of Protestant, Catholic, and Orthodox believers in various countries and regions of the world. What a goldmine! Here's what this map, more than a century old, revealed:

- France had the most Roman Catholics (35.5 million), followed by Austria, the nations of South America, Italy, Spain, and Germany.
- The United States, with 30 million Protestants, led Germany, Great Britain, Sweden, Russia, Austria, and the Netherlands.
- Russia was the dominant Orthodox country, maintaining the allegiance of over 54 million adherents, followed by Turkey, Austria, and Greece.
- The continent of Africa had a mere 709,000 Protestants (fewer than Polynesia) and 1.1 million Catholics.
- India had only 300,000 Protestants, and the Arabian region, Turkey, Persia (Iran), and China had a paltry 89,000 altogether.
- Christianity's center of gravity was the United States and Europe.

But interestingly, 1886 was a time when God began to wake up the church in the West to the needs of the world. A year earlier, the "Cambridge Seven" packed their bags for China. In 1886, the Student Volunteer Movement launched as one hundred university and seminary students at D. L. Moody's conference grounds at Mount Hermon, Massachusetts, signed the Princeton Pledge, which says, "I purpose, God willing, to become a foreign missionary." By the following year, those hundred students were serving in the four corners of the globe. In 1888, Jonathan Goforth sailed for China and John R. Mott was appointed chairman of the Student Volunteer Movement, whose motto was "The evangelization of the world in this generation." In 1890, Central American Mission (CAM) was founded by C. I. Scofield, for which the Scofield Reference Bible was named. In the same year, Charles Gabriel wrote the missionary song "Send the Light" and John Livingston Nevius of China launched the ministry in Korea. In 1891, Samuel Zwemer went to Arabia and Helen Chapman sailed for the Congo. And in 1895, Africa Inland Mission was formed by Peter Cameron Scott, the Japan Bible Society was established, and Amy Carmichael arrived in India. The missionaries had started their work, and their work made a global difference.

Phillip Jenkins, in his 2002 book *The Next Christendom,* writes, "Until recently, the overwhelming majority of Christians have lived in White nations, allowing theorists to speak smugly, arrogantly, of 'European Christian' civilization. . . . Over the past century, however, the center of gravity in the Christian world has shifted inexorably southward, to Africa, Asia, and Latin America. Already today, the largest Christian communities on the planet are to be found in Africa and Latin America."[5] Kenyon scholar John Mbiti notes that "the centers of the church's universality [are] no longer in Geneva, Rome, Athens, Paris, London, [and] New York, but Kinshasa, Buenos Aires, Addis Ababa, and Manila."[6] The largest churches in the world are not in southern California or Texas. In fact, "None of the fifty largest churches in the world are found in North America."[7] "The Full Gospel Central Church in Seoul now has over half a million members, earning it a place in the *Guinness Book of World Records* as the world's largest single congregation on earth."[8] Megachurch does not describe a church of this size. Today, "there almost twice as many Presbyterians in South Korea as in the United States."[9]

Missionaries from Other Countries

According to a 2006 article in *Christianity Today,* "South Korea sends more missionaries than any country but the U.S. And it won't be long before it's number one."[10] This is not just a dream but a plan. The Korea Mission Association plans "to send 100,000 full-time Korean missionaries by 2030. "Currently over 3,700 Nigerians are serving as missionaries with a hundred agencies in more than fifty countries . . . [and] now it's becoming a major missionary-sending country. For every missionary who now enters Nigeria, five Nigerians go out as missionaries to other fields of service."[11] In our own community of Boulder, Colorado, we welcomed an Anglican missionary from Africa who had come here to reach people with the gospel. The center of gravity has shifted.

The Big Shifts

To address the changing face of missions, God is raising up churches and leaders of those churches who are painting a different picture of missions. They are telling a different story. They are making the shift from top down to mutuality, from proclamation of the gospel to proclamation and demonstration of the gospel, from local and global missions being separate to global and local residing under one ministry department. These leaders are the new generation of missional leaders in the iteration of missions from long-term expatriates to long-term commitments with short-term vocational teams. These entrepreneurial leaders have long-term relationships but travel in and out of countries as easily as leaders drove across town a generation ago. With the flattening of the world and the immediacy and economy of global communication, leaders are figuring new ways to influence the world. Missionaries that try to have a "business cover" are being replaced with businesspeople who are living out the gospel. Single missionaries are being replaced with small groups of people that are living missionally. Innovative, leading churches find themselves partnering not around denominations but with those who share a like commitment. Church leaders are no longer raising mission funds just from the congregation, but churches are raising resources from the community to help sponsor hospitals, water projects, and other ventures of common concern.

The cultural ethos of missions back in the late twentieth century went something like this: we in America have everything—the tools, strategies, technologies, and training to reach the world. We just need to mobilize our people and go. So we went—sending people out as long-term missionaries, short-term missionaries, and sending others on *Jesus* film and vision trips, and it worked, but something was shifting underfoot in missions.

Interviewing Leaders

In 2009, Eric interviewed around fifty leaders of large churches that were engaged in global outreach. Each interview lasted about an hour and covered what the person was doing globally. It was a fascinating educational experience to hear what these externally focused leaders were thinking and doing. Each leader brought passion and insight to the conversation. Each of them was eager to explain what they were doing but also expressed a desire to learn from others who walked in their global shoes. It was a new world, and they were eager to learn.

The Present Future

William Gibson observes that "the future is already here—it's just not evenly distributed."[12] We agree. All around us are examples of innovators and early adopters who have discovered new principles—more effective ways of thinking, being, and doing that have yet to become the dominant or prevailing way of living. But it is only a matter of time. From our experience, reading, and interviews with missional leaders, we'd like to introduce you to eight trends that we think will shape the future of missions.

Mutuality

The future of missions will be shaped by mutuality between East and West, North and South, and sending and receiving nations. Because there are now vibrant believers and thriving churches in Africa, Asia, Latin America, Eurasia, and even the Middle East, we in the West don't have to think of ourselves as the saving force in world missions. This fact is underscored by the observation that the gospel is growing in nearly every part of the world *but* the United States! This means, consciously for the first time, we now have the opportunity to learn from others as well as others learning from us. Can we learn anything from Korea on prayer, from China on house churches, from Africa on worship? Mutuality reflects a shift from the one-up, one-down relationships stemming from a colonial approach to missions. Bishop Desmond Tutu complained that "when the missionaries came to Africa, they had the Bible and we had the land. They said, 'Let us pray.' We closed our eyes. When we opened them, we had the Bible and they had the land."[13] Hopefully, those days are behind us. Today there is a need for mutual respect and mutual learning. We from the West come not just to give but also to receive as true peers. And that's the challenge. As one mission's pastor said so well, "My biggest opportunity is to be a resourced, educated white guy and submit to a God-called foreigner who needs you."

Matt Olthoff, senior director for community development at Mariners Church in Irvine, California, notes that

> there is a paradigm shift toward reciprocity that is taking place. What does it mean to come to the table as equals? The West is typically loud, directive, and the one that leads by bringing resources to the table. But with 40 percent of our wealth disappearing overnight, we've lost our biggest tool to bring us to the table. Secondly, the church is growing in leaps and bounds in developing countries while the Western church is dying. We in the West have always been givers, but we need to learn to be receivers. Reciprocity is not about missions, but this is about the church in community. When you come to the global table, you realize that Africa and Asia have different inroads for reaching those people groups. African pastors reaching Africans in England. . . . For us, it is partnerships.[14]

Stacey Campbell, executive pastor at Christ Community Church in Greeley, Colorado, is surprised by how much he and people from his church learn from their international partners through mutuality and partnering. He tells of one of the church's partners whose vision is to plant a million churches; he has been arrested multiple times for his faith and fully expects to die for his faith. Stacey continues, "We have strong partnerships with strong leaders in these countries—people on the ground—and we follow their lead. We probably learn more, are challenged more, and are provoked more by our partners than they are by us. They get the raw end of the deal. One of my buddies just got back from Syria and told me, 'Over here we live for Jesus. Over there they die for Jesus.'"[15]

Scott White, pastor for global outreach, Lake Avenue Church in Pasadena, California, tells how he navigates in the new world of mutuality and partnerships:

> I like to ask questions, listen, and learn because of the incredible challenge we in the Western missions church face in terms of humility. This past century has been our era of missions through the organizations like the IMB [Southern Baptist's International Missions Board] and Campus Crusade, but now we need new humility. In the past, partnership was us leading and you walking two steps behind us. In our post-Christian world, the opportunity to be a missional church is to learn from the missional churches overseas. They can teach us to be a pilgrim people. We can be their student as we have been their teacher. Models are not as transferable as before, but principles like humility, availability, and incarnational are eternal. We have the opportunity to be blessed by them and learn from them if we are willing. Most of training we have is for a different era. We need to think differently, or we will be confined to making missionary buggy whips.[16]

Tim Senff of Crossroads Church in Cincinnati, Ohio, unpacks what mutuality looks like in its partnership with Charity and Faith Mission Church in Mamelodi, South Africa, a township of a million people northeast of Pretoria. Moved by the AIDS crisis in Africa, Crossroads stepped up to the plate by raising $750,000 to build the largest AIDS hospice in South Africa, providing free medical care for AIDS patients. Although the church led with a project, it followed up with relationships. "Relationships changed the game by knitting our hearts together, and this really changed us," says Tim. "We've had three big trips and have sent fourteen hundred Crossroads folks to Mamelodi, who spend the nights as guests in the homes of people in the township. This changes everything. No white people had ever done that before. Just as important, over one hundred people from Mamelodi have come to Cincinnati to help us accomplish our local mission. We do a pulpit exchange with our lead pastor, Brian Tome, exchanging pulpits with Mamelodi's Pastor Titus."[17]

Tim told us that the Mamelodi church had strengths and resources that Crossroads lacked. "They are so strong in prayer and pray for hours at a time. Recently we sent the church scores of Polaroid photos of ourselves along with our prayer request written in permanent marker on the front of the picture." Tim then showed me a picture of a Mamelodi woman, eyes closed with tears streaming down her cheeks, holding the picture of a young woman of college age with the prayer request that she would be 100 percent for Jesus. Welcome to the world of mutuality.

Partnering

Partnering is different from mutuality. Mutuality is needed for true partnering to exist, but whereas mutuality has to do with the equality of those who come to the table, partnering pertains to the purposes or projects that require the need of real partners. Tom Mullis, director for global outreach at Perimeter Church in Atlanta, points out that "the age of pioneering of Western mission is over, but many don't realize it. Local people are more effective in reaching local people. But they do need training. We in the West started as pioneers, but over the years, we have deteriorated into patrons of projects. Now we need partnerships around shared values rather than bringing in our separate agenda or program."[18]

Partnering is not about bringing prescribed programs with us but begins with what indigenous leaders in the country are trying to accomplish. Mike Kenyon of Rock Harbor Church in Costa Mesa, California, understands this well: "There are still structural things the West can bring, but our posture is always to come as equal partners, . . . as brothers and sisters. Our overseas friends don't want great Western partners to come and save the day. This new reality provides an opportunity for collaboration."[19]

Ian Stevenson, pastor of Go Ministries at The Crossing, also in Costa Mesa, is pioneering mutuality in missions. Leaders from The Crossing recognize that people in each of the five countries they are ministering in have something to offer their church in suburban southern California. In the summer of 2007, teams of people from The Crossing crossed the border to help their partner church accomplish their goals, and thirty people from their partner church in Mexico crossed the border to work with congregants of The Crossing in southern California during their Serve Day. It's a whole new world of missions.

Almost all the pastors interviewed mentioned the absolute importance of long-term relationships. They are the singular key to sustainable and fruitful partnering. Matt Olthoff, of Mariners Church in Irvine, also shares a helpful insight on partnerships: "There is a big shift occurring now in missions. It's no longer ministry *to* or ministry *for* but ministry *with*. If you look at partnership from the West, it is very business-oriented and transactional. The rest of world defines partnerships in terms of marriage—dating and courting—it's a relationship. We talk in terms of "transactional." They talk in terms of "communal." Our challenge is communicating reciprocity in greater means and measures."[20]

In the spring of 2009, Mariners brought its overseas partners together in Irvine, where together they formulated their global strategies. Many leaders commented that this was the first time in their lives that they were treated as peers by those from the West.

Steve Hanson, global impact pastor for the Church of the Open Door in Maple Grove, Minnesota, develops the analogy of dating and forming partnerships: "We support missionaries whom God sends out from our church, but we also have what we call 'focused partners,' of which we have five. I sometimes refer to our focused partners as marriages because we pursue them in the same way—we talk, date, hold hands, walk together, hug and kiss, get engaged, get married, and have kids. These are long-term partnerships, and we don't marry everyone we date."[21]

Bob Roberts of Northwood Church for the Community cogently sums up what is most needed. He advises that churches "don't go in as the 'savior' but as a partner. Realize that you are going to receive as much from getting to know them and experiencing them as you will give them. Don't forget, you're a pilgrim, not a missionary. A missionary goes and gives with an end-game in mind or a project to complete. A pilgrim simply gives and receives on a journey."[22]

Investing in Leaders

In 2009, jockey Calvin Borel defied the 50-to-1 long-shot odds and rode an unknown horse named Mine That Bird to victory in the Kentucky Derby. A couple of weeks later, running in the second leg of the Triple Crown, the Preakness, Borel switched horses and this time rode Rachel Alexandra to finish first. In the third leg of the Triple Crown, the Belmont Stakes, he again put the riding crop against the flanks of Mine That Bird and, though riding valiantly, came up short and finished in third place. Not too bad of a feat, running in the money in the three most prestigious races in the world. Sometimes it's better to bet on the jockey than on the horse. What's the point? Leadership is everything. Wherever good things are happening, there will be a capable and passionate man or woman leading the way. Churches that are effective overseas have learned to bet on the jockey. Keith West, pastor for missions at Lake Pointe Church in Rockwall, Texas, says:

> We focus on a key leader of an indigenous church who shares our values and is getting the job done. We realized that if we came along-side these leaders, we could accelerate what they are doing so they could become a regional influence. It's like the parable of talents. We resource those who are doing the most with what they've been given and help them excel even more. We want to find a few key partners, stay with them, and pour into them to multiply their effectiveness.[23]

Durwood Snead, director of GlobalX at North Point Church in Atlanta, says, "Our model is to work with indigenous leaders to help them develop, reproduce, and multiply from there. These multiplying churches then become models for other churches that become movements of churches."[24]

Eric Hanson, director of international impact at Christ Community Church in Saint Charles, Illinois, works with indigenous leaders who are doing church planting multiplication in six countries around world. He says, "We are doing things the hard way. It is easier for us to find a Western missionary who could integrate our people there, but we're led to indigenous leaders who have not been exposed to Western leaders. But we are seeing great fruit. We're always working uphill."[25] Since 2005, in Sierra Leone alone, they have seen over eleven hundred churches started with over forty thousand new believers and sense that God is pouring out his spirit. Partnering with indigenous leaders does not mean they don't send their own people, but the people they send are in service to the local leader.

How do you recognize good leaders who make great partners? The most obvious sign is that they are already engaged in ministry without any outside help. Steve Hanson of the Church of the Open Door says, "When I go into a village, I don't know how to dig a well or build a building, but I do know relationships. When I walk into a local church in southern Uganda that is missing a roof because the people are using their monies to build houses for grandmothers to take care of AIDS orphans, I pay attention. They have a bigger God than I do."[26]

Mariners' strategy is simple: Matt Olthoff understands that a country's ability to receive outside help is based on the country's leadership capacity. The church begins by asking a potential partner, "Tell us what God is doing in your ministry. Can you take us to places where this is working? How can we help you make this sustainable? How can we help you leverage what you do well across everything?"[27] For Ian Stevenson of The

Crossing, God-sized goals distinguish one potential partner from another. "Our partner in northern India is working to plant five hundred churches by 2015 and a thousand churches before he dies."[28]

Keith West of Lake Pointe Church uses the "dating" process to identify the right leader: "First we send a scout team to see what is going on. If the team likes what they see regarding the work and leadership and something we need to investigate further, I'll bring another pastor with me and vet further. This begins our dating process. We look for leaders who share our values and are getting the job done. We respond to responsiveness of the local leaders."[29]

Combining Good Deeds and Good News

Externally focused churches, by definition, are churches that believe that the gospel is and has always been a message that is best expressed in both words of love and works of love. Good deeds *verify* the good news, and good news *clarifies* the good deeds.

Evangelistically, we believe that good deeds create goodwill, and goodwill is a great platform for sharing the good news. Combining good deeds and good news is not novel in foreign missions. This has always been a strength of the sending church—to add a component of physical blessing to the people it is trying to reach. Cinderblocks and paintbrushes fit neatly and comfortably alongside jungle mime and backyard Bible clubs in the tool box of the short-term missionary. What is new is the level of problem solving that externally focused missional churches are engaged in. What is new are the influential people who are speaking out for global holistic solutions.

In 2003, Saddleback Church's pastor, Rick Warren, was in Africa where he had just finished a Purpose Driven Seminar that connected to ninety thousand pastors on the continent. Afterward, he was taken to a remote village where he met a local village pastor who faithfully downloaded Warren's sermons from Pastors.com at a post office ninety minutes away on foot. Meeting this obscure pastor proved to be both catalytic and providential as Warren began to pray what he was to do with the influence God gave him. Under the African sky, he began to articulate the big "giants" facing humanity around the world. He came up with five global giants:

1. Spiritual emptiness. "[People] don't know God made them for a purpose."
2. Egocentric leadership. "The world is full of little Saddams. Most people cannot handle power. It goes to their heads."

3. Poverty. "Half the world lives on less than $2 per day."
4. Disease. "We have billions of people dying from preventable disease. That's unconscionable."
5. Illiteracy. "Half the world is functionally illiterate."[30]

To take on the global giants, Warren came up with his PEACE Plan. As the Saddleback Web site explains, "The PEACE Plan is a massive effort to mobilize Christians around the world to address what Pastor Rick calls the 'five global giants' of spiritual emptiness, corrupt leadership, poverty, disease, and illiteracy by promoting reconciliation, equipping servant leaders, assisting the poor, caring for the sick, and educating the next generation."[31]

The goal of the PEACE Plan is to mobilize the body of Christ— the churches of the world—to engage the five big giants, and thousands of churches of all stripes are signing on to be a part of this global effort. Warren invites all comers. "We need to mobilize a billion Catholic and Orthodox believers. I'm really not that interested in interfaith dialogue. I am interested in interfaith projects. . . . We do have different beliefs, but the fact is we serve the same Lord. Let's work on the things we can agree on."[32]

Today, churches are engaging the broken places of the world simply because these places are broken. "I like to ask people from developing countries what they think heaven will be like," says Steve Hanson of Church of the Open Door, "Most of them say, 'It will be a place where I don't need to worry about food and I won't hear my children cry because they are hungry.'" This is a far different view of heaven from most Westerners, who may view heaven as a mix between a nice beach and a country club. Having enough food doesn't even cross our minds. "'Give us this day our daily bread' is a prayer I've never had to pray," Hanson goes on to say. But for the two billion people on earth living on less than two dollars a day, this is their daily prayer, and the church has the opportunity to be an answer to that prayer.[33]

Churches are taking on big projects and going to places where the church has never gone before. Churches are engaged in providing alternatives for young children enslaved in sex trafficking in Thailand and India. Mark Connelly, senior pastor of Mission Community Church in Gilbert, Arizona, is passionate about what his church is doing globally. "We don't have members; we have missionaries. In the church foyer, we don't have a map with pictures and yarn; we are the ones who are going. Initially, we asked ourselves, who are the most broken and hurting people on the planet? Sex trafficking came to our attention. What can we do to rescue these women and children and bring them to Jesus?"[34]

Mission Community Church found a partner in former congress-woman Linda Smith, founder of Shared Hope International (http://www .sharedhope.org). Mark said, "Point us in the right direction," and she pointed to Fiji in the South Pacific and a holistic village called Homes of Hope. Homes of Hope is a 43-acre village that rescues girls and their children from the streets and the brothels and gives them a safe place to live, be educated and discipled, learn to run a business, earn their own money, buy their own home, and get physical, emotional, and spiritual healing and restoration in the name of Jesus. Mark explains, "We send teams with resources every six to eight weeks to help them build out that village. This month, we made space for eleven more girls to be rescued." To the people of Mission Community Church, this is not just missions. It's the beginning of a movement. To give legs to the movement, they started Vision Abolition (http://www.visionabolition.org) so that other churches could join in this transformational ministry. One new church partner raised $81,000 on Easter Sunday, during the same hour Superstition Springs was raising another $20,000. Other than Homes of Hope, there is no safety or escape for women captive to sex trafficking. Because of the success the church is seeing in Fiji, it feels that this model could be replicated throughout the South Pacific.

What was happening in Fiji opened church members' eyes to what was happening in the Phoenix area—a hub for child prostitution, where the average age of a child prostitute is thirteen years.[35] Mark Connelly and other pastors began meeting with government officials to work toward ending sex trafficking in the Phoenix area. In the spring of 2009, thirty pastors from the greater Phoenix area churches started StreetLight Phoenix, a cooperative effort between the faith community and other domains of society to end child prostitution and establish safe houses in the community. "We believe that when churches come together, people will come together and share resources that serve the greater good of the community. It is then that it is possible to change the world in sustainable ways."[36] And that's what they want to do: change the world.

David Thoresen of Pantano Christian Church in Tucson, Arizona, is committed to community development as an integral part of holistic ministry. In its simplest form, community development is of two types: *need-based*, regarding the community as filled with needs, and *asset-based*, regarding the community as filled with assets to solve its own problems. With their dual focus on church multiplication and community transformation, Pantano founded an organization called Community Health Evangelism (CHE; http://www.cheintl.org). The basis of CHE is that transformation comes from within the community.

The community decides what the problems are and what a better future would look like. It finds local assets and does its own transformation. This approach really doesn't require much from the outside. "We've already heard about how communities have been figuring out transformation with their own resources—what they always thought only others could do. If church decides it wants a building, money comes from the church."[37]

Good news and good deeds are great traveling companions. Jonathan Martin of Good Shepherd Church, in Boring, Oregon, says that even in the toughest of countries, the mission teams they send don't want to leave Jesus at the immigration booth. Jonathan says, "When we are asked if we intend to proselytize people through service, we tell them, 'We're here to make Jesus known, and Jesus gets known through his followers' doing good' as opposed to 'We are not here to get followers of Jesus.' So far that has worked for us."[38]

Greater Financial Accountability

American churches are incredibly generous. "U.S. church donations to both humanitarian and evangelistic transnational ministry now total about $4 billion annually."[39] However, churches that engage in global ministry are thinking differently about whom they support, what they support, and how they support missional engagement. One thing is clear: the days of cutting a check and hoping for the best are nearly over. With all the needs and opportunities in the world, global missions leaders of the future are trying to maximize every dollar expended on global outreach. The paradigm of funding partnering is challenging. Mike Robinson, unleashing pastor at Fellowship Bible Church in Little Rock, Arkansas, says, "Our challenge is to develop sustainable and healthy partnerships with indigenous people without enabling those who need help. When a gringo walks through the door, the nationals see a dollar sign, which only leads to paternalism and dependence. The untold story is this: when Americans leave and take their money with them, the churches fold. All around the world, we see the skeletons of the great intentions of Americans."[40]

After ten years in East Asia, Jonathan Martin was invited to be the pastor for global outreach at Good Shepherd Community Church. Living overseas as a supported missionary, he had seen the effects of well-intended but misplaced finances. This trail of financial havoc led him to ask, "How can we get behind indigenous works without destroying them? How can we be lavishly generous yet incredibly wise in our giving?" Meeting with a group of other like-mined leaders, Jonathan came up with four guiding principles that inform all overseas giving decisions, summed up in the acronym RAISE:[41]

> R—*Relationship:* We cannot bypass relationships and must always lead with relationships—real, viable, and incarnational relationships. This is why we must have people on the ground, since money follows people.
>
> A—*Accountability:* Never give to an individual pastor or indigenous missionary. Give to organizations that provide oversight and accountability. Good people are ruined by easy access to money, no matter how well intentioned they are.
>
> IS—*Indigenous Sustainability:* This is all about helping locals do ministry without money. If it won't go on without Western money, we don't do it. "Ask yourself: Will the project I give to require ongoing and continual foreign funds to keep it alive, or are these funds seeding a plant that can eventually be watered and grown by locals?" If the project cannot be funded, maintained, and multiplied by locals, don't invest in it.
>
> E—*Equity:* We as Americans can create entities that destroy local life. If we build orphanages where children get better care and education than a parent can provide, parents will often bring their children to the orphanage. "The financial gift should not create economic inequities in the place it is given." We may think, "This pastor shouldn't have to live in this shack. Let's build him a house." That may be the right thing to do, but we need to do so with the knowledge that his congregation may never learn to support that pastor financially. Why should it? "The Americans will cover for us and come to the rescue."

Externally focused churches of the future support mission-critical projects that their global partners deem important. This type of giving can only come from a trusted relationship. Kirk DeWitt, of Calvary Community Church in Westlake Village, California, says:

> I think it is important to have a trust relationship with our partners in other countries. For example, if we come and say, "We want to sink a well," sinking a well may be the partner's seventh priority. On the other hand, if we go and ask what is needed, the partner may come up with something off the wall—like two SUVs—because the thinking goes, "We have just one shot at this American money." But as we get

to know each other in a trusted relationship, we can discover what we can do to empower people to accomplish their mission. "This is very different from "What can we give you?"[42]

Our interviews revealed that although most church global budgets were substantial, there was some anxiety regarding the future of giving. One pastor said, "We know how forty-year-olds respond to giving opportunities, but we haven't figured out how to motivate twenty- to thirty-year-olds to give." John Chung, minister of the Mission at Park Street Church in Boston, notes that "in this age of missions, our twenty- and thirty-year-olds are more excited about AIDS orphans and water than about evangelism and church planting. How do we combine these?"[43] Dave Hall, of Emmanuel Faith Church in Escondido, California, provided this insight:

> All models are based on older patterns of giving. Younger people respond to being invited into a movement, not a program or a bureaucracy. Members of the older generation were content to give money to a church as they would invest in a mutual fund. They give a check to the church and trust that the church knows best how to invest this money. Younger people think more like investment bankers, who look for specific singular investment (giving) opportunities, like helping to dig a well in southern Uganda or caring for AIDS orphans."[44]

This is a new reality that churches will need to navigate. The age of the mutual fund may be over.

Business as Mission

An emerging possibility for funding is attached to the effectiveness of business as mission. Northpoint's Durwood Snead explains:

> Our biggest challenge is a funding crisis that existed before the recent economic downturn. "Business as mission" is a new model for funding. A well-run business will provide salaries for people doing business as mission. In an unreached world, business as mission is a big thing God has for this time in history. All countries desire economic development, so we're trying to figure out kingdom business. If we are employing people, we have great freedom to use the Bible as a management textbook to do this in countries closed to traditional missionaries. These are authentic businesses, and government welcomes them.[45]

Emmanuel Faith's Dave Hall says, "My challenge is figuring out how to maximize these entrepreneurs for the kingdom. Whereas before the inroad was teaching English, now God is raising up a whole new group of people from the business domain. The traditional missionary who dabbles at something else will fade away, while professionals with kingdom mentality are the future."[46]

Joey Shaw, minister of international missions at Austin Stone Church in Austin, Texas, is trying to demystify global engagement and intentionally engaging businesspeople in the church's ministry to Turkish Christians. "The energy we have here is for being global. We have a church full of what we call 'cosmocrats'—people who will fly overseas to attend a wedding or who regularly travel overseas for business. We are trying to make them cosmocrats for the kingdom." Desire is translated into strategy. Shaw notes:

> On our first trip to Turkey, in January 2008, I took a group of CEOs and businessmen. I did this intentionally to show that I wanted to engage the body beyond doctors and nurses. We investigated a business idea—a cheesecake factory. Interestingly enough, there is a market; Turks love cheesecake! Half the members of this team have developed business as mission, and they are now investors. Another group is looking to set up a Curves business in Istanbul. We are sitting on a gold mine of people to send, and we're racking our brains how to do this.[47]

Lake Avenue's Scott White notes that "as we become post-Christian, our funding model needs to be different. Much of our ministry's footprint is not sustainable the way it is. Most cultures around the world do not have a charity ethos regarding asking and giving, so most churches in these places don't ask and give. We must train in different ways to make bivocational funding the new norm of sustainability."[48]

Focus

There is a power of focus. On the flipside, the most frustrated pastors interviewed were those whose churches supported scores of legacy missionaries they inherited, scattered all over the map. Much of the time, these missionaries were not the homegrown variety but nephews of former staff or friends of friends or a missionary tied to a designated gift. In the past, the often unstated missions goal was to have representatives from the church on every continent of the globe. The more yarn and pictures, the better. This is changing. Churches that seem to be most effective in making a global impact are focused churches. When asked what Central Christian Church of the East Valley in Mesa, Arizona, was doing globally, Neil Hendershot did not hesitate:

> We are focused on holistic transformation through the expansion of the kingdom of God throughout northeastern Africa. We focus on unreached and unengaged people groups. Unreached people groups include those who may have an expression of Christianity but no church. An unengaged people group has no known believers with no one trying to reach it. Unengaged people will die without ever meeting a believer or hearing the gospel. All our efforts are along this focus.[49]

It doesn't take long to figure out what these folks do and don't do.

Fellowship Bible Church in Brentwood, Tennessee, describes its dual strategy: "We are committed to reaching the nations with the good news of Jesus Christ, building people up in the faith, and launching people into kingdom service . . . primarily through the ministry of the local church. We're also committed to compassionate love for people who suffer from disease, war, famine, and neglect."[50]

Ian Stevenson, from The Crossing in Costa Mesa, California, says:

> For us, the biggest thing is focus. A lot of churches have a full menu of stuff they keep adding to. We encourage individuals to go where they want to go, but as a church, we partner with five places to go and make a difference. Organizationally, we just do five. We have folks that go to France and a person in Zimbabwe, but as an organization, these efforts are not what we promote from the pulpit. For the sake of focus, we stick with our five partners.[51]

David Thoresen, director for international outreach at Pantano Christian Church in Tucson, Arizona, outlines the power of the church's dual focus:

> Our focus is church planting movements coupled with community transformation. We believe that wherever Jesus' church is present, lives and communities should be improved. God has brought us into relationship with some great indigenous partners who share our vision and passion that each church would have within its DNA the tools and desire to multiply itself. Wherever we plant churches, we want to transform communities, and clean water has been very big for us because it is tied to so many other areas of transformation. Our partner in India has started 750 churches, and our partner in Nigeria has planted over 400. Multiplying churches and transforming communities— that's what we're about.[52]

For Tim Senff, director of ReachOut at Crossroads Church in Cincinnati, focus adds synergy to global engagement with Mamelodi, South Africa:

> Our church loves to be able to focus our prayers, our thinking, our going, and our giving on one massive need in a specific location of the world. We've discovered the power of focus—going deep rather than wider. How we approach money, prayer, worship, and spiritual warfare is changed by focus. Our focus even caused us to change our mission from "Connecting seekers to a community of growing Christ followers" to "Connecting seekers to a community of growing Christ followers *who are changing the world.*" . . . People want to be part of a movement—a social force to change the world.[53]

Technology

With every breakthrough in communication technology, people have exploited that technology to advance the gospel. The printing press, radio, TV, and the Internet have allowed the church to increasingly enter a world without boundaries. All around us are glimpses of churches that are discovering the power of technology—of having an impact in a country without ever physically visiting that country. At Rock Harbor Church, a group of folks committed to Uganda developed an advocacy team and used Facebook raise $6,000 to build three wells.

Dave Gibbons of Newsong Church in Irvine is also big on technology. He told us:

> How do we use technology and innovate to be more effective and efficient in what we are trying to do? As a whole, the church is way behind the culture. We need to take technology to the next level and be more like Google, which has dedicated part of its budget for R&D. At Newsong, we have an innovation lab where we are birthing new ideas for the church. We have top-level business and Web developers in this room thinking about breakthrough ideas. We just started a site called YangDang.com where we connect churches who want to serve with service opportunities that fit their passion and DNA."

Northpoint's Durwood Snead found out how useful and seamless technology can be on a recent trip to eastern Europe. "Europe is like plowing concrete. I met a guy named Stephan in Dubrovnik who asked lots of questions about Christ." Stephan had traveled to Dubrovnik looking for answers, and so he and Durwood exchanged e-mail addresses. Soon they connected via Skype, and Durwood initiated a weekly Bible study over Skype. Eight weeks later, Stephan came to Christ and is "growing like a weed and says he knows hundreds of others like himself." North Point uses technology to train global church leaders. Lead Pastor Andy Stanley hosted five live Web events in the first three months of 2009 for pastors all around the world (at http://www.driveinternational.org) "We want to identify leaders in Europe and then help them."

Our changing world calls for a radical change in how we communicate in that world.

The Leadership Challenge

We actually have two leadership challenges for you. The first is corporate, and the second is personal. We hope you'll take both challenges and watch how God shapes your church to change the world as you look and ask.

Look

Take a look at what you are doing globally. Going forward, do you need to stop doing, start doing, continue doing, or measure in view of the new realities of global missions in the eight areas we have discussed in this chapter? Table 5.1 will help you conduct an overview.

Ask

Sometimes asking people to engage globally can be a daunting task for leaders. There is a financial concern, and most places are a long way

Table 5.1

	Stop	Start	Continue	Measure
Mutuality				
Partnering				
Investing in leaders				
Combining good news and good deeds				
Greater financial accountability				
Business as mission				
Focus				
Technology				

from comfortable. We believe we do a great disservice to people's faith development and the work God has for us in changing the world if we don't take risks and ask people to engage globally. We admit that we have sometimes fallen short of asking people to take on the more daunting task of global engagement because of perceived barriers. All you can do is ask, and sometimes that's all it takes.

Dick Herring didn't need another task added to his list, but as a result of a Bible study for busy executives and a challenge from Rick to do more, Dick added something big to his life and is changing the landscape of a nation. As the senior executive for Ball Aerospace, Dick traveled around the world. Rick asked him if he could manage a few days in Thailand during one of his trips. Rick wanted him to check out a missionary LifeBridge had been supporting in Chiang Mai. That one trip got hold of Dick's heart and his ability for problem solving. He not only assisted LifeBridge's missionary, Joni (pronounced Johnny) Morse, in creating a strategic plan for his work among the hill tribes in northern Thailand, but he also became a vital partner. Joni's long ministry and family history in that region had earned the respect of the national government, the tribal leaders, the city officials in Chiang Mai, and even the king of Thailand. This laid the foundation for Dick to organize trips from both the church and the community, helping more than thirty communities in Thailand.

The initial tasks were building projects (community buildings, schools, medical clinics), and they were completed by local U.S. churches taking groups of people over on short trips. Not long after retiring from Ball Aerospace, Dick was invited to lead Engineers Without Borders. This group is made up of engineering students from universities around the United States. They would also take short trips but would be designing clean water systems, buildings, and agricultural support in the field. Although this group was not necessarily Christian in its orientation, Dick found a way to connect the students to the work Joni was doing, and thus both practical and spiritual help was provided.

Dick has also assisted Joni in helping many of the villages set up microenterprises to provide jobs and resources for communities that had formerly been nomadic. The Thai government assisted and supported this effort, as it had a strong desire to have these tribal communities become stable and economically viable. Entire communities along the northern Thai border have been dramatically changed as a result of one really busy person finding a way to be a really busy kingdom-minded global servant.

Who are *you* going to ask to check out what God is doing in the world?

CHAPTER 6

Partnering: They Build Wells, Not Walls

If you want to go fast, go alone. If you want to go far, go together.

African proverb

PROBABLY ONE OF THE MOST PROVOCATIVE STATEMENTS and suggestions we made in our first book, *The Externally Focused Church*, was that the church could and should partner with any organization that is morally positive and spiritually neutral.[1] Should churches serve alongside local community agencies or other churches with which they don't always agree? We continue to get more questions about "partnering" than just about any other topic. The partnership challenge is discussed, explored, and debated in almost every venue we attend. We also hear some of the most inspiring and amazing stories from churches that jump into partnering with both feet—sometimes with very unlikely partners! We hope that the externally focused questions we've been asking of you to this point have been valuable. We hope that the questions we pose next will stir things up even more. What "partnership" questions you ask can make a world of difference to your scope of impact. Partnering and collaboration are not essential for becoming the best church in the community but absolutely essential if you want to be the best church *for* the community.

Do You Believe What I Believe?

In 1978, Paul Hiebert of Fuller Theological Seminary developed a construct that helps leaders think about whom they can and cannot align themselves with. Hiebert makes the distinction between a "bounded set"

Figure 6.1

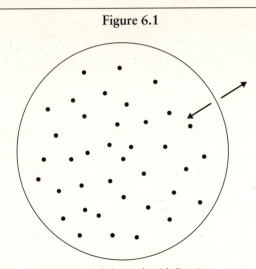

Do you believe what I believe?

and a "centered set." Picture a bounded set as a circle. Inside the circle are the distinctive beliefs and practices of the "insiders" regarding the right way to baptize or the proper view of spiritual gifts or sacraments. It is this set of distinctive beliefs that determines who is in the group and who is outside the group. Traditionally, this is how denominations have defined themselves—by how they are *different* from everyone else. The primary question of those in the bounded set is "Do you believe what I believe?"— and people are either inside or outside that circle (see Figure 6.1).

Some churches define their potential for partnership with other agencies or churches around that question. Thinking in a "bounded set" way, what is the size of the circle? How big—or rather how small—would our influence and impact be if we sought only partners who responded in the affirmative to "Do you believe what I believe?"

Do You Care About What I Care About?

As Hiebert pointed out, there is another way to look at unity: through the eyes of a "centered set." A centered set consists of persons who share a common affection, interest, pursuit, or allegiance. The centered set can be depicted as a dot in the center of a sheet of paper, representing Jesus, without any boundary determining who is "in" or who is "out." Individual lives are depicted by arrows moving toward the dot or away from it (see Figure 6.2). This indicates that some people may be more or

Figure 6.2

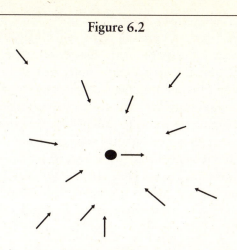

Do you care about what I care about?

less passionate or committed than others, but they are all directing them-selves toward the same center. Hiebert even suggests that it is not distance from the center that is most important but the direction of the arrow. It is better to be far away and moving toward Jesus than to be next to Jesus but moving away.

If you are old enough to have attended a Promise Keepers conference in the 1990s, you will remember Bill McCartney welcoming the men by saying something like "It doesn't matter if you are Baptist or Catholic or charismatic or nothing at all, but if you want to get closer to Jesus, you belong here." And all the men would cheer. Bill was describing centered-set theology. So in respect to Christianity, the primary question of the centered set is "Do you care about what I care about?" Hiebert's construct is an expression of the seventeenth-century sentiment "In essen-tials, unity; in nonessentials, liberty; in all things, charity."[2]

Recently, a couple of Australians, Michael Frost and Alan Hirsch, came up with a good illustration of the difference between a bounded set and a centered set:

> In some farming communities, the farmers might build fences around their properties to keep their livestock in and the livestock of neighbor-ing farms out. This is a bounded set. . . . In our home in Australia . . . ranches are so vast that fences are superfluous. Under these conditions a farmer has to sink a bore and create a well, a precious water supply in the Outback. It is assumed that livestock, though they will stray, will never roam too far from the well, lest they die. This is a centered set.[3]

Churches that are transforming their communities think in terms of sinking wells rather than building walls. Theologically, the "well" is Jesus, of course, but the diagram also serves to define what people in the community mutually care about. Churches that are transforming communities don't divide over their differences but unite with other churches and community service organizations (faith-based or not) around their common love for the community. We can unite and work together with other churches and other groups in our communities not because we share the same theology but because we care about the same things. As we move throughout this chapter, you will read about both kinds of partnerships. Whether it is a church-to-church collaboration or a church-community partnership, it's always about the well and not about the wall.

Churches Sinking Wells

Churches that are working together have discovered the biblical truth that there is really one church in the city that meets in different locations and at different times. There may be many congregations, but there is only one church. When the apostle Paul wrote his letters to groups of believers, it was to the church in a city that met in several locations. So he writes about the church in Cenchrea, the church in Corinth, the church in Rome, and so on. Understanding the "church in the city" concept may help explain verses like 1 Corinthians 12:28: "And in the church God has appointed first of all apostles, second prophets, third teachers, then workers of miracles, also those having gifts of healing, those able to help others, those with gifts of administration, and those speaking in different kinds of tongues." As you look around your individual congregation, especially if yours is a small one, you won't necessarily see all those gifts, but you will certainly see them distributed to the church in the city. Understanding that there is one church in the city allows us to experience the unity of family that we share as belonging to the same father (Ephesians 4:3–6), the unity of fellowship as we accept one another and worship together (Romans 15:4), and the unity of purpose as independently or cooperatively we seek to let the world know that God sent Jesus and God and loves every person on earth as much as he loves his own son (John 17: 23). Congregations are discovering that sometimes we can publicly express our unity, not through parades or marches but through service to bless our communities.

Catalytic Days of Service and Unity

In many communities around the country, churches are uniting around serving their communities for one- or two-day serving events. The advantage of such weekend events is that churches can jump-start their externally focused ministry by giving large numbers of people the opportunity to stick their toe in the water and get their feet wet in a well-planned, well-defined, time-bound opportunity that requires little preparation and training. Many churches in Omaha, Nebraska, have come together under the name of Step Out and Serve, "a joint effort of dozens of churches to bless the city through service projects in order to practically demonstrate our love for Jesus and for the people of the Omaha metro" area.[4] In August 2008, 6,200 volunteers from thirty-one churches invested 27,000 hours serving and loving their community, which city officials estimated was a half-million-dollar gift to the city.[5]

Eric Marsh, of Grace Brethren in Long Beach, California, is one of the leaders of Serve Day (http://ocnorth.serveday.org), an Orange County–based day of service started by Rock Harbor Church in 2000. In 2008, more than five thousand people from forty-five churches served at over 320 community organizations, businesses, and other locations. Eric says, "How does the movement of the gospel break out? I believe so much can be done when we are not being petty but unified. There is one church in this city, and if we put aside the things that are negotiable, then we can actually be a unified front for the gospel of Christ. More often than not, unity is developed shoulder to shoulder rather than face to face."[6]

In May 2009, sixty-five hundred volunteers from twenty-five churches worked in three hundred different locations throughout Cincinnati to transform neighborhoods, serve the homeless, refurbish Habitat homes, plant ecogardens, pray with the broken, paint schools, clean up empty lots, and help make a difference. GO Cincinnati (http://www.gocincinnati.net) is a one-day community service blitz started by Crossroads Community Church in 2005 to encourage believers to make serving a lifestyle, not a one-day event. After the work was done, the leaders of GO Cincinnati invited the community to a dinner in the park, prepared by nine of the best chefs in Cincinnati. It was a party and celebration as hundreds of people danced the electric slide in the park. Tim Senff, director of ReachOut at Crossroads Community Church, said, "This is what it looks like to give the best to those who have the least. . . . We're hard-wired by God that when you go out and serve someone selflessly, . . . there's no way that's not going to affect you, no matter where you are in your relationship with the Lord. It doesn't matter."[7]

Rural Transformation

Unified events don't need to be confined to cities or metropolitan areas. In Massillon, Ohio (population 35,000), RiverTree Christian Church (http://www.rivertreechristian.com) has pulled together more than thirty Stark County churches to provide a rallying point for the congregations of the county who share a common passion to see the county grow into the healthy and vibrant community that all locals want it to be. Leaders at RiverTree are committed "to invest in our community at least as much as our property tax assessment would be."[8] Ohio has been hit hard by the current recession, but the Christians of Stark County are thinking and acting differently. In November 2009, dozens of local pastors taught a common series of messages about the role of God's people caring for people on the margins of society. Over a thousand people served and worked together in countywide projects at schools and human service agencies. They culminated their month of prayer and service with a community Thanksgiving service where they raised $236,000 to retire the debt of the Canton, Ohio, homeless shelter and soup kitchen.

Most Popular Ways to Partner

In 2006, Leadership Network conducted a survey with the nearly seventy churches involved in the Externally Focused Churches Leadership Communities. Church leaders were asked how they had partnered with other local churches in community service ministry. The following are the primary ways in which these churches have collaborated in community service:

- Food programs (food pantry, Meals on Wheels, and so on)
- Emergency assistance (providing food, clothing, or short-term financial assistance)
- Child and youth programs (tutoring, youth sports, and the like)
- Housing programs (Habitat for Humanity, homeless shelter work)
- Prison ministry
- Medical and dental programs
- Immigrant ministries
- Special one-day project work

A couple of other interesting findings emerged. First, churches reported that they came together for prayer just as much as they gathered for community service work, and 96 percent of churches reported that "kingdom building" is their goal for working with other churches.[9] And one can expect this trend to accelerate. In May 2008, *Leadership Journal* surveyed nearly seven hundred evangelical pastors, asking "how their perceptions of the gospel and mission currently compare with their understanding a decade ago." Seventy-five percent of the respondents stated that partnering with other churches is essential to accomplishing their mission, compared to just 51 percent in 1998.[10]

One additional finding from the Leadership Network survey pertained to how churches in partnership measured the effectiveness of their collaborative efforts. Acknowledging the difficulty and need for improved metrics, the following list shows the most widely used forms of measuring success. (Survey participants could choose as many as applicable.)

- Witness of unity to the community (71 percent)
- Total number of people served (52 percent)
- Total number of volunteers (52 percent)
- Number of new relationships formed (47 percent)
- Number of service events (31 percent)
- Number of first-time volunteers (33 percent)[11]

Sometimes churches can unite under the leadership of a neutral kingdom-minded convener even if serving only the local community. Extreme Community Makeover is an initiative begun by Confluence Ministries in Denver, Colorado, to facilitate area churches and businesses to serve the people of metro Denver by assisting underserved people on one block with home improvement projects such as home repair, yard work, or painting. On the day Eric visited Confluence Ministries, 280 Lutherans were doing an extreme community makeover on one block in the West Colfax area. To date, the group has deployed over three thousand volunteers and refurbished more than 180 homes.

Why It Hasn't Always Been This Way

Before we move on to discussing other powerful partnerships—such as between church and community and church and state agencies—we would be remiss if we didn't take a moment to learn from the past. Why hasn't it always been this way? Why haven't churches engaged their communities in collaboration and with greater effectiveness? Here are some perspectives that we hope will help the church avoid repeating the past. Before Martin Luther, a priest and theology professor, tacked his Ninety-Five Theses on the wooden door of the Castle Church in Wittenberg, Germany, in October 1517, there existed only one true and apostolic church. This might be hard to comprehend, but a passionate believer could not start an "alternative service" or do "house church" in the name of conviction or effectiveness. To do so was to invite excommunication, charges of heresy, and even burning at the stake, as John Wycliffe and Jan Hus can readily testify to. The priesthood of all believers was yet to be realized, and so independent religious thought had great consequences. Luther himself understood the importance of unity, expressing a desire to reform the corruption of the church, not abandon the church, but his resolute conviction regarding justification by faith alone led to his eventual break from the church. This rift was not an amiable "Let's agree to disagree"; it was a standoff regarding who was right and who was wrong.

With the Reformation came the fragmentation of the protesting church. The South African missiologist David Bosch writes, "When the Reformation shattered the ancient unity of the Western church, each of the fragments into which it was now divided was obliged to define itself over against all other fragments. . . . The reformational descriptions of the church thus ended up accentuating differences rather than similarities. Christians were taught to look divisively at other Christians. Eventually, Lutherans divided from Lutherans, Reformed separated from Reformed, each group justifying its actions by appealing to marks of the true church.[12]

Did you get that? Churches split not because they wanted to establish a creative alternative to what the existing church was but because they were so convinced that they were "right" and the existing church was "wrong." It wasn't just differences—it was about right and wrong, about who had the truth and who didn't. To protect itself from false doctrine, each brand of church built walls that separated it from believers of any other ilk. With the priesthood of all believers (God does not have a hierarchy in his family), each believer had not just the right but also the responsibility to decide individually what the Scriptures said. Authority was decentralized to the extent that today there are an estimated forty thousand churches, each believing that it is the closest expression of what God wants a New Testament church to be.[13] And aren't you glad you found yourself in the right one? Most pastors will say something like this: "We're not a perfect church, but we do believe we are the closest expression of what a New Testament church should be." We've never met a pastor who said, "We feel we're about eighty-seventh in what God want us to be, but it's our five-year goal to move up another ten or so notches."

All leaders think their doctrine is correct, and the way they do church is the way Jesus wants them to. If there were a better way, they'd do it!

By asking "Do you care about what I care about?" we can bypass the issue of who is right and who is wrong and head straight toward kingdom solutions to community and world problems. We said this in *The Externally Focused Church,* and it bears repeating here: we form our partnerships not around our statements of faith or doctrine but rather around our common love and commitment to our community.[14]

Who Else Cares?

Many local individuals and entities care about the community. This common ground of concern and care provides the opportunity to work with unlikely partners to achieve something greater than the church itself could do. People of good faith can partner with people of goodwill around things they commonly care about. So you might ask, "Who else cares about underperforming schoolchildren?" or "Who cares about single moms or fatherless children?" We can build wells, not walls.

Rather than creating new faith-based entities, which take up kingdom resources, why not partner with others in the city who share a common concern for things you care about? Churches are finding tremendous leverage when they discover that partnering possibilities exist with almost any organization or entity that is morally positive and spiritually neutral. Working with groups outside our normal spheres puts us in face-to-face and shoulder-to-shoulder relationships that spawn a thousand unlikely conversations through which people come to faith. We need to tap in to the power of cross-sector networks; it's about common care for the city.

Embracing the same sentiment, the venerable Christian statesman John Stott writes, "God created man, who is my neighbor, a body-soul-in-community. Therefore, if we love our neighbor as God made him we must inevitably be concerned for his soul, body and community. . . . And there is no reason why, in pursuing this quest, we should not join hands with all men of good will, even if they are not Christians."[15]

Most churches and leaders tend to think about creating new opportunities rather than partnering. It's almost as if it is a knee-jerk reaction. Let's suppose that the local church in Anycity, USA, feels compelled to address an issue in its community—say, assisting the homeless (a huge need in any city). The typical path is to get a committee together to study the issue, appoint a task force, and set up a church homeless ministry. Needs are assessed, volunteers are recruited, money is spent, and we launch our effort to care for the homeless in our community.

It's likely that in your community, regardless of the issue, there is someone who is addressing it at some level. Having participated with hundreds of churches in all kinds of communities, we can offer a lesson learned by accident: those agencies, groups, nonprofits, and government coalitions see the church as competition. Despite its efforts to do good, the church is often perceived as an enemy or as "too good" to collaborate with others. We know this isn't a very good reason to start a ministry, but it does reflect that we have often been blind to what others are doing.

In our local community, we have a group that addresses the homelessness issue. It's become a cooperative effort of churches, government, businesses, and nonprofits. The needs are assessed, volunteers are recruited, and the community comes together to address the issue. It isn't perfect, doesn't always lead to success, and requires a great deal of flexibility, but the church becomes part of the solution and engages in the conversation.

Vision San Diego

In San Diego, California, 3,700 believers from fifty churches, flying under the banner of Vision San Diego (http://www.visionsandiego.com), came together the last weekend of April 2009 to serve the local community by completing one hundred different projects: cleaning up schools, nursing homes, military housing complexes, mobile home parks, and a fire station through a national service campaign sponsored by World Vision and Outreach Inc.'s Faith in Action (http://www.putyourfaithinaction .org), whose working motto for the weekend was "Don't go to church this Sunday. Be the church." But after the weekend, the groups wanted to do more. So they began to meet with government and city officials and asked, "What if we were able to pull together two hundred churches to serve the city? What could we do for you?" The city leaders identified five main problem areas where the church could step in to help.

• *Elder care.* With the cutback of state and local budgets, the twenty-two thousand seniors and adults with disabilities formerly visited by workers from the county health and human services department monthly were now being visited only once a year. They were relying on meter readers and mail carriers to look for signs of distress as a stopgap measure. The city volunteered to send out a questionnaire to seniors in need of county services, asking if they would like to be assisted by the church. One official predicted that twenty thousand of the twenty-two thousand people would request a monthly visit from the faith community.

The church was invited to make on-site monthly visits to as many seniors as the church could adopt.

• *Foster care.* The county health and human services department invited the church to adopt one of 102 group homes near the church's location to meet the needs of foster kids and their providers.

• *Military.* San Diego has the largest military population of any city in the world. The chaplain's offices identified over a thousand military families that desired and requested a church-based support group to help them out. The church was also asked to get training to provide help to work with the Veterans Administration in ministering to veterans with posttraumatic stress disorder.

• *Tutoring.* Working through the county office of education, which runs a program called Every Child a Reader, the church in San Diego was asked to help children in grades one through three learn to read at grade level. This is critical to long-term success in school and in life. Educators tell us that learning to read at grade level is the most determinative component of a child's future because until the third grade, a person learns to read; after that, a person reads to learn. Volunteers are given three hours of training and then volunteer locally at one of the 150 schools where the majority of kids are not reading at grade level.

• *Mentoring.* The juvenile court system is working to provide mentor training and to match mentors with kids in the juvenile justice system who need them—former gang members on probation or kids that have gotten into some type of trouble but have yet to be incarcerated.

Sometimes God puts ministry opportunities right in front of our eyes but we miss them because we are thinking and praying about other things or our own ways of doing things. But reread these five invitations from the city to serve the people of San Diego; clearly, when the city is inviting the church to serve, something has fundamentally changed.

Street GRACE in Atlanta

In Atlanta, Unite! serves as a network of over 140 churches led by pastors and faith leaders from a wide variety of denominations and cultural and ethnic backgrounds who work and serve together throughout the city through unified prayer, along with deeds of kindness, mercy, compassion, and justice. Together they are focusing on four impact areas: justice, education, poverty, and families. One key initiative that came out of the Atlanta

Externally Focused Leadership Community was Street GRACE (Galvanizing Resources Against Child Exploitation) (http://www.streetgrace.org). Atlanta is a major hub for child prostitution, and Street GRACE is working with churches, social services, law enforcement, other faiths, and government to eliminate the commercial sexual exploitation of children.

People of good faith have come together with people of goodwill to work on problems they all care about. Of the unlikely partnership, Stephanie Davis, policy adviser on women's issues for Atlanta Mayor Shirley Franklin, says, "Being a self-proclaimed feminist, I haven't had much chance to work with the far right . . . but the issue of commercial sexual exploitation of children creates an automatic response in any human being. No one has personal ownership of that issue."[16] Unite! leader Chip Sweney says:

> It's pretty amazing. There have been people outside the church working on child exploitation for a few years, but they were running out of steam. This is a billion-dollar industry, and those in control won't give it up without a fight. We've come alongside them with fresh fighting power. We're not trying to dictate anything but just trying to be a player at the table and a good teammate. Going after this issue is a good example of multisector collaboration. The resources from the faith community have really helped. As Christ followers, how can we not be involved in this and fight for these children? The small victories, such as fixing up homes for these children and getting kids off the street, have been really positive.[17]

StreetLight Phoenix

Churches in the greater Phoenix area have come together under the banner of StreetLight Phoenix (http://www.streetlightphx.com) "StreetLight was founded to provide opportunities for young girls to experience God's unconditional love, forgiveness, and life-transforming power."[18] Dozens of churches are working together to meet the physical, spiritual, and social needs of children affected by sexual exploitation. Currently, these churches, working together with marketplace leader, nonprofit organizations, government, and passionate individuals, are establishing homes in which these children can be cared for, educated, loved, and vocationally trained.

"When I Was Hungry . . ."

Most communities have a free or reduced hot lunch program to nourish children whose parents' income falls below the poverty line. This is a needed program, but here's a question that few people have asked: What do these same children eat on the weekends? The people of Titus County, a two-hour drive east of Dallas, did ask that question and came up with an innovative program called Titus County Cares (http://www .tituscountycares.org) that distributes more than nine hundred backpacks filled with child-friendly food for kids to take home as part of a holistic effort to prevent childhood hunger and give the greatest opportunity for children to succeed in school and in life. Each Friday, the elementary school children of Trinity Baptist Church fill the backpacks with food and pray for each recipient. One young recipient asked, "Could I get another backpack for my grandpa? He doesn't have any food either." Trinity Baptist Senior Pastor Mike Kessler says, "We are . . . working with government, business, and social service domains . . . to have a common purpose within our community, and everyone appreciates the disappearance of the church walls."[19]

Omar Reyes, from Northwood Church in Keller, Texas, discovered there were fifty to sixty kids in Haltom City that don't have supper because they live in motels without kitchens. So at night they have a soda and potato chips or other snacks. Omar prayed, "OK, God, here's a need. What do we do with it?" The answer was found in a partnership with one school district, two churches, and the Tarrant County food bank. "We came together around the common purpose of getting these kids a hot meal every night." Together they installed a kitchen at the Haltom City Christian center, their after-school tutoring program location, to feed fifty kids at Kids Café. Omar says, "Every week, eighty volunteers from Northwood feed and love on these kids. It's here that they meet kids and their families, relationships are built, and God takes it from there— and we see that life-on-life transformation."[20]

Season of Service in Portland

Imago Dei's Rick McKinley began the church not through Sunday service but through selfless service to the people in the city center of Portland, Oregon. Each year, Imago provides hundreds of volunteers to spruce up several schools and provides hundreds of families with school supplies, clothing, food, and Christmas gifts. In 2007, the mayor of Portland gave Imago Dei the Spirit of Portland award for its work at six underresourced schools in southeast Portland.[21] In the summer of 2008, the people of Imago Dei joined together with scores of Portland area churches and with the Luis Palau Association for a "summer of service" that culminated with a gift to the city of $100,000 for the benefit of homeless families and the education of recent high school dropouts. On the day when the check was presented at a city council meeting in March 2009, Nick Fish, Portland's housing commissioner, made the following comment:

> Something has happened here that I think needs to be acknowledged. As long as I've lived in Portland, there has been . . . a divide between the faith community—particularly what I would call the more fundamentalist, evangelical wing of the faith community—and the city of Portland. It has been my impression that what has frequently been accentuated in that relationship is the differences. And there have been some people both in government and in the faith community . . . who have been very effective in emphasizing those differences, and we know it's easy to pick a fight and much harder to find common ground. . . . So I have watched this relationship evolve . . . with some skepticism, and I think this skepticism was shared by many in the faith community. . . . But what has happened through this season of service has such a powerful resonance with all of us regardless of our faith or regardless of our path, that this has provided for us a new baseline for a new relationship of mutual understanding and respect. And "season of service," as I'm fond of saying, are three of the most beautiful words in the English language. If the season of service is a rose, we hope that it is a perennial and not an annual. And I'm so pleased the Palau organization and Pastor Rick McKinley and all of the folks involved who have said this is going to be an annual event.[22]

How Influence and Impact Can Grow

In the spring of 2004, leaders from Eric's church, Calvary Bible Church of Boulder, inspired by Little Rock's Sharefest (http://www.sharefest.com), met with the superintendent of schools for the Boulder Valley School District and asked what they could do to help and serve. "Give us the three schools that are in the worst shape, and we'll see what we can do." District officials identified an elementary school, a middle school, and a high school that budget cuts, time, and use had not been kind to. Seven hundred of the approximate one thousand people who attend Calvary Bible worked all day Saturday and three hours Sunday morning painting classrooms and hallways, scraping gum off of the undersides of desks and handrails, washing windows, striping parking lots, cleaning vents and sprinkler systems, landscaping and weeding, painting murals, and writing hundreds of letters of appreciation to the teachers and staff of these three schools.

The principal of the middle school beamed when she told Eric, "What you people have done today is an absolute miracle! You have accomplished more in a day than we could have done in three months." After cleaning the paintbrushes and storing the supplies, all of the volunteers met with school district officials at the high school for a celebration and barbecue. School officials were incredibly grateful for the $150,000 in labor and materials that were donated to the three schools. In tough economic times, $150,000 may mean that the music program, the art program, or the band won't be trimmed.

Once word got around, other Boulder area churches asked to come on board, so in 2005, fourteen hundred people from three churches did extreme makeovers at more schools. During this year, church leaders and school leaders celebrated at Mackey Auditorium on the University of Colorado campus, followed by a catered barbecue on the sprawling lawn. School officials gushed in gratitude for the $212,000 the church had provided in service to these schools.

Year after year, under the talented leadership of local pastors and volunteers, Sharefest has grown (see Table 6.1). By 2009, so many churches and so many people had volunteered to serve in the 130 projects, Sharefest had to be spread to six different Saturdays as part of a "summer of service." Churches praying together and working together can make a huge difference.

What Sustains Partnerships

Phill Butler, in his book *Well Connected,* defines a partnership as "any group of individuals or organizations, sharing a common interest, who regularly communicate, plan, and work together to achieve a common vision beyond the capacity of the individual partners."[23] People or entities don't partner together unless they really believe that they can

Table 6.1. Sharefest History in Boulder County, Colorado.

	2004	2005	2006	2007	2008
Churches involved	1	3	7	19	35
Schools and agencies served	3	5	8	19	50
Number of volunteers	1,000	1,400	1,700	2,200	3,500
Financial impact for schools and organizations	$150,000	$212,000	$258,000	$260,000	$600,000

accomplish more together than they can accomplish by themselves. And partnerships don't last unless each partner is gaining something from the relationship that they couldn't attain by themselves and seeing results that they would not be seeing working alone. The new thing God is doing is through unlikely partners working on common ground to achieve astonishing results.

Lessons Learned

LifeBridge has established fifty-four partnerships in the community, with school districts, social service agencies, government programs, nonprofits, other churches, and community projects. The church has also partnered with some local businesses on things they are doing in the community. Through the years, there have been plenty of lessons, much success, and a few failures. While there are some guiding principles, LifeBridge doesn't have any formal procedures for partnering but rather evaluates each opportunity on its own strengths and weaknesses. The church has, however, discovered some informal guiding principles that are true of partnerships.

Release Folks Outside

Most of the time, when people say "service" in the church, they mean "serve us." There have been some tough LifeBridge staff discussions about this over the years, especially when the church first began encouraging people to volunteer with community organizations. Will it take people away from serving inside the church? At the end of most weeks, Rick admits that LifeBridge still has internal recruiting needs. LifeBridge has discovered, though, that somehow God does the math and people find their best place to serve. As long as they are honoring God and helping to meet needs in the church or the community, Rick is content with that. So LifeBridge lists its internal ministry needs right alongside the community service opportunities and counts on good things to happen.

Every Partnership Requires Understanding the Rules

Put two people together, and you are bound to have conflict or misunderstanding sooner or later. Put more than two together, and the chances increase exponentially.

LifeBridge has improved its ability to clarify and understand expectations when it comes to partnering. Improvement mainly comes with time and experience. Every partnership needs defining boundaries and established communication channels. No matter how large or how small, each partnership has a LifeBridge "go-to" person. This person helps ensure that the church is doing what it said it would do and that the organization or other church is keeping its end of the deal. If there is a problem or someone falls short or more direction is needed, the LifeBridge liaison has the responsibility to communicate and help resolve the situation.

Most of the time, the church is simply helping a community group meet an existing need. For example, schools are regularly in need of volunteers for all kinds of things. They let LifeBridge know, and the church makes the need known. Rick is sometimes asked how many volunteers his church has in the schools. The correct answer is none. The several hundred the church has helped recruit are actually not LifeBridge volunteers; they are school volunteers. To that end, Rick and other LifeBridge leaders encourage these volunteers to play by the rules in that environment. As much as Rick would love for those volunteers to be able to read Bible stories during a tutoring session, volunteers use the materials the school provides.

You Don't Have to Wear Shirts

Several years ago, a TOMA study was done in our community. TOMA stands for Top of Mind Awareness. It is basically a marketing study to see what businesses or agencies were known for certain things. When it was completed, the group doing the study called to tell Rick that even though this wasn't being measured specifically, LifeBridge was consistently mentioned as "caring for the community." Of course, he was glad to hear that!

Rick remembers early discussions about how people would know it was LifeBridge people serving if volunteers didn't have some way to identify themselves. It isn't that volunteers from the church were or are purposely trying to go unnoticed; they are, however, intentionally attempting to do service for the sake of serving and not for getting a headline in the paper. If the group LifeBridge partners with has T-shirts, volunteers will wear them (Sharefest, March of Dimes, and so on), but they would prefer simply to serve.

Now here's a little side note about marketing: let service be service and marketing be marketing. Of course, as a pastor, Rick wants to see the church grow, and he cares about getting the message of grace and hope to the community. One of his personal pet peeves, though, is when Christians do marketing and call it service. We have all seen the bottles of water given out at some community events that have the service times of the local church printed on them with Scripture about never being thirsty. Rick is all for marketing, and there are ministries and activities that LifeBridge certainly wants to make the community aware of. There are plenty of ways to market, though, and at LifeBridge, they prefer to keep marketing *marketing* and service *service*. We'll talk more about marketing in Chapter Eight.

It Doesn't Matter Who Gets the Credit

Admittedly, this one is tough. When LifeBridge does something good, Rick wants people to know. Several years ago, a community agency had a big event to collect food for the local food bank. The agency had been doing it for years but each year was collecting less and less. The organizers came to LifeBridge and asked if the church could drive the event and give new life to it. LifeBridge went about working toward this community food drive. The result was a record (by double) of any previous year of food collected. The next day, the local paper had a huge headline about the successful drive and listed a number of the businesses that participated, mentioned the hospital employees and the Rotary Club and even schools that participated. But there was not one mention of LifeBridge, not even a hint that it was the result of some very capable church leaders and their volunteers who recruited those businesses and clubs. Who planned, worked, sweated, and basically did all the heavy lifting? Rick admits that he read the article and moaned. He notes, "Of course, I never got a complaint from one of the LifeBridge folks that we didn't get mentioned. I guess I forgot that we don't care who gets the credit."

Not Every Partnership Works Out

There are times when things simply don't work out. LifeBridge has had times when the parameters of the organization it was connecting with simply weren't in line with things that the church valued or created moral issues that church leaders and volunteers couldn't live with. Other times it was just a matter of personalities. For example, LifeBridge had a long-term partnership with a community organization that had been going quite well. It was very beneficial for both the church and this organization, which often called on LifeBridge to provide physical labor, painting, cleaning, repairs, and even child care and counseling. "The organization even found ways to assist in ministry activities we were doing," Rick recalls. "Unfortunately, when there was a change in directors, the partnership changed. The new director had no use for the church, Christians, or anyone who remotely thought God might be out there. In short order, this person found ways to make volunteering incredibly difficult. While we still cared about the same things the organization cared about, we couldn't find ways to work together." So a positive relationship ended up no longer being possible. While this scenario is not the norm for LifeBridge, Rick admits that some days you do have to take your ball and find somewhere else to play.

There have also been times when LifeBridge has been responsible for a failed partnership. The church had one community organization that provided computer skills classes for the working poor. Volunteers from the church were asked if they could help out. "We said yes when we should have examined the situation more carefully. We thought we could get some of our local business connections to donate computers. We didn't manage to get the number or quality that was needed and had to scramble to cobble together equipment—not quite what we had communicated could happen." To add to that disappointment, LifeBridge had several volunteers who said they could give a few hours each week to teach. Suffice it to say not everyone who volunteers for a task is suited to that task. LifeBridge was again embarrassed by the inability to do what the church said it would do. "It was early in our partnering experience, and it provided some painful lessons for us. It is better to underpromise and then overdeliver—a lesson we learned the hard way on this occasion," says Rick.

There Is Value in the People and Partnerships Themselves

Of course, tackling an issue in the community—large or small—and seeing any results is rewarding. LifeBridge has also learned that the relationships formed through partnering with other community benefit organizations or churches are of value in and of themselves. To come alongside others in the community who care is a blessing. Many relationships have lent themselves to conversations, not debates, about the things partners don't see eye to eye on. LifeBridge is constantly building relational capital and care for the people behind the partnerships as much as the initiatives they work together to solve.

Changing Who Waits in Boulder

One of Rick's fellow laborers in ministry is Brian Mavis. He serves as the externally focused director at LifeBridge Christian Church and for the Externally Focused Network. Brian and his wife, Julie, are passionate about finding homes for foster care kids. Brian and Julie know from firsthand experience the joys and heartaches of foster parenting, and the more they know, the more God leads them to leading others. "In virtually every county in the country, there are more foster children waiting for families than there are families with open homes, and there are more 'orphans' waiting for forever families than there are families willing to adopt," says Brian.

Although LifeBridge could have set up a center or children's home to provide group housing, the church chose to partner directly with Boulder County Social Services to achieve the department's goal, "Change Who Waits." Brian explains, "We don't want the kids to wait for families. We want to see families waiting for the kids! This was actually the expressed goal of the county, and LifeBridge embraced it." After a year of working with social services, Brian received this e-mail from the recruitment specialist of the Boulder County Department of Human Services:

> I wanted to share with you some very exciting news. With your help, dedication, long hours of volunteering, calling, referring, and bringing in families, we certified 104 families in 2008—that's 89% MORE than last year. . . . From myself, the Family Enrichment Team, and Boulder County, we'd like to thank you. You Rock!!!

December 2008 was the first time in almost three decades Boulder County had enough homes and families for all kids. "Together we turned the tide and reached our initial goal of changing who waits," says Brian.

What was the biggest asset that LifeBridge provided the Boulder County Social Services? Communication. Social services introduced Brian to a recent study documenting where people learn about foster parenting and where they would like to hear about it. Most people (65 percent) say that they hear about fostering through social services and child welfare agencies. Where they'd *prefer* to hear about fostering is their place of worship. Seventy-five percent of African American families surveyed said they wanted to hear about fostering at church; so did 59 percent of Caucasians and 61 percent of Hispanics.

Social services told Brian, "People prefer to hear about foster care and foster-to-adoption in their place of worship, due to the community, comfort, and support, as well as the fact that often, in the worship setting, people are more open to things they might not consider while at work or while watching football at home."

When he crunches the numbers, Brian notes that the church in America, in partnership with social services, has the capacity to change who waits all across the United States. "Some 500,000 children are in foster care in this country, and about 130,000 are available for adoption. There are approximately 350,000 churches in the United States. If every other church would adopt one child, no more children would be waiting for forever families. Furthermore, if every church would just *foster* one child, it would more than double the current network of foster families, giving every child a temporary home until a permanent reunification or placement occurred." Can you just imagine the church rising up together to build a well like that?

Fellow Workers

The expression "fellow worker" is used twelve times in the Apostle Paul's writings. Logically enough, Paul calls his vocational Christian friends Timothy, Mark, and Luke his "fellow workers," but this title is not reserved for the professional Christians but applied to his other partners from other parts of the community. The tent makers, Priscilla and Aquila, are his fellow workers (Romans 16:3), as is Philemon, the businessman from Colossae, and Urbanus, perhaps a government official from Rome, along with a host of others. The expression "fellow worker" is a translation of the Greek word *synergos,* from which we get our English word *synergy.* Synergy implies that the whole is greater than the sum of the individual parts: $1 + 1 = >2$. When we partner with others outside the walls of our church or ministry, synergy happens. We accomplish more together than we could ever accomplish alone. When synergy is present, we not only accomplish more but also become better people in the process. To become the best church for the community, we need to learn to work well and play well with others.

The Leadership Challenge

In the next ninety days, have lunch, coffee, or a break with six pastors in your city. If you are a pastor, you might initiate by saying something like this: "I feel a bit embarrassed that we've been ministering in the same town for all these years and yet haven't really sat down and talked. Could I take you to lunch?" While at lunch, you might initiate with the following questions: "Where have you seen God at work in our city?" "Where do you see the pain of the city?" "Is there anything God might have us do together that would make a bigger impact for the kingdom than we are presently doing by ourselves?"

(Continued)

(Continued)

In the ninety days after that, have lunch, coffee, or a break with six executive directors of human service agencies in your city. You might say something like this: "Hi, this is Pastor Harold Wong from First Community Church here in the city. I know you've been serving the city for decades, and as a pastor, I am painfully aware of how little I know about what you great people do. Can I take you to lunch?" While at lunch, ask about the history and mission of the organization and then ask, "What can we as a church do for you?" "As you were talking, I realized that you care about a lot of the same things we care about. Is there something we could do together?" "If we had twenty-five people available for four to six hours with no strings attached, how could we help you?"

In a third period of ninety days, do the same with school or government officials, asking these leaders to identify the biggest needs of the schools or cities. In the fourth ninety days, have lunch, coffee, or a break with six leaders from the business world in your city—CEOs, company presidents, other executives. You might initiate by saying something like this: "What do you see as the biggest needs of our city?" "If you could change one thing about the future of our city, what would it be?" After listening and jotting down responses, you might say something like this: "Over the past nine months, I've been meeting with church leaders and leaders of government, schools, and nonprofits to try to identify the biggest needs of our community. Here's what we've come up with. I think we'd all agree that to solve these problems, it will take the cooperation among all sectors of our community—the public sector (government), the private sector (business), and the social sector (human service agencies and churches). How can we work together to solve some of these issues?"

CHAPTER 7

Systems: They Create Paradigms, Not Programs

No good tree *bears bad fruit, nor does a bad tree bear good fruit.*

Luke 6:43

HOW DOES A CHURCH on an aisle slide over to a window seat? How does a church consistently engage in strength training rather than bodybuilding? How does a church become the kind of church that the community would not just miss, were it to leave, but would fight to have it stay? How does a church become both internally strong and externally focused? How does a church become the best church *for* the community? The answers to these questions are found not in programs but in paradigms. A program has a beginning and an end. A paradigm is a pattern or model from which many programs and initiatives will flow, but they will emerge from your strengths, from your capacities and calling. This chapter, then, is about creating structures and systems that enhance, strengthen, and sustain externally focused ministry. This may be the most important chapter in this book. Leadership is not just about finding leaders but also about creating good systems. An average leader in a good system will produce more than a great leader in an average system.

Most churches say that service, mercy, and love for those outside the church are import aspects of the Christian life. But this chapter is not about what people say but about what people do. You must create structures that operationalize your values; otherwise, they are not really values—they are merely sentiments. For many Christ followers, service and ministry are sentiments but not values. How can we make externally focused ministry a part of who we are, part of our DNA?

Creating Structures for What We Value

Externally focused churches create systems that continually reinforce their values. To align our beliefs with our behaviors, we create structures for everything that we value in church. For example, if your church values the teaching and exposition of God's Word, you would never have a service where the Word of God is not opened and read. Because you value prayer, you would never have a service where you would not pray. If you value the sacraments of baptism and the Lord's Supper, these are also regularly scheduled on your church calendar. Why do we structure these elements into the life of our church? At least partly because these are the very things that define us as a church, and to stop doing these things means that we stop being the church that God wants us to be. So if we didn't open God's Word, we'd cease to be the church. If we stopped praying, we wouldn't be the church. So we create systems and structures to help us live out our values and beliefs—and that's a good thing.

If we want the people we lead to "get into the game," we must create structures for them to engage. Systems and mechanisms are the link between our values and our behaviors. The right mechanisms cause good things to happen even when we are not paying attention to them. For example, if you have a system set up to pay your bills through some type of automatic transfer, think about how that simplifies your life (assuming that there is money in your account, of course). Somewhere around 2:00 A.M., while you are enjoying a good night's sleep, money is withdrawn from your checking account and your bill is marked "paid in full." The mechanism caused good things to happen even when you weren't paying attention.

In the book of Acts, for example, the Greek widows were being overlooked in the distribution of the groceries. This was a problem that was not going to go away. The early church leaders chose not to address this on a behavioral level ("You women should stop complaining; maybe a little fasting would do you good") but rather on the systems level. They instituted a mechanism—the diaconate—that would look out for the physical needs of the church, not just for that day, but for nearly two thousand years now. Good things have been happening even when no one was paying attention to them.

What Would Jim Do?

Jim Collins, teacher, researcher, and writer, elevates systems even above strategy. Writing in the *Harvard Business Review,* in an article titled

"Turning Goals into Results: The Power of Catalytic Mechanisms," Collins writes:

> Take 3M. For decades, its executives have dreamed of a constant flow of terrific new products. To achieve that end, in 1956, the company instituted a catalytic mechanism that is by now well known: scientists are urged to spend 15 percent of their time experimenting and inventing in the area of their own choice. . . . No one is told what products to work on, just how much to work. And that loosening of controls has led to a stream of profitable innovations, from the famous Post-it Notes to less well-known examples. . . . 3M's sales and earnings have increased more than 40-fold since instituting the 15 percent rule.[1]

Writing for *Inc.* magazine, in an article titled "The Most Creative Product Ever," Collins poses a question:

> What was Thomas Edison's greatest invention? Not the light bulb. Not the phonograph. Not the telegraph. I agree with many Edison observers that his greatest invention was the modern research-and-development laboratory—a social invention. What was Henry Ford's greatest invention? Not the Model T but the first successful large-scale application of a new method of management—the assembly line—to the automobile industry. What was Walt Disney's greatest creation? Not Disneyland or Mickey Mouse but the Disney creative department, which to this day continues to generate ingenious ways to make people happy.[2]

John Wesley and His System

If we can borrow from a chapter in church history, the contrast between George Whitefield and John Wesley serves as an important lesson for us regarding the power of structures that affect behavior. England in the early 1700s was in an abysmal state—economically, socially, and spiritually. Many children began "at four or five years of age to work in the mines, the mills, and the brickyards. . . . Less than one in twenty-five had any kind of schooling, and . . . [in] 1736 every sixth house in London was licensed as a grogshop. . . . This epidemic of drunkenness eroded what little decency was left among the working people, leaving them adrift in hopeless despair. . . . The English populace was gripped in a vise of poverty, disease, and moral decay."[3]

In London a couple of years ago, on an eight-hour layover between planes, Eric took a taxi to the British Museum. Among the fascinating

British Museum, London/Bridgeman Art Library

William Hogarth, *Gin Lane* (engraving), 1751

displays was an exhibit of life in London in the 1700s. It was appalling. One engraving, *Gin Lane* by William Hogarth, depicted the times well. One woman is pouring gin into the mouth of her baby. Another woman is sprawled on a set of stairs, with a baby falling out of her arms to the street below. There is a man in front of a pawnshop gnawing a bone with his dog. Many people lie about, passed out. One man is being placed into a coffin, and another has taken his life by hanging. Hogarth was a social commentator, and he captured well the moral state of London.

Into this environment stepped George Whitefield. Whitefield began what he called "field preaching." He was the finest preacher of his time. During a time when possibly only 1 percent of the British population were affiliated with the Anglican Church, Whitefield could draw crowds of several thousand coal diggers and mine workers. Even Benjamin Franklin sang his praises when Whitefield came to America. "Franklin calculated that Whitefield could easily address 30,000 people standing in an open place."[4] Although it was Whitefield who popularized open-air mass evangelism, it was Wesley who figured out how to preserve the fruits of such gatherings. Whitefield hoped that his converts would follow through on their decision, but Wesley, by contrast, created a method, or mechanism, to preserve the fruits. "He made sure that those who were serious about leading a new life were channeled into small groups for growth in discipleship. . . . The class meeting [small group] turned out to be the primary means of bringing millions of England's most desperate people into the liberating discipline of the Christian faith."[5] After several years of ministry, Whitefield lamented, "My brother Wesley acted wisely—the souls that were awakened under his ministry he joined in class and thus preserved the fruits of his labor. This I neglected, and my people are a rope of sand."[6] Wesley's methods were so distinct that his followers came to be called Methodists.

Jim Collins says that good systems cause good things to happen even when no one is paying attention to them. That means that once a system is in place, like Wesley's classrooms, he could easily (or at least efficiently) oversee thousands of believers. One thing we are learning about systems is the place of small groups in externally focused ministry. If service outside the church becomes part of the DNA of every small group in a church, then the ministry of each small group takes on a life of its own. Without this, someone always has to be pushing programs. That's just one example. What other *externally focused* systems could there be?

Creating Systems That Influence Behavior

Externally focused churches are churches whose effectiveness is not measured merely by attendance but also by the transformational effect they are having on the community around them. They share the gospel in word and deed; otherwise, for them, it's really not the gospel. How does a church build external focus into its DNA? We'd like to suggest six things any church can do to scoot from the aisle seat to the window seat. These are six different practices that externally focused churches consistently engage in to extend and reinforce who they are and strive to be. These are the habits of externally focused churches. These are the vital signs and benchmarks of externally focused ministry.

Start with a Strong Scriptural Foundation

Fundamental to an externally focused church is a strong theological foundation. To use a coaching analogy, the foundation consists of the basic skills of a sport that must be mastered before players can begin improvising. When God first began giving guidelines and statutes to his followers, such commandments included laws on justice and mercy. So as early as Exodus 22, God gives guidance for just and merciful compassion toward the poor, widows, orphans, and strangers. In the books of Leviticus and Deuteronomy, God, through Moses, is more specific in how all people should be treated, regardless of their physical condition or social status. The teachings are clear. One author and practitioner noted that injustice was "the second most prominent theme in the . . . Old Testament—the first was idolatry. . . . One out of every sixteen verses in the New Testament is about the poor or the subject of money."[7]

What then should you do? Saturate yourself in the Gospels. As we asked in Chapter Five, what did Jesus do? Christology (the life and teachings of Jesus) informs and shapes our missiology (what the mission of the church should be). Missiology then shapes and guides our ecclesiology—how we structure church to accomplish our God-given mission. Many churches are started with the usual mission, vision, purpose, values, and exercises and then illustrate them from the life of Jesus or the book of Acts. But all mission is really rooted in and begins with the mission of Jesus.

In 1984, a small leadership team at Mariners Church in southern California spent an entire year immersed in the study of God's Word, endeavoring to discover what God had to say about the poor and those in need in the community. These leaders were startled to find out how much God had to say about caring for the poor, the widows, the strangers, and the orphans that God has placed around us. References to helping people in need were found in both the Old Testament and the New. It took them aback to see how directly God spoke about how he wanted the poor treated and what he expected of the church in fulfilling their needs. The church leaders felt a burden to heed God's direction and accept the responsibility to bring their findings to their bourgeoning church of four hundred members. It was time to take action. It was time to take the field. Their theology informed their vision: "The vision of Mariners Local

Outreach is to help every poor and needy person in Orange County. We want to bring God's kingdom to these people by sharing through word and deed the message of the Gospel." The vision then shaped their threefold goal: "First, we teach our members what the Bible has to say about serving those in need. Second, we encourage them to become personally involved. And finally, we provide opportunities to serve."[8] As the leadership team brought its findings to the congregation, the congregation enthusiastically responded, with one fourth of the members signing up to be involved and donating $12,000 to jump-start what would become Lighthouse Ministries.

Today, Mariners Outreach, as it is now called, has an externally focused budget of nearly $2 million dollars. Each year, thousands of Mariners' people give of themselves in service to others—working in after-school programs on Minnie Street in neighboring Santa Ana or mentoring moms who permanently live in motels as part of the Miracles in Motion ministry. Because love, compassion, and service are "who they are" when Hurricanes Katrina and Rita struck in fall 2005, Mariners bought vans (that later would be donated to Gulf Coast churches) and mobilized scores of rotating teams to clean up and help rebuild lives and homes in the devastated areas. It's who they are. They could do no less. And in addition to sending helpers, special offerings allowed them to donate tens of thousands of dollars. It's who they are. They could do no less. To the people of Mariners, externally focused ministry is not a program or an emphasis. It is who they are, and to stop serving, giving, and loving would jeopardize their very existence. But it all began by looking at the heart of God.

Preach About It Regularly

Build God's heart into the rhythms of your preaching and teaching regarding those on the margins of society and the absolute need for service and ministry as it pertains to our own spiritual growth. The message of good news and good deeds resonates not only with believers but with seekers and unbelievers as well. A strong theological base forms the foundation for implementing every other strategy. The Scriptures are rich with God's heart for the less fortunate. Jesus' first public words, when he explains the purpose of his ministry in the gospel of Luke (4:18, 19), are from Isaiah 61:

> The Spirit of the Lord is on me,
> because he has anointed me

to preach good news to the poor.
He has sent me to proclaim freedom for the prisoners
and recovery of sight for the blind,
to release the oppressed,
to proclaim the year of the Lord's favor.

Jesus' kingdom mission was to be one of good news and good deeds—combining words of truth with works of grace. Of course Jesus loved and nurtured those who were closest to him (John 13:1), but he was always going after what he didn't have, not just preserving what he did have. He spoke about the shepherd who was willing to "leave the ninety-nine in the open country and go after the lost sheep until he finds it" (Luke 15:4). When pressed to stay in a place where he was appreciated and lauded, "Jesus replied, 'Let us go somewhere else—to the nearby villages—so I can preach there also. That is why I have come'" (Mark 1:38). Jesus taught about loving one's neighbor by telling the story of the Good Samaritan (Luke 10:25–27). He explained that one day God would judge our truest spiritual condition by how we treated those most unlike us—the hungry, the thirsty, the prisoner, the sick, and the stranger—and he punctuates his message by saying, "I tell you the truth, whatever you did for one of the least of these brothers of mine, you did for me" (Matthew 25:40). The early disciples were so captivated with the teachings of Jesus that they too lived them out. Paul was eager to help the poor (Galatians 2:10), and James was concerned that the poor be elevated to honor (James 2:1–13). The first decision the early church made regarded the care of widows (Acts 6:1–7). The disciples fully grasped the teachings of Jesus.

One of the responsibilities of leaders is to communicate vision. There was a time when Rick taught that vision was a clear, compelling magnetic image of a preferable future. It was something he'd read or heard, and it sounded good. After a few decades, however, he realized that vision is a glimpse of the future, and every time it goes by, a bit more becomes clear. As leaders, it is our job to help communicate the vision we see, and that means we must tell the story, tell the story, tell the story. Rick Warren is right: we preach to a parade. We can never share the vision too much.

In Chapter Three, Rick introduced you to the newest LifeBridge language: *discovering grace, growing in grace,* and *living gracefully.* He has that message everywhere and encourages staff and volunteers to develop their ministry initiatives around those three things. The LifeBridge elders—whose responsibility is to gauge the spiritual and missional health as well as the integrity of our ministry—are always asking staff and themselves these questions:

- How is this program or initiative helping people discover eternal change through God's grace?
- How is it helping people grow and see change in their lives?
- How is this program helping people change the world through graceful living?

There are times when Rick and his staff create a specific series of messages to address one of those questions. There are times when they infuse those values and that language into an existing series. The bottom line is that Rick and his LifeBridge leaders are constantly finding ways to reinforce those three messages of grace and change.

SUMMER OF LOVE

The fortieth anniversary of Woodstock and the other events of 1969 inspired LifeBridge staff to mount a "Summer of Love" series from June through August 2009. The entire series came from 1,2,3 John, and it was broken down into three parts. The first month's theme was "Love God," and every message was about helping people find their hope in Christ (Discovering Grace). Believers were encouraged to become engaged in a growth opportunity, small group, or other activity (Growing in Grace). At the end of those four weeks, LifeBridge held a baptism service. Rick explains, "We set up pools in our parking lot, and that weekend more than one hundred people climbed into those pools and gave their lives to Christ. It was wonderful to see people lined up waiting to get in between services. They went in with their clothes on, were baptized, were given a towel and a Bible, and drove home wet—but renewed."

The next month, LifeBridge did "Love Others," encouraging simple acts of kindness, and the last month, the church did "Love the World" and spoke about being world changers (Living Gracefully). Creative LifeBridge leaders also found a 1974 Volkswagen van that was painted up all hippie-ish, and every day all summer, groups of people from our church took the van out to perform a variety of services. People were innovative in what they did with the van. Some groups passed out cold water to construction workers; others cleaned city parks or bought gas for people behind them in line. Wherever the van was, something good was happening!

A YEAR WITH JESUS

In 2007, Rick preached through the Gospels for the entire year. The series was called "A Year with Jesus." As you can imagine, this provided regular opportunities to speak of being externally focused. Truth is, there is so much in the Scriptures about caring for those around us that it isn't too tough to have externally focused language be a part of any message or series.

Like so many other congregations, LifeBridge has developed some additional sites. There are currently two venues in different towns within half an hour of the main LifeBridge campus. Both of these venues use video as a primary way of presenting the message. Rick says, "Our campus pastors do a great job of making sure that we get their part of the body serving in their own, unique communities. In fact, before either site launched, we led with months of serving." This set the stage for an external focus from day one of these new communities of faith. Campus pastors and lead volunteers connected with the local police and government officials to learn what needs existed. The first partnership and service opportunities in those venues have come with the schools LifeBridge is renting on weekends to hold worship in.

No matter what campus you visit, LifeBridge is big on sharing stories. The best way to communicate vision is storytelling: stories of people serving, of people being served, and how God is using each of us to make a difference. Everyone has a story, and LifeBridge has created systems to collect and share them as often as possible.

Make It Part of Your Plans

Many large churches have what is called an executive pastor—a fancy title bestowed in exchange for doing what the senior pastor didn't want to do: hire staff, do performance reviews, plan, evaluate, and so on. Regardless of whether or not your church has such a position, every church has someone who aligns people and resources against the mission. The big idea here is that every person, program, or financial resource that is not helping further the mission is a waste of resources. Most churches have a planning cycle in which each ministry leader or volunteer is asked to submit plans for the next cycle of ministry (quarter, semester, or year). If we want to maximize the opportunities to get everyone in the game, we need to think of creative ways and strategies to engage everyone in externally focused ministry. Because we staff and budget around what we value in every planning cycle, each ministry department, from children to senior adults, can be asked to submit a plan for what it will do to get its people ministering and serving outside the walls of the church. Structures and systems help transform values and intentions into reality. Because we want to build ministry and service into the life of our church and into the life of every person, we need systems that help bring that about. If our values and objectives are right and the behavior is lacking, the problem is normally there are no systems in place that operationalize the values and influence behaviors and habits. Programs and tactics are what help people live out and experience the values of the church.

Frazier Memorial United Methodist Church has figured out how systems and structures encourage engagement. Ninety percent of its congregation of roughly five thousand is engaged in some type of volunteer service, either inside or outside the walls of the church. Missions Pastor Rudy Heintzelman explains how the church captures the energy and heart of its members to get them in the game:

> Each member fills out a commitment card on which they pledge their prayer, presence, gifts, and service—the basic United Methodist Church discipleship questions regarding spiritual stewardship. We offer 274 different volunteer opportunities, with number 275 being "anything the church needs done" and number 276 being "something I want to do but don't see listed." That's how new ministries are started around here. Other churches use these types of commitment cards but never follow through. We take these commitments so seriously that around here, not following through with a volunteer request is grounds for dismissal.

Rudy continues by explaining the effects that ministry and service to others have on the church. "People really grow as they get involved in service, and as they grow, they get excited and tell others and the church grows, which causes more people to grow. It's like a snowball rolling downhill. We never recruit for anything. . . . There are so many areas to choose from, and people simply self-select and do what God tells them to do." Rudy believes that people who become ardent followers of Christ need to be living out all four elements of their commitment—prayer, presence, gifts, and service. "We need all four elements . . . like the spokes of a bicycle wheel. A wheel without any one of the supporting spokes will collapse."[9] Frazier UMC has figured out how to get almost everybody into the game.

Infuse Service into Small Groups

John Wesley always viewed service and ministry to others as an integral part of his "class meetings" of small groups, home groups, or community groups. Interestingly, he was greatly influenced by a French Catholic nobleman from a century before, Gaston-Jean-Baptiste de Renty. De Renty dedicated "his whole life to caring for the poor and encouraging his countrymen to a devout and holy life." Among the practices that Wesley took from de Renty and incorporated into his small groups was "the establishment of little gatherings of devout people who met weekly for prayer, reading devotional books, distribution of food to the poor, and discussion of personal religious experience."[10] Wesley did not use small groups for personal Bible study. He felt they got all the Bible they needed to act on during the weekly gathering of the church. Again, following de Renty's belief that personal and spiritual growth came through service to others rather than careful attention to and introspection of self, Wesley put thousands on the playing field.

The way we get people into the game is to infuse service and ministry to others into the life of every small group as Wesley did. Every small group that is started has regular engagement in ministry or service outside the church or the small group. For churches that employ this tactic, service and ministry are part of what it means to be in a small group. So to identify with a small group in these churches is to identify with action, with getting into the game. Your question to anyone in such a small group could be "Tell me about your ministry," not "Are you doing anything outside the group?" For most benchwarming small groups, the biggest challenge is "What should we study next?" What will it be? A topical study? A book of the Bible? Some book by Eldridge? By infusing service and ministry into the life of every small group, think of the difference it would make in the lives of your members and the lives of those in the community. Think of the impact for the kingdom.

Service not only benefits others and helps us grow as believers but also builds community among the members of a group. One externally focused pastor put it this way: "Community is like sweat: it happens when you work."

Chase Oaks Church Plano, Texas, has been known for its internal health since its inception thirty years ago. Its pastor of adult ministries, Glen Brechner, says, "What we've been known for is not what we want to be known for." Six years ago, the church began turning its focus outward. "We don't want to be disconnected from our community. The mission is out there," says Glen.

To get away from the "subculture of church," Chase Oaks began with a lot of simple things, such as abandoning church-league softball and joining community-league softball. It started building relational bridges— bridges of compassion into the community. Four years ago, the church launched the Community Service Impact (CSI) Ministry. This has been a huge catalyst to develop partnership throughout the Plano community to serve and minister to local needs. A year after CSI began, Glen says, he called all the small group leaders together for a meeting and summarily fired every one of them—but then rehired all of them before they left for the evening. Their old job was leading a weekly or biweekly home Bible study. That job no longer existed. Going forward, Glen was asking each small group to have an external focus. "It's been absolutely electric," Glen says. Each group now commits to an externally focused ministry for one year and develops relationship with the people the group members are serving and working alongside. The expectation is that every fourth or fifth meeting, the group forgoes chips and dip for serving in its compassion ministry. "This has lit our people up," says Glen. With over sixteen hundred adults in eighty small groups, that's a lot of ministry taking place each year. Because they were posed for service and wanted "to respond to the needs of the community," each of the small groups also adopted a displaced family from Hurricane Katrina. Chase Oaks also has fifteen other externally focused ministry initiatives and continues to look for additional ways to serve.

What is different now about Chase Oaks Church? For one thing, what's "normal" at church is different at Chase Oaks. With an abundance of churches in the Dallas area, people in the community have plenty of options for their church experience. People come to Chase Oaks because the church is active in the community. Sixty percent of the congregation has been at Chase Oaks for less than three years—not because people are leaving but new people (especially those who want to be where the action is) are showing up. People are attracted to the church because of its community involvement. One man put it this way: "I don't know why I'm here in church, but last week you guys painted my neighbor's house, and I thought, 'I should check this church out.'"[11] Second, a new group of leaders have emerged at Chase Oaks. Previously, most folks thought one needed to be a Bible teacher to be a Life Group (small group) leader, but now leaders tend to be more entrepreneurial. Each Life Group has four leadership positions—the group leader; a "connect champion," responsible for creating community within the Life Group; a "growth champion," responsible for biblical content; and a "bridge champion," who leads the Life Group into making a difference in the community. The structure, depicted in Figure 7.1, is simple. Each Life Group has three goals: connect relationally, grow spiritually, and make a difference—belong, believe, and bless.

Figure 7.1

Chase Oaks Life Group Structure

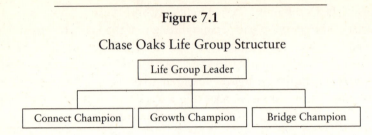

Here's something else Glen has discovered. As much as we'd love to have every person in our bailiwick living out his or her missional, Ephesians 2:10 passion, most people arrive at that passion through a process. Finding one's individual passion may begin with an annual churchwide service event like Sharefest, Serve Day, or Faith in Action Weekend. These events are highly organized and usually staff-intensive. These are easy entry "y'all come" events that require little preparation on the part of volunteers. Folks just need to show up and get their feet wet. Small groups (missional communities, Life Groups, and so on), then, with a regular ongoing externally focused missional expression, are a great intermediate experiences that helps people discover their individual passion and purpose. Figure 7.2 shows how Glen envisions people moving from organized service to organic service.

Notice that churchwide annual days of service are programs for the church. As commitment to love and serve outside of friends and family increases, eventually people can operate from personal passion, but missional communities are a wonderful way to regularly engage the community so that service becomes a habit and a lifestyle.

What are the other benefits of externally focused small groups? Here are a few things that we've discovered along the way:

SMALL GROUPS HELP PEOPLE LIVE MISSIONALLY

You're already familiar with our belief that good deeds create goodwill and that goodwill is a wonderful platform for sharing the good news. But something must come first. It is good friends who help turn good intentions into good deeds, which in turn creates goodwill. What we've found is that as much as we'd love for every individual to be living out his or her Ephesians 2:10 calling, it is service with our friends that is the critical path to get there. We've discovered that most people are more likely to do something they don't really enjoy doing (cooking for the homeless,

Figure 7.2

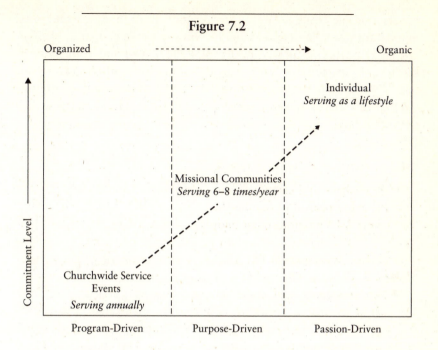

Organized   ----------------------→   Organic

Individual
Serving as a lifestyle

Missional Communities
Serving 6–8 times/year

Churchwide Service
Events
Serving annually

Commitment Level

Program-Driven   Purpose-Driven   Passion-Driven

after-school mentoring, handing out Snuggies to the elderly) with people they like being with than they are to discover that place of individual service by themselves.

We are often like one of the three paratroopers getting the once-over from the company commander:

"Soldier! Do you like jumping out of airplanes?" he asked the first soldier.

"Yes, Sir! I love jumping out of airplanes, Sir!"

And to the second: "Soldier! Do you like jumping out of airplanes?"

"Yes, Sir! I love jumping out of airplanes, Sir!"

Then he stepped in front of the third soldier. "Soldier! Do you like jumping out of airplanes?"

"No, Sir! I do not like jumping out of airplanes, Sir!" he replied but then quickly added, "but I love being with men who love to jump out of airplanes, Sir!"

Volunteer guru Don Simmons reminds us that "93 percent of North Americans are not self-initiators, so we really can't say, 'Here I am; send me.' Rather we must say, 'Here we are; send us.'"[12] Serving with others you like being with is a greater motivator than spiritual gifts. Sometimes when Eric is speaking, he will say to the audience, "If after taking a spiritual gifts test and being exhorted to find your place of service, if you actually went and did something, please raise your hand." Of the hundreds of people he's asked that question, only one woman in Canada raised her hand—and it turned out that she was only stretching.

SMALL GROUPS CREATE COMMUNITY

Community is a by-product of something greater. Speaking at Leadership Network's I-3 conference in Dallas in 2009, Matt Carter, lead pastor at Austin Stone Community Church, told of the Stone's journey into missional small groups:

> As much as we tried to build community through community groups, we had to admit that we stunk at building community. Most were inwardly focused and had trouble getting along with each other. We had to ask ourselves, "What is it in life that forms authentic community?" Our answer was "mission." That was the "aha" moment for us. Isn't that how Jesus built community? "Follow me and I will make you a fisher of men." We took that principle and applied it to our small groups. What if we didn't center our small groups around chips and dip, Bible study, and hanging out together and centered instead around mission? What if we changed to missional communities around a cause? So we began casting vision for missional ministry. One of our most dysfunctional small groups began to look around the city and saw thousands of international students at the University of Texas—most of whom will not spend time in an American's home. They are from every corner of the world. So this small group bought a smoker and got permission from UT to host a "Welcome to Texas" party. Over one thousand international students showed up, ate barbecue, and square-danced. This was step one. Then the group asked . . . , "How do we engage them in the gospel?" So they gathered other missional communities and began to recruit them to other events. Now families from other communities adopted these students to have dinner, do laundry, and have conversations about Jesus. It has made such a difference. Here is the crazy thing. If you were to go to this small group, what was once ugly, dysfunctional, and asking, "How are you going to meet my needs tonight?" you now have a group that is walking in mission together, . . . loving, walking, and serving together. It's happening all

over our church. We have over three hundred missional communities. Now here's the thing: when we aimed simply for community, we got neither community nor mission. When we aimed for mission, we got mission and community almost every single time.[13]

Writing about social movements in his book *The True Believer*, Eric Hoffer addresses the importance of action, not thought, as the catalyst that brings people together:

> Action is a unifier. There is less individual distinctness in the genuine man of action—the builder, soldier, sportsman and even the scientist—than in the thinker or in one whose creativeness flows from communion with the self. . . . Those who came to this country to act (to make money) were more quickly and thoroughly Americanized than those who came to realize some lofty ideal. The former felt an immediate kinship with the millions absorbed in the same pursuit. It was as if they were joining a brotherhood. . . . Men of thought seldom work well together whereas between men of action there is usually an easy camaraderie. Teamwork is rare in intellectual or artistic undertakings but common and almost indispensable among men of action. The cry "Go, let us build us a city, and a tower" is always a call for united action"[14]

EXTERNALLY FOCUSED SMALL GROUPS REALLY HELP PEOPLE

Missional communities have sufficient critical mass to make a sustainable difference. In 2008, Eric was in Alor Star, Malaysia, meeting with pastors and talking about externally focused ministry and the potential of small groups as the most underleveraged resource for externally focused ministry. In Malaysia, most churches work from a "cell group" model, and without a mission, even the best cell groups can turn inward. When Eric returned to the country six months later, Pastor Kuilan of Trinity Baptist Church in Alor Star asked Eric to lunch. He explained that after the first conference, he returned to his church and asked all the cell group leaders to begin loving and giving themselves to others who could do nothing in return for them. They threw themselves into the mission. Pastor Kuilan then brought out a three-ring binder and leafed through page after page of pictures and stories of what the cell groups had done. Some had adopted single moms; others, disabled children and adults. Others served in an apartment complex, and some worked with orphans. Serving others had totally transformed the church, but even more important, the church was really making a difference in the community.

Robert Moffitt, founder and president of Harvest Ministries, writes about the transforming power of small groups in a Ugandan church pastored by Gary Skinner:

> Skinner said that cell group members find a problem, take ownership of it, and engage and love the community. One seed project his church did was to fix and clean wells so the water was potable again. At a home for the poor, a cell group replaced a roof that was leaking so badly those living under it were wet, cold and sick. Another seed project raised food for orphans. "We are looking after twelve hundred orphans," Skinner said. "Half of them live in homes we have built." Every cell group of Kampala Pentecostal Church has been asked to take ownership of a family with AIDS, a major problem in Uganda. The groups do whatever family members need: a visit, a hug for the sick, someone to sit by their beds or help in getting medicine. Nearly all the patients come to faith in Christ. When a patient dies, instead of the drunken orgy that commonly follows death, the group holds a worship service with family members, who come to faith in Christ because they have seen and experienced Christ's love.[15]

We believe that small groups are the very best way to help a church live out its externally focused, missional DNA. Imagine what your church would be like and the impact you'd have on your community if every small group served and loved the city? What would it be like if every few weeks, instead of three hours of hospitality, snacks, Bible study, and prayer, the small group acted to meet the needs of something God cares about in the world? When small groups become missional, the church changes. . . . the world changes.

Engage in Regular Churchwide Projects

To provide opportunities for those who are not part of a small group or age-segmented ministry, regularly scheduled churchwide community projects help everyone get into the game. Every church could provide an annual day or weekend when everyone can participate in a community service project. Such projects don't require previous screening and can include the contribution of people of all ages—from babies in backpacks to senior adults. This is an opportunity for parents and grandparents to serve alongside their kids and grandkids. Having experienced these types of events in our own churches and hearing countless stories from other churches, we see the value of children working alongside their elders as they together seek to be Christ followers in practical ways.

Often good things happen just because believers are showing up. One of the pastors at Pantano Christian Church in Tucson, Arizona, told us, "During our annual Serve Tucson event, one of our members met a lady at a Laundromat and engaged her in conversation. This lady was trying to get a loan to attend nursing school. Our member, who was a supervisor at a local hospital, told this lady to come to the hospital and she would be hired, and the hospital would pay for her schooling—and that's just how it happened."

The outreach pastor at Fellowship Bible Church in Nashville, Tennessee, sent the following note:

> We called the weekend of May 19–20 "The Church Has Left the Building." We canceled all four of our worship services that weekend and told folks rather than *going* to church, spend the day *being* the church. We did not organize service "events" for the body. Instead, we had every Community Group go through a four-week series leading up to the weekend that focused on how to "lift their eyes" to see the relationships and opportunities God has place in front of them (like Nehemiah surveying the walls of Jerusalem). And we challenged them to go do it—to begin rebuilding the walls in front of their own homes. Some went out and served as Community Groups, others as individuals. We had people visiting nursing homes, providing meals at fire stations, riding the metro bus system passing out free bus tickets (with doughnuts, of course!), cleaning homes of single mothers, holding church services in some inner-city parks, cleaning up and stocking food banks, etc., etc. It was unbelievable. The following Sunday was a day of sharing what God had done. It was awesome—and we're already seeing Community Groups spurred on toward an externally focused lifestyle, not just events.

Having an annual service event is a great way to encourage intergenerational service. Wouldn't it be great to serve together year after year? Research shows that many young people walk away from their faith after high school. Wouldn't it be great if we could raise up a generation whose testimony might be something like this: "When I graduated high school, I tried to walk away from the faith, but I couldn't get over the reality of the good that my family and my church did in the community." Faith content may vary from young person to young person, but the church can definitely model what it means to live life as a giver and not just a taker.

Think "Kingdom," Not "Church"

In 2007, members of the Crossroads Christian Church adult pastoral team were feeling frustrated by the increased number of walk-ins of people requesting financial assistance and feeling helpless in what they could do. The Evansville, Indiana, church had a modest fund designed specifically for church family members; and it constantly ran to empty. "It elevated our awareness of need, and because we were all thinking the same thing, we felt that perhaps a movement of God's Holy Spirit was at work in our hearts. We've always believed that a church is not to be measured by numbers but by its impact on the community," says Todd Bussey, associate pastor. Church leaders wondered what kingdom impact they were really having on this very basic need. Leaders at Crossroads moved over to the window and started asking new "kingdom" questions:

- What should our church do in response to poverty?
- How do we know we are really helping people and not enabling unhealthy behavior?
- Is the solution only a matter of raising and giving money, or does it require a deeper investment of ourselves?

They really didn't have any immediate answers, just a lot of questions. This led Crossroads' leaders to a season of thoughtful dialogue and prayer. Each minister did personal research, and they all came back with these conclusions:

1. Poverty is a spiritual as well as a physical issue.
2. Christ came to preach the good news to the poor, and we have a clear mandate to minister to them.
3. How we choose to address the need is a necessary step in our personal discipleship.
4. Unity among interested agencies and congregations in strategic partnership is essential.
5. Poverty will probably never be eliminated, but the gospel brings hope.

The next step in their journey led to prayer and education. "Besides setting aside specific personal and corporate prayer, we took our whole team to a two-day-long "Bridges out of Poverty" seminar. We also sent a few of us to visit and see what Eric and Rick were doing in Colorado! It was here that we were given definitions on situational and generational poverty," says Todd.

The good news was that Crossroads saw that it was doing fairly well at helping people who had hit a rough patch. The bad news was that the church didn't have any meaningful investment in addressing those who have spent two or three generations in poverty. That led to a big step. Todd explains, "We reassigned Eric Cummings, a member of our pastoral team, to invest more of his ministry time to work on strategic partnerships with other congregations and agencies and to develop a blueprint for how Crossroads would be invested for the long haul." Eric's job description was simple: teach people, get them to pray, mobilize them for action, and figure out how to support those who are meeting the needs of the poor. In a short amount of time, Eric developed an impact team from church and managed to get around the table of nearly every agency in the city. He asked agencies:

- What are you doing?
- How can we help?
- What voids are there in meeting the poverty initiatives of our city?

He also orchestrated a series of van tours, filling them with members of the church and Bible study groups. "As the buses weaved their way to the inner city, he told our 'story,' explaining the comprehensive nature of poverty and what was being done to solve it. At several points along the way, Eric would stop to talk about a specific group of people serving the poor, pray for them, and then provide information on how they could get involved," Todd explains.

In a very short time, the agencies were being flooded with Crossroads people! The tours now occur monthly and are the single most effective training tool that Crossroads has discovered. The church also celebrates these victories by sharing stories in weekend worship and challenging people to live "great lives of service." Not long ago, a stranger identified Eric as a pastor who serves at "the church that cares." Crossroads didn't just create new programs; it changed paradigms. Good programs may help you be the best church in the community, but it is your paradigms that will help make you the best church *for* your community.

The Leadership Challenge

Rate your church's commitment and progress in the following basic areas of externally focused ministry (EFM) using this 5-point scale by circling the number that most accurately reflects the church's current circumstances.

No scriptural understanding	1	2	3	4	5	Strong scriptural foundation
No preaching about EFM	1	2	3	4	5	Preaching about EFM regularly
EFM not reflected in plans	1	2	3	4	5	EFM integrated into every ministry plan
EFM not part of groups	1	2	3	4	5	EFM infused into every small group
No churchwide EFM projects	1	2	3	4	5	Regular EFM churchwide projects
Thinking "church" over "kingdom"	1	2	3	4	5	Thinking "kingdom" over "church"

What is your score? If you found yourself circling 4s and 5s, you were most likely reflecting the externally focused nature of your ministry. If you averaged 3 or below, you know you have lots of potential for growth. What areas are within your power to influence or correct? Make it your goal to move up at least one number in those areas in the next three to six months.

CHAPTER 8

Evangelism: They Deploy Kingdom Laborers, Not Just Community Volunteers

The harvest is plentiful but the workers are few. Ask the Lord of the harvest, therefore, to send out workers into his harvest field.

Matthew 9:38

A COUPLE OF YEARS AGO, Eric was meeting with a number of externally focused church leaders. They were engaged in creative exercises and brainstorming around the topic of volunteers and how to get more people engaged in purposeful service and ministry in the community. Volunteers do a lot of good in the community (regardless of their religiosity—or lack thereof). So the question was "How can we get more church volunteers serving in the community?" We really have a long way to go when it comes to serving and ministering outside the walls of the church. George Barna reported in 2005 that "approximately one out of every four adults claims to volunteer their time to help their church's ministry during a typical week."[1] That's a good thing, since churches are run by volunteers. But what about the impact outside the walls of the church? In an article titled "Seven Sins of Dying Churches," the researcher Thom Rainer writes, "In a recent survey of churches across America, we found that nearly 95% of the churches' ministries were for the members alone. Indeed, many churches had no ministries for those outside the congregation."[2]

The discussion of externally focused leaders was progressing nicely when one of the leaders asked a perceptive question: "When Jesus asked us to pray for laborers for the harvest field, is putting more volunteers in the community the answer to his prayer for laborers?" Wow! What a zinger! Jesus didn't ask us to pray for volunteers for the community but to ask him for workers for the harvest field.

The group divided into a number of working groups where volunteers in the community and workers in the harvest were compared and contrasted. And finally it was concluded that "a volunteer in the community becomes a laborer in the harvest field when he or she combines the good news with the good deeds." Wow! Now that is a big idea that we can attach ourselves to.

Please don't misunderstand our point. We want to say from the onset that the world needs multiple times more compassionate, good-hearted volunteers. They are the instruments of God in his redemptive process. But we also want to make a distinction between community volunteers and kingdom workers. Kingdom workers always have an eye for introducing people to the king. They are convinced that real and abundant life is found in a relationship with the living God.

The Ministry of Jesus: Good News and Good Deeds

When the apostle Peter preached the good news for the first time to a group of non-Jewish people, he chose to summarize Jesus' ministry in a few short sentences found in Acts 10:36–38: "You know the message God sent to the people of Israel, telling the good news of peace through Jesus Christ, who is Lord of all . . . [and] how God anointed Jesus of Nazareth with the Holy Spirit and power, and how he went around doing good." All that Jesus did was summarized in good news and good deeds. First let's look at how Jesus went about doing good.

Ministry of Mercy

First of all, Jesus did good through his ministry of mercy. Mercy is God's attitude and action toward people in distress. Mercy is distributed without qualification. Their qualification is not their worthiness but their distress. Like grace, mercy can be neither merited nor deserved. When received, mercy makes someone's life better, if only for a day. Mercy is expressed in giving people a fish so they can feed themselves for a day. When Jesus fed the five thousand or when he fed the four thousand, he gave them the loaves and fishes, not because they were worthy but because they were hungry. "I have compassion for these people; they have already been with me three days and have nothing to eat. I do not want to send them away hungry, or they may collapse on the way" (Matthew 15:32). Notice that Jesus wasn't fearful that people would die but that people might collapse or faint along the way. So after multiplying the loaves and fishes, he sent them on their way.

Now if they were like many of us, they'd probably be hungry again when they got home. This act of mercy did not cure world hunger. He didn't take a systemic approach to their hunger by giving them tips on reaping a bigger harvest or seed planting techniques. He also didn't shame them by saying, "You should have known that this was going to be a long time of teaching, and you should have brought your own food, so to teach you all a lesson, I'm sending you home without any supper." No, he multiplied the food, and everyone had more than enough. That's what mercy is; that's what mercy does.

Think of when Jesus and his disciples stopped by the home of Peter and Andrew. Most likely Peter said something like this: "Hey, we're pretty near my house. I'll bet my mother-in-law will whip us up a good meal if we hurry." So the text says, "When Jesus came into Peter's house, he saw Peter's mother-in-law lying in bed with a fever. He touched her hand and the fever left her, and she got up and began to wait on him" (Matthew 8:14–15). Peter's mother-in-law probably had many fevers in her lifetime and would probably have many more to come, but for that evening, Jesus made her life better. That's what mercy does. So she fixed supper and had a great evening of fellowship with Jesus, her son-in-law, and his buddies.

Mercy is expressed in the deeds of the Good Samaritan (Luke 10:25–37). Where others had passed the bruised and beaten man, the Samaritan saw him, went to him, bandaged his wounds, put him on his donkey, took him to the inn, spent the night with him, and paid the innkeeper in the morning with the promise to cover any additional expenses. Mercy is as simple as medical help, transportation, companionship, lodging, and perhaps a little well-spent cash.

Eric's son Andy, along with his wife, Natalie, and their two children, have lived in East Asia for the past five years, sharing their faith in Christ and building spiritual movements. Recently Andy told his dad that before he does Bible study each week with groups of students, they go into the streets and serve the poor and the migrants. When Eric asked him how he decided to do this, here's how he replied: "Remember how Jesus ends the parable of the Good Samaritan? He says, 'Go and do likewise'—not 'Go and think likewise' or 'Go and value likewise.' It's our goal to help students become like Jesus, and I can't tell if they are becoming like Jesus by the answers they give me in Bible study, but I can tell if they are becoming more like Jesus when they serve and love as Jesus did."

Churches have figured out that mercy is a wonderful expression of what it means to be like Jesus to the world. Sometimes you may wonder, "With all the need in the world, what difference could we possibly make?" Perhaps you have heard the story of the boy walking along the beach with his father. A recent storm had washed thousands of starfish up onto the beach, and many of them were dying. The boy began stooping over and tossing the starfish back into the surf. The father, somewhat puzzled, asked his son, "With the thousands of dying starfish stranded here on the beach, what difference do you think you can make?" Without breaking stride, the young boy picked up another starfish, lobbed it into the sea, and said, "Well, Dad, I just made a difference for that one"—he tossed another—"and for that one"—he tossed another—"and for that one." Mercy is about making a difference for "that one."

If you are wondering where you might get started in your ministry of mercy, turn to Matthew 25:31–46 and review the story of the sheep and the goats. In this passage, Jesus commends people for how they responded to the hungry, the thirsty, the sick, the stranger, and the prisoner. Being merciful is as simple as providing food or clean water or medical attention, hospitality, or visitation to people in distress.

Recently, Eric received an e-mail from a Leadership Network coworker who had just returned from Healing Place Church (HPC) in Baton Rouge, Louisiana. He wrote:

> I'm just finishing up a great trip to Healing Place Church in Baton Rouge. Healing Place is not a place to go if you want to play church. . . . Pastor Dino Rizzo and his staff are committed to reaching out to hurting and poor people in the area. For example, yesterday, our group took a 40-minute trip over to the Donaldsonville Campus to visit and feed the widows. I'm quite embarrassed to say that this was my first experience actually doing something that God commands us specifically to do. Each Thursday, HPC feeds close to 70 widows in this small, very poor community (the average income in this neighborhood is just $8,900 per *year*). At each house, we went in and prayed with these women and gave them something to eat. These are people that the world has forgotten, but HPC is ministering too. And you should have seen how much these women appreciated the visit. A lot of ministry took place in those two short hours. It stretched me and was a great experience. This type of ministry goes on each and every day here at Healing Place. Last year alone, they gave over $1 million to missions and outreach, prepared 65,000 meals for hungry people, provided medical care to 1,300 people, made 1,200 hospital visits, gave away 1,800 $25 Christmas vouchers to underresourced people, and saw over 1,400 people make first-time decisions for Christ.[3]

Jack Jezreel recently challenged Eric with a new iteration of an old question we've been asking externally focused churches. He asked, "If your church disappeared, would the poor notice?"

Ministry of Empowerment

Jesus went about doing good not just through his ministry of mercy but also through his ministry of empowerment—Jesus' healing ministry. Anytime Jesus healed someone of a debilitating disease or caused the deaf to hear, the blind to see, or the lame to walk, he was improving the recipient's life not just for a day but for the rest of the person's life. He was helping people move from dependency (most of these people had to beg to make a living) to sufficiency. Whereas mercy gives people fish so they can feed themselves for the day, empowerment teaches people how to fish so they can feed themselves for a lifetime.

After reading Psalm 68:5—"A father to the fatherless, a defender of widows, is God in his holy dwelling," Pastor Robert Gelinas of Colorado Community Church in Aurora, Colorado, asked himself, "If God is the father to the fatherless, who is the mother to the fatherless?" His answer was "the bride of Christ: the church." As a cofounder of Project 1.27 (http://www.project127.com), Robert is excited to see the results of this way of empowering children. Working with twenty other Colorado churches, Project 1.27 has found permanent families for eighty-five children, with another fifty-seven families about to complete the adoption process. Another hundred families are queued up to adopt children. The result is that there are fewer adoptable children today in Colorado than there were in 2005.

Mercy tends to deal with the symptoms of a person's life. Empowerment deals with the underlying causes of those symptoms, and we are called to work on both. Jesus said, "Make a tree good and its fruit will be good, or make a tree bad and its fruit will be bad, for a tree is recognized by its fruit" (Matthew 12:33). If you want to change the fruit, you've got to change the tree. Mercy is giving people a fish so they are fed for the day. Empowerment is teaching people how to fish, how to own the pond, and even how to zone the pond for fishing.

Believers can make a powerful difference in the lives of others, but it may take a different kind of thinking regarding the best way to help. Robert Lupton writes:

> Ancient Hebrew wisdom describes four levels of charity. At the highest level, the giver provides a job for a person in need without that person knowing who provided it. At the next level, the giver provides work that the needy person knows the giver provided. The third level

is an anonymous gift. At the lowest level of charity, which should be avoided whenever possible, the giver gives a gift to a poor person who has full knowledge of the donor's identity. The deepest poverty is to have nothing of value to offer. Charity that fosters such poverty must be challenged. We know that work produces dignity while welfare depletes self-esteem. We know that reciprocity builds mutual respect while one-way giving brews contempt. Yet we continue to run clothes closets and free food pantries and give away benevolence funds, and we wonder why the joy is missing.[4]

Ministries of mercy and empowerment reflect the value of physical well-being. It can be argued that the soul will outlive the body, but the well-being of both the body and the soul are equally important to God—and should be to us.

Sometimes people ask, "But what if the people we serve don't respond the way we'd like them to?" The truth is that many people won't come to faith regardless of what evidence they have (Matthew 11:20). So in Luke 17:11–17, we read of Jesus and ten lepers. Lepers were the outcasts of society. Jesus did what only he could do: he cleansed all ten of the lepers. Interestingly, only one in ten returned to Jesus and made the God connection by giving praise to God. We think Jesus knew all along that only one would make the God connection, and yet knowing that nine would go on their merry way didn't prevent Jesus from healing them. He healed them not because they would convert but because they were broken. Likewise, although we believe there is no more fertile ground for evangelism than selfless service, we serve not to convert but because we have been converted. We serve not to make others Christian but because we are Christians. People are worthy recipients whether they become Christ followers or not. Evangelism is our *ultimate* motive, but it can never be our *ulterior* motive for serving.

John Stott shares his insight regarding motives in service:

> To sum up, we are sent into the world, like Jesus, to serve. For this is the natural expression of our love for our neighbors. We love. We go. We serve. And in this we have (or should have) no ulterior motive. True, the gospel lacks visibility if we merely preach it, and lacks credibility if we who preach it are interested only in souls and have no concern about the welfare of people's bodies, situations and communities. Yet the reason for our acceptance of social responsibility is not primarily in order to give the gospel either a visibility or a credibility it would otherwise lack, but rather simple uncomplicated compassion. Love has no need to justify itself. It merely expresses itself in service wherever it sees need.[5]

Ministry of Evangelism

Whereas mercy makes a person's life better for a day and empowerment improves a person's life for a lifetime, evangelism makes people's lives better for eternity. Jesus always kept people's eternal destiny in mind. So with Nicodemus, the religious man, Jesus directed the conversation toward his need for spiritual birth—and Nicodemus was transformed. Through her encounter with Jesus, the woman at the well was transformed from a serially husbanded adulterer to the first person to introduce her entire city to Jesus. When Zacchaeus climbed down from the sycamore tree, he was changed from a cheating tax collector to a philanthropist. Think of the thief on the cross. He had done nothing to deserve salvation, but his simple prayer of faith—"Lord, remember me . . ."—garnered the response from Jesus, "Today you will be with me in paradise." Evangelism changes people for eternity. It is well and good to want to be "the hands and feet of Jesus" by what we do, but we also need to be the voice of Jesus by what we say and how we say it. Romans 10:17 expresses the need for words in our evangelism: "Faith comes from hearing the message, and the message is heard through the word of Christ." How do deeds of mercy and empowerment affect evangelism?

How do mercy and empowerment connect to evangelism? Here's how we make the connection. We say "Good deeds create goodwill, and goodwill is a wonderful platform for good conversations about the good news." A couple of years ago, the pastor of a large multisite church in Sacramento, California, told us of his church's mentoring and tutoring program with an underresourced middle school. One day, the principal of the middle school called the pastor and asked, "Would you start a church here at our school?" The pastor excitedly agreed but then asked what would prompt such a request. Here's what the principal said: "We notice that every time you people show up, good things happen, and we just want more good things to happen on a more regular basis." Good deeds create goodwill.

What are good deeds, exactly? Jay Lorenzen, of Campus Crusade's Faculty Commons ministry, points out that good deeds are those that are perceived as good by both the receiving culture and the church. Working from the words of Peter, Christ-followers "live such good lives among the pagans that, though they accuse you of doing wrong, they may see your good deeds and glorify God on the day he visits us" (1 Peter 1:12). It is only in the overlap of what we perceive as "good" and those outside the church perceive as "good" that we let our light shine. So Jesus parades and personal spiritual disciplines may be good works, but these are not necessarily perceived by the culture to be so. The diagram in Figure 8.1 helps explain this life-giving intersection.

Figure 8.1

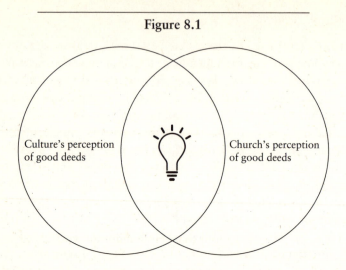

It is within this space of mutually perceived good where the light shines that conversations move toward God. New Song Church's Dave Gibbons says, "Justice, advocacy, and compassion have to lead the conversation, or it won't be authentic to the next generation."[6] Campus Crusade's Ben Ecklu, from a predominantly Muslim country in Africa, says, "In our country, if you come and tell about Christ, you are stoned. If you come to dig a well, the government gives you the land to build a church and protects you from others, and if someone tries to attack you, the government steps in and says, 'No, these are good people.'"[7]

Riding on the shuttle bus to the airport not long ago, Eric sat next to the principal of one of the elementary schools where his church, Calvary Bible Church, held its annual Sharefest event. When Eric asked if she had been involved in Sharefest, she replied:

> It brought tears to my eyes to see hundreds of people showing up and working at our school. A youth pastor met with us a few weeks before and asked me, "What is it that you need? What do you want done? Go ahead and dream. I can't guarantee we can do it, but we'll try." Being from Hawaii, I have always wanted an outdoor classroom where teachers could take their students and sit under a tree. And you know what? They did it! By eleven o'clock on Sunday morning, the outdoor classroom was built. The church was amazing!

Good deeds created goodwill, and in this atmosphere of goodwill, it was very easy to talk about her story, Eric's story, and God's story.

Two Questions

When people are recipients or observers of undeserved mercy or grace, they always ask two questions: "Who are you?" and "Why are you here?" A couple of years ago, Eric got a call from Randy Chestnut. Randy had moved to Cleveland to plant churches as part of a city initiative called Strategic Cities. Over the phone, Randy explained that he had gone to the mayor of Cleveland and asked the Jesus question, "What can we do for you?" After some justified hesitation, the mayor said, "Can you guys paint houses?" Randy assured him that they could mobilize lots of people to paint houses. The mayor told Randy that the government gave the city a grant to paint houses of elderly or disabled people, but the grant barely covered the cost of the paint, let alone the labor. Randy assured him not to worry about that. How did it all work out? "Well," Randy said, after four months, we've painted around thirty houses and seen nearly that many people come to Christ." The initiative came to be called Fresh Coat Cleveland.[8]

Eric asked Randy how the evangelism works. "We're very intentional about evangelism," Randy explained, "since we believe that we're never more like Jesus than when we are serving. So we expect God to show up in unusual ways. So sometimes the people who live in the house come to Christ. We have people prayer-walking through the neighborhood, and sometimes the people they talk to and pray with come to know Jesus. The last person who came to Christ was a man who lived next door who had to figure out why a dozen people would take a week of vacation to paint a house for a person they didn't even know." Randy's team had started a Bible study in that man's home and hoped to turn it into a church plant.

In Omaha, Christ Community Church partnered with public schools and others to help pack and ship three hundred thousand food packets through the Meals for Mali program. After working side by side with church people, one public school teacher commented, "I want to be part of a church that is making this type of difference in the world."[9]

At Crossroads Christian Church in Cincinnati, the church partnered with Habitat for Humanity and provided the labor to build a home for Michelle, a single mom who had no place to live. As Michelle got to know the people of Crossroads, she decided to "try God out" for the first time in her life and began attending Crossroads. Through the love shown to her and the truth of the gospel lived out and explained to her, both Michelle and her daughter gave their lives to Christ. It was through her new friendships at Crossroads that Michelle landed a well-paying job at a local hospital.

More Pearls for Single Moms

As an executive who helped build a successful company and then transitioned to an executive role in a large aerospace concern, Hal Bagley was given the benefit of a significant amount of leadership training. Like many successful people, he felt a calling to apply his leadership to the benefit of his local community. He just wasn't sure what to do or how to do it.

A group of business leaders brought together by common faith began to meet and assess various community challenges (meth addiction, high recidivism rates, economic issues, gangs) and finally chose to tackle the growing single-parent challenge, which they felt undergirded the other community challenges. It was sobering to these executives to realize that 24 percent of children in the county lived in a single-parent household and that the majority of those households were headed by women.[10]

The Pearl Group was formed, and Hal was given the opportunity to lead. Pearl initially focused on single moms, providing them with an opportunity to get "unstuck." The group wanted this to be a ministry of mercy, empowerment, and evangelism. The empowerment goals were training for higher-income employment, formal education, housing, low-cost or free car repairs, emergency microloans, child care, parenting classes, financial management classes, and affordable housing. Hal explains Pearl in greater detail:

> Our focus is to seek solutions that are built on self-sustaining business models and partner with existing businesses and agencies. We don't wish to duplicate services that already exist. Thus far, we have put in place the car repair service, The Closet (free but high-quality clothing for moms and their children), financial management and parenting classes, and nonmandatory Christian-based weekly support meetings. We are in the process of establishing a multipartnership solution to supporting education with the county department of human services, the local community college, existing licensed child care facilities, and ourselves. Affordable after-hours child care was a big barrier to a single mom's decision to go back to school.

This LifeBridge Christian Church ministry offers all components: mercy, empowerment, and evangelism. The Closet gets fifty-eight customers per week, 70 percent of them nonmembers of the church (the mercy component). Some of these nonmembers have joined the Wednesday night single moms group. The car repair service accepts donated vehicles, some of which are sold to generate the funds that pay for the "free" repairs. The remaining vehicles go to single moms in need of transportation for employment or education (the empowerment component). To date, the Pearl Group has seen seventy-five cars repaired and provided eight free cars to clients. The voluntary Wednesday night single moms group, which provides Christian-based classes, meals, child care, and fellowship has doubled over the past twelve months, and one of every three new members was not previously associated with the church or even the faith (the evangelism component). Hal's greatest piece of advice? "Get started! We didn't know all the answers—or any answers, for that matter—but you just have to start the journey, and God will work through you."

Driving or Putting?

Doug Pollock refers to himself as a recovering evangelist. As the evangelism trainer for Campus Crusade's Athletes in Action, he has trained thousands of people on six continents in effective evangelism. In his younger days, he did what he called "bar evangelism," inviting students to follow him into crowded bars and holding conversations about Jesus with all who would listen. "It was exciting and a whole lot of fun. The problem was that although students admired my boldness, very few followed me. I was a leader without followers."[11]

Doug began to look for a more effective approach to evangelism, more in concert with the way God has wired people. In a book that he wrote with Steve Sjogren and Dave Ping called *Irresistible Evangelism*, Doug employs the metaphor of golf to help us think clearly about evangelism.[12] He notes that the most highly used evangelistic tools, such as *The Four Spiritual Laws*, *The Bridge*, and the *Roman Road*, were designed when many (if not most) people in our culture shared a common worldview and intellectually knew a lot of the Bible story. They were on the green, very near the hole, and just needed to know how they could take the next step and become a Christian. What the evangelist needed was an evangelistic putter to help with the decision. As recently as a decade ago, the majority of non-Christians aged sixteen to twenty-nine were "favorably disposed" toward Christianity's role in society. Today, only 16 percent of non-Christians in that age group are favorably disposed toward Christianity, with a mere 3 percent favorably disposed toward evangelicals.[13] This means that today people are farther from the green and we need more than one golf club to be effective. What is important is that everything we do moves them closer to the pin. Doug points out that one of the greatest golfers of all time, Tiger Woods, as of 2007 had scored only nineteen holes-in-one![14] Even the best golfers take more than one shot to put the ball in the hole. Evangelistic hole-in-one stories are the exception, not the norm. We need to add more clubs to our bag if we want to effectively play today's golf course. Unexpected mercy, grace, or service is a great tee shot that puts the conversation on the fairway. Doug contrasts approaches that are more effective:

LESS EFFECTIVE	MORE EFFECTIVE
Monologue	Dialogue
Compelling proof	Compelling stories
Presentations	Conversations
Words	Images
Our language	Their language
Us versus them	Fellow travelers
Number of conversions	Number of conversations
Front-door approaches	Back-door approaches
Fishing from the bank	Swimming with the fish
Believing to belong	Belonging before believing
Driven by events	Driven by context
"Come and see"	"Go and be"
Scripted	Spontaneous
Winning	Nudging
Gospel presentations	Gospel experiences[15]

We really like the approach Doug is taking. (You can find out more about his ministry at http://GodsGPS.com.)

Good Deeds and Goodwill

If you study the ministry of Jesus, you will note that almost invariably his good deeds created goodwill among the people around him. After observing the kindness, mercy, and love of Jesus, the Gospels tell us that people in the crowd were in awe or wondered or were astonished or marveled or held Jesus in high esteem. Good deeds almost always create goodwill with others. Deeds get people's attention as few words can. Nevertheless, goodwill alone does not lead people to faith in Christ, so it is important that we not mistake goodwill for good news.

As we wrote about in *The Externally Focused Life*,[16] people on their own often come to erroneous conclusions by just observing the work of God. When the Holy Spirit came upon the believers in Acts 2, the writer records that the onlookers were "amazed and perplexed" and "asked one another, 'What does this mean?'" Others concluded that "they have had too much wine." They needed the words of God to explain the work of God, so Peter stood up and began his explanation: "Let me explain this to you; listen carefully to what I say" (Acts 2:14). The result was three thousand people putting their faith in Jesus. In Acts 3, when God healed the beggar through Peter and John, the crowd was "filled with wonder and amazement at what happened to him" (Acts 3:10). Peter again had to give them understanding, "Why does this surprise you? Why do you stare at us as if by our own power or godliness we had made this man walk?" (Acts 3:12). Scriptural example after example leads us to believe that God will tee up the conversation through the good deeds but there is still good news to be shared. We must keep in mind that "faith comes from hearing the message, and the message is heard through the word of Christ" (Romans 10:17). Good deeds may *verify* the good news, but we need good news to *clarify* the meaning of the good deeds.

Water of Life Community Church in Fontana, California, is living out its slogan, "Passion for God, Compassion for People." For the past few years, the church has hosted WOW JAM, (http://www.wowjam.com), a neighborhood festival designed to create community and make Jesus visible in the toughest of communities. At the 2008 WOW JAM, more than four thousand neighbors showed up to eat hamburgers, slurp snow cones, and listen to great local bands. Church people repaired bikes and cooked up 4,100 hamburgers. Pastor Danny Carroll called it "an amazing day" as the good deeds created enough goodwill to create space for over six hundred people to commit their lives to Christ and eighty of those being baptized over the weekend of WOW JAM.

Pastor Hal Seed of New Song Community Church in Oceanside, California, sees hundreds of people come to faith every year at his church. Being so close to the Marines' Camp Pendleton allows it to be actively engaged in ministering to military families—especially those whose loved ones are deployed. The people of New Song are very committed to both showing their love and telling of God's love. Hal says:

> Events like Operation Yellow Ribbon ("welcome home" parties for returning soldiers) are almost always pre-evangelism events. People can smell inauthenticity a mile away. So if we hold an event to bless a certain people group, and then we program ten or fifteen minutes in for a gospel presentation, they see it as a bait-and-switch and it actually serves as a negative gospel influence for most attendees. The purpose of a special event like Operation Yellow Ribbon is to extend love, in hopes that the recipients will want to join us. Once they join us, we help them experience the love of Christ and then respond to it. John's gospel tells us that Jesus was full of grace and truth. Most people need grace before they buy our truth. Most churches only offer truth, no grace. That's why we are so intrigued with the externally focused concept. It offers grace. It's about showing and telling.[17]

Why You Don't Have to Wear a T-Shirt with Your Church's Name on It

Pittsburgh's Reid Carpenter has said, "As a church, we have no attraction, so we have to resort to promotion."[18] Sometimes we have the tendency to think that if we do some acts of kindness, ministry, love, or service, we have to remove all doubt as to who is doing it. So if we give something away, we should make sure it has our church's name and possibly service times printed on it. We are too quick to answer the first question that comes to people's minds: "Who are you?" But if everything we do is attached to a name, smart people figure it out rather quickly. "Oh, I get it! This is a marketing campaign for the church! It's good all right. But it's really just marketing." Contrast that approach with how Jesus interacted with people after he performed a miracle: he didn't hand out his business card and say, "Now make sure you let them know who did this." No, often he said, "Now don't tell anyone" (Matthew 8:4). People eventually found out it was Jesus who did it. But the power and impact were greater (and far less self-serving) when others pointed to Jesus as the source of the life change. By intentionally not seeking to advertise ourselves, we make space for others to glorify God.

Apologetics Today

Today we no longer have the home field advantage. In most social situations, we are the visiting team, so we need to rethink what compelling evidence looks like for those outside the faith. Of course, apologetics (a defense for the reasonableness of Christianity) is still needed today, but most likely the best apologetics will be demonstrated as much as postulated. We think that in many circles, good apologetics is a combination of healthy agnosticism coupled with absolute certainty. So many times we, as Christians, feel that to be credible, we have to have all the answers; after all, we do have the truth, don't we? Embracing healthy agnosticism means that we have the freedom to say, "I don't know." So how do we couple agnosticism with certainty? In response to a question about why God would allow or cause an earthquake, tsunami, or other tragedy that takes or breaks innocent lives, we could say, "I could give you some philosophical or religious answers, but I really don't know for certain. But I do know with absolute certainty how Jesus would respond to such a tragedy because there are four books of the New Testament that describe how he did respond to pain and loss and suffering, and that's what my family, friends, and church are trying to do in this situation—to be the hands, feet, and voice of Jesus to those who are hurting."

For younger believers, authenticity trumps certainty in apologeti David Kinnaman, president of the Barna Group and coauthor of *UnChristian*, said, "For your generation, your verse was John 3:16; for our generation, it is John 3:17: 'For God sent his Son into the world not to condemn the world but that the world through him might be saved.'" Matt Wilson, director of the Message Trust in Manchester, England, said something similar regarding Christ followers in England. "For you, it is John 3:16; for us, it is 1 John 3:16–18: 'This is how we know what love is: Jesus Christ laid down his life for us. And we ought to lay down our lives for our brothers. If anyone has material possessions and sees his brother in need but has no pity on him, how can the love of God be in him? Dear children, let us not love with words or tongue but with actions and in truth.'"

It seems that most people would still rather see a sermon than hear a sermon most days of the week.

The Role of Expectancy

Ministering to, loving, and serving others are avenues to the grace of God and invites him into a situation. God is showing up and will be at work. We can expect him to create that curiosity and unanswered questions in the people we are serving or those we are serving alongside of. We need to approach these opportunities looking for God to be at work by looking for things that only he can do—creating curiosity, prompting questions, and so on. When someone asks, "Who are you?" and "Why are you doing this?" you can expect that God is at work. Our expectancy does not cause God to work but makes us aware that he is at work.

Expectancy doesn't cause anything different to happen but simply makes us aware of what is happening. It doesn't cause things to happen but allows us to take advantage of them when they do. Let us explain. Bob Swenson, a friend of Eric's since college, was one of the first individuals hired for Promise Keepers in the early 1990s. As a "walk-on," Bob also had a ten-year career as an outside linebacker for the Denver Broncos, even making All-Pro. He was part of the fabled "Orange Crush" defense that took Denver to the Super Bowl in the 1970s. Eric remembers watching the team play and thinking, "The Broncos are the luckiest team! The defense recovered another fumble."

Here's where expectancy plays its role. Eric asked Bob how the Broncos seemed to manage always to be in the right place at the right time. Bob answered, "If you watch other teams tackling a runner, the defensive players start slowing down because they assume the play is over. We taught ourselves always to be thinking, 'He's going to fumble and

I'm going to be there when it happens." That expectancy didn't cause the fumble, but when the occasional fumble occurred, the Broncos were there to catch it on the bounce and run with it. Bob still holds the longest fumble return in Bronco history—a record that has stood for more than twenty-five years. In 1979, against San Francisco, Bob scooped up a fumble and galloped eighty-eight yards for a touchdown. His expectancy didn't cause the fumble—All-Pro Louie Wright did—but expectancy of the fumble led to the return and the touchdown.

If we fully expect that when we are serving and loving, God space is being created, we will be more in tune with people and their needs and unanswered questions. Expectancy doesn't cause people to come to Christ, but it makes us aware of what God is doing and wants to do in a person's life.

What Can We Learn About Evangelism from "Evangelists"?

Guy Kawasaki is recognized as one of the leading thinkers in marketing. He's also a committed Christ follower. In a blog posting, Kawasaki notes that out of curiosity, he searched a job-posting site for jobs using the keyword *evangelist*. He reports, "Amazingly, there were 611 matches—and none were for churches. It seems that 'evangelist' is now a secular, mainstream job title." Reading through the different job descriptions he sums up the ten "fundamental principles of evangelism":

1. *Create a cause.* The starting point of evangelism is having a great thing to evangelize. A cause seizes the moral high ground. It is a product or service that improves the lives of people, ends bad things, or perpetuates good things. . . .

2. *Love the cause.* "Evangelist" isn't simply a job title. It's a way of life. It means that the evangelist totally loves the product and sees it as a way to bring the "good news." A love of the cause is the second most important determinant of the success of an evangelist—second only to the quality of the cause itself. No matter how great the person, if he doesn't love the cause, he cannot be a good evangelist for it.

3. *Look for agnostics, ignore atheists.* A good evangelist can usually tell if people understand and like a product in five minutes. If they don't, cut your losses and avoid them. It is very hard to convert someone to a new religion (i.e., product) when he believes in another god (i.e., another product). . . .

4. *Localize the pain.* No matter how revolutionary your product, don't describe it using lofty, flowery terms like "revolutionary,"

"paradigm shifting," and "curve jumping." . . . People don't buy "revolutions." They buy "aspirins" to fix the pain or "vitamins" to supplement their lives.

5. *Let people test drive the cause.* Essentially, say to people, "We think you are smart. Therefore, we aren't going to bludgeon you into becoming our customer. Try our product, take it home, download it, and then decide if it's right for you." . . .

6. *Learn to give a demo.* An "evangelist who cannot give a great demo" is an oxymoron. A person simply cannot be an evangelist if she cannot demo the product. . . .

7. *Provide a safe first step.* The path to adopting a cause should have a slippery slope. For example, the safe first step to recruit an evangelist for the environment is not requiring that she chain herself to a tree; it's to ask her to start recycling and taking shorter showers.

8. *Ignore pedigrees.* Good evangelists aren't proud. They don't focus on the people with big titles and big reputations. Frankly, they'll meet with, and help, anyone who "gets it." . . .

9. *Never tell a lie.* Very simply, lying is morally and ethically wrong. . . . If one always tells the truth, then there's nothing to keep track of. Evangelists know their stuff, so they never have to tell a lie to cover their ignorance.

10. *Remember your friends.* Be nice to the people on the way up because one is likely to see them again on the way down. Once an evangelist has achieved success, he shouldn't think that he'll never need those folks again. . . .[19]

We think Kawasaki's insights are particularly valuable and fit completely with how evangelism works.

"These Church People Are Different"

Rick's church has "adopted" a middle school that is a few blocks away. One of the things the church does is provide a weekend of maintenance when the school year ends, painting, fixing, and cleaning the building. Rick and a friend were replacing ceiling tiles, and when they ran out of tiles, Rick asked George, the lead maintenance person for the school, to take him to get more. They had never met, so George had no clue that Rick was the pastor of the church, and that was just as well. On their way back to the storeroom, George said, "I really appreciate all the things that the church does to help our school, especially all the cleanup and fixing. It saves us a lot of time and money." He also added that it made the school's appearance so much nicer for the students. Then he asked, "I'm curious. Why do you guys do this?"

"Well," said Rick "first, we care about the students, and second, we believe that God has been gracious to us and we want to be graceful, which means we want to help others." George said, "I am not a church-goer and I am not from this country, but I told my wife, 'These church people are different. Maybe we should check the place out.'"

The Leadership Challenge

As a leader, you can really help people move along the continuum from good deeds to good news. In evangelism, teach your people to recognize the "God moment"–the time that God enters a conversation. God moments are characterized by curiosity and questions. When a person asks questions like "Who are you?" and "Why are you doing this?" you can be certain that God has entered that conversation. A second thing you can do is teach people how to pray evangelistically. A couple of years ago, Eric was at Christ Community Church in Saint Charles, Illinois. Senior Pastor Jim Nicodem was preparing people for evangelism as they were going out to serve their community. Jim read from Colossians 4:2-6:

> Devote yourselves to prayer, keeping alert in it with an attitude of thanksgiving; praying at the same time for us as well, that God will open up to us a door for the word, so that we may speak forth the mystery of Christ, for which I have also been imprisoned; that I may make it clear in the way I ought to speak. Conduct yourselves with wisdom toward outsiders, making the most of the opportunity. Let your speech always be with grace, as though seasoned with salt, so that you will know how you should respond to each person.

Jim said there were three things we needed to pray as we went forth to serve: Open the door.

> Open my mouth.
> Open their hearts.

This type of prayer goes along with recognizing the God moment.

A third way you can influence those you are leading is by modeling and telling others what you do. A few months ago, Eric received an e-mail from Monte Schmidt of Rolling Hills Community Church–an externally focused church in Tualatin, Oregon, that desired to be more intentional in recognizing the God moment and initiating spiritual conversations. Monte wrote:

> Our focus has been primarily on initiating "exploring" conversations, knowing that in this area of faith, baby steps seems to be the key. To date

we have recorded just shy of 1,000 "exploring" conversations, and more are coming in all the time. The key catalyst in this has been our senior pastor, Dale Ebel. This has really awakened the evangelistic fires of Dale's heart. The true momentum for us has been Dale sharing his own personal stories of engaging with people on their spiritual journeys.

Sometimes when you serve, you are serving in the context of an all-church weekend event, like a Sharefest or Serve Day, and you are not serving beside unbelievers. You can still create hundreds of evangelistic conversations simply by saying, "This week tell five people, 'I had a great weekend,' and then just shut up. If God is in the conversation, people will respond with curiosity and questions and say something like 'What did you do?' You can then tell them, 'I just served alongside three hundred other Christ followers painting, washing windows, and landscaping the local elementary school. We're just trying to figure out what Jesus would do if he were walking among us and do that. And we do a lot of other things like that to serve our community,' and let God take it from there." If three hundred people had five spiritual conversations that week, that would be fifteen hundred conversations that might otherwise never have taken place.

CHAPTER 9

Creativity: They Innovate, Not Replicate

The real acts of discovery consist not in finding new lands but in seeing with new eyes.

Attributed to Marcel Proust

FOR THE PAST SEVERAL YEARS, Eric has taken a number of groups through an exercise based on what we wrote about in Chapter One to discover what kind of day we live in. He marks on a fifteen-foot length of butcher paper the six STEEPR categories: Society, Technology, Economics, Environment, Politics, and Religion. Along the top of the butcher paper he writes a timeline, with 1990 (twenty years ago) at the far left, 2010 in the middle, and 2030 on the far right. He then asks participants to grab a marker and write out on the butcher paper the milestone events that occurred in these six areas in the past twenty years, what is happening in these areas today, and what events will shape the next twenty years. It's a great exercise. The exercise concludes with a vigorous discussion on the rapidity and unexpected nature of change and the reality that we can't be wedded to any currently successful methodology if we want to create a different kind of future. We will need to change in view of our changing world. Perhaps to be the best church in the community, we can replicate what a church in another community has done. But to be the best church *for* the community we live in, we will need to learn to innovate.

Innovation and Growth

In 2009, Leadership Network, in partnership with the Hartford Institute for Religion Research, conducted a study to find out how large churches

174

that describe themselves as "innovative" differ from other churches. The results were both revealing and enlightening. Highly innovative churches

- Grow faster than other churches
- Have a higher rate of new believers than other churches
- Put more emphasis on personal Bible study and tithing than other churches
- Experience less conflict than other churches

Ninety-one percent of the people attending highly innovative churches strongly agree their church "has a clear mission and purpose" and see themselves as "a positive force for good in our community." They have more volunteers and are significantly more likely to invite friends and family to church. The author of the survey, Warren Bird, makes some insightful observations: "Churches that welcome innovation tend to embrace creativity, ingenuity, and divergent ways of thinking *inside* the box. They have a willingness to change their practice in order to improve performance. Their bent is to solve problems that will generate better results—such as more and better disciples of Jesus Christ."[1]

Warren's insights are important. Churches don't innovate simply to be novel, cute, or clever; they innovate to achieve their God-given mission.

Ideation, Creativity, Inspiration, Invention, and Innovation

We want first of all to clarify what innovation is *not* on the way to discovering what innovation is. Innovation is *not* the same as inspiration, ideation, invention, or creativity. To be certain, creativity, inspiration, and ideation are important to the innovative process, but innovation always pertains to the productive application of creativity. Tom Kelley of the global design company Ideo reminds us that "all good working definitions of innovation pair ideas with action, the spark with the fire." Drilling down further, he quotes the 3M company's definition of innovation: "new ideas—plus action or implementation—which result in an improvement, a gain, or a profit."[2] Thomas Edison is said to have pointed out that "an idea is called an invention. Converting an idea into something that is useful to the customer and profitable for the company is called innovation."[3] Elaine Dundon defines innovation as "the profitable implementation of strategic creativity."[4] It is innovation that brings ideas to life.

Innovation deals with being not simply novel or different but "better." And it is important to think about where we put our innovative energies and not mistake innovation for uniqueness, creativity, or cleverness. Innovation needs to be tied to results that matter in regard to your mission. So having a children's area that looks like Disneyland may be creative, but it may not be innovative. Having candles in the back of the church may be creative but not necessarily innovative. Writing your own follow-up or discipleship materials may be creative but not necessarily innovative—if they do not change the outcomes compared to using materials that already exist. In areas that are non-mission-critical, we can replicate what has been done. Creative and innovative energy should be reserved for the growth plates that are crucial to accomplishing your mission.

Results and Effort

Innovation always pertains to the relationship between inputs and outcomes—between effort and resources expended versus the result or fruit of the outcome. Look at the quadrant diagram in Figure 9.1. Many churches are in the upper-right quadrant—they are getting results according to their effort. Their budgets, programs, and staff are accomplishing what they were intended to accomplish. In the lower-right quadrant are churches that spend much but accomplish little against their mission. In the lower-left quadrant are churches that expend little and accomplish little. They are simply in survival mode. To be honest, all of us would like to

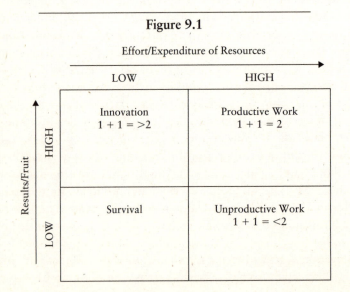

Figure 9.1

Effort/Expenditure of Resources

	LOW	HIGH
HIGH	Innovation $1 + 1 = >2$	Productive Work $1 + 1 = 2$
LOW	Survival	Unproductive Work $1 + 1 = <2$

Results/Fruit

accomplish more and use fewer resources and expend less effort to do so, as depicted in the upper-left quadrant. To do so requires innovation.

Innovation and Entrepreneurship

All innovation is ultimately tied to entrepreneurship. You may not think of yourself or your church as entrepreneurial, but the ability to think like an entrepreneur is not limited to people who describe themselves as "entrepreneurs." In fact, we think that entrepreneurship and corresponding innovation are what is desperately needed to take the church into the future—to accomplish more with less.

Let's start by tapping into the writing of Peter Drucker. Drucker is widely recognized as the father of modern management. He was a prolific thinker and writer about human behavior and organizational effectiveness. He was the first to distinguish between managers and leaders. He was fond of saying, "Managers do things right. Leaders do the right things." To define entrepreneurship, Drucker takes us back to a French economist named Jean-Baptiste Say, who explained, "An entrepreneur shifts economic resources out of an area of lower and into an area of higher productivity and greater yield."[5]

Using this as a simple baseline definition, you have probably done some entrepreneurial activities in your lifetime. If you have moved money from a checking account to a money market account or switched phone companies to get a larger bundled package of minutes and options for a lower price or shopped at Sam's Club or Costco for bulk items, you are already thinking about shifting your economic resources to an area of higher productivity or yield. You are thinking like an entrepreneur. Is it possible to ratchet up your thinking to include areas of greater kingdom impact and consequence? We think it is not just possible but necessary for the world we live in.

Innovation is the entrepreneur's tool necessary to shift resources to from lower to higher yield. Drucker proposes that one does not need to wait for moments of inspiration to innovate but can "learn to practice systematic innovation." He writes, "Successful entrepreneurs . . . try to create value and to make a contribution. . . . They are not content simply to improve on what already exists, or to modify it. They try to create new and different values and new and different satisfactions . . . or to combine existing resources in a new and more productive configuration."[6]

For now, we leave Drucker behind, but we have enough to build on in our quest to learn better how to innovate and be more entrepreneurial. We just need to think like an entrepreneur.

Trading Up from a Paper Clip to a House

One of the great entrepreneurial feats of the last ten years was how one man shifted the value of his lowly paper clip to a full-size three bedroom house. Twenty-six-year-old Kyle McDonald advertised on Craigslist .com that he wanted to trade his red paper clip for something bigger and better. He then offered to trade the received object for something more. He found a succession of people who were willing to trade—a doorknob, a camp stove, a recording contract, a free year's rent, and finally, fourteen swaps later, landed himself a house in Kipling, Saskatchewan, valued at nearly $50,000.[7]

The One Condition for Innovation

Anyone whose goals are bigger than their resources can be an innovator. If you are content with the status quo, there is no need to innovate. Innovation thrives under the conditions of scarcity or opportunity, but it never happens unless the leader has a goal. Genuine innovation occurs not because a person is trying to be original but because a person is attempting something difficult. Let's take a look at Moses in Deuteronomy 1. Deuteronomy is the record of three speeches given by Moses to prepare the Israelites to enter the promised land. In his first address, he said to the Israelites, "At that time I said to you, 'You are too heavy a burden for me to carry alone. The Lord your God has increased your numbers so that today you are as many as the stars in the sky. May the Lord, the God of your fathers, increase you a thousand times and bless you as he has promised!'"

You have just read about the heart of a leader "You are way more than I can handle. I don't think I can do this job one more day, but my prayer is that God would multiply you *a thousand times more!*" As burned-out as he was, he still wanted God to do a thousand times more. Leaders have a way to hold two seemingly contrary things in their mind until they discover the solution. Moses didn't succumb to "either-or" thinking. He wanted more time in his schedule and space in his life *and* he wanted to see God multiply the Israelites by a thousand times more. It is only when we want to accomplish something great and seemingly impossible that we are open to solutions and creativity from any source. Do you remember what happens next (as recorded in the parallel passage in Exodus 18)? Moses' father-in-law, Jethro, a pagan priest from a rival tribe, came up with the solution regarding appointing and training leaders. Leaders have the capacity to embrace "both-and" rather than "either-or" thinking. Think of what Moses wanted: he wanted space in his life and time in his schedule, and he wanted the community to multiply a thousandfold. It was only by simultaneously holding on to both pieces of his desires was he open to a creative solution. Solomon reminds us that "it is good to grasp the one and not let go of the other" (Ecclesiastes 7:18). If Moses had given up on one idea or the other, he would not have seen the genius of Jethro's solution. Creativity (new ideas) and innovation (the implementation of creativity) come at the intersection of two contradictory ideas. If Moses had let go of either aspiration, he most likely would have told Jethro to take a hike. He could solve his own problems.

Feeding the Fifty Thousand

In July 2006, Eric flew to southern California to be part of Serve Day, a one-day service project involving dozens of churches and more than five thousand volunteers. Serve Day was begun as a single church initiative by Rock Harbor Church in Costa Mesa, California, as an alternative to worship service because the usual meeting place had been double-booked on Sunday morning. Serving on Sunday was an innovative alternative to Sunday service. After Serve Day, a good friend, Eric Marsh, took Eric around to see some of the externally focused initiatives in the Long Beach area. One of the most amazing people he met was Arlene Mercer, founder and executive director of Food Finders in Long Beach (http://www .foodfinders.org). In 1989, Arlene became aware of all the hungry people in this community near Los Angeles. But what could she do by herself? She had no warehouse in which to store or distribute food. But what she did have was an innovative idea. What if she was able to connect the restaurants and grocery stores that threw out clean, edible food every day with agencies that fed hungry people? "What could be" was converted to "what is." From her thrift store, Food Finders now works with 230 human service organizations and, using her innovative storefront model, feeds some fifty thousand children and sick, elderly, and homeless people in Orange County and Los Angeles every day! Over the past twenty years, Food Finders has been responsible for distributing over 72 million pounds of food—without ever having to store one item. Arlene's probably a person you have never heard of, but she is cutting a huge swath for the kingdom.

What Do You Want to Accomplish?

So what is it that you want to accomplish that is so big that currently you don't have the resources to accomplish? Leaders always have the ability to create something that doesn't currently exist with resources they don't currently have. What keeps you awake at night? What do you find yourself thinking about? Where do your thoughts gravitate? What peppers your conversation with other kingdom-minded believers? How do you want to change the world? How will people, communities, relationships, and cities be different if God granted you the desire of your heart? Having a compelling dream pulls you forward and allows you to say yes to people and opportunities to get you where you want to go (think of Nehemiah before the king) and say no to things that would derail your mission (think of Joseph before Pothiphar's wife). A big, compelling dream is the criterion by which you measure opportunities for innovation. If entrepreneurship involves shifting resources from lower to higher value, what is it that you really value? Rich Nathan, senior pastor of the Vineyard Church in Columbus, Ohio, expresses his dream:

> We need a larger target than simply building a great church. We want to live in a great city. We don't want the church to simply be an oasis in a great desert. We would like to live in a city where people are not shredded as they go to work in their companies because the moral environment of their companies is so dehumanizing. When people walk out the doors of this church, we don't want to send them back to places in our city that are plagued by gangs. We don't want to send our kids back to schools where they have to be afraid of being attacked or where very little learning actually takes place. We want to send people of this church out into a city that has access to medical care, where there is an availability of jobs, where the races are getting along and there is racial understanding.[8]

How can we make the shift from trying to be the best church *in* the community to being the best church *for* the community?

Shifting Resources

When you make the switch from wanting to be the best church *in* the community to being the best church *for* the community, you have made a shift of tectonic proportions in moving all of your resources from a lower to higher value and greater yield. Within your church, you have the same resources at your disposal to become the best church for the community as you have for being the best church in the community. What resources are we talking about? As we mentioned in Chapter Four, Reggie McNeal and Eric have been spearheading a Leadership Network movement called Missional Renaissance.[9] The idea comes from the cross-pollination of ideas that began in fifteenth-century Florence, Italy, that resulted in the Renaissance. Reggie and Eric and their colleagues bring together cross-domain leaders from church, government, business, and human services to work toward the missional transformation of a community. These "leadership communities" meet four times over a two-year period, each session ending with a determination of what each city team plans to do in the next six months, and each gathering begins with a report of what they have accomplished in the previous six months.

Making the shift from an internal to an external focus involves shifting the value of the resources at hand. What resources are available to us, and how can we raise their value? Reggie helps us see that all churches have the exact same resources at their disposal: people, facilities, prayer, finances, technology, and time. It is how these resources are expended that makes the difference.

People (Leaders and Others)

People are a church's most important resource, yet most churches view people as "consumers of religious goods and services" and the church as the vendor of those same religious goods and services. How can we raise the value of the contribution of people? Let's start with leaders. The contribution of leaders is enhanced as they take on the responsibility to equip the saints for service (Ephesians 4:11) and also help people discover and live out their Ephesians 2:10 calling. They ask people, "What do you love to do? How can God use that for ministry?" In this role, they are operating like Home Depot, proclaiming, "You can do it. We can help."

Here's the point: the contribution of people greatly increases when they move from Ephesians 2:8–9 to Ephesians 2:10, from coming to Jesus to hear his words and to be healed of their diseases to serving and giving, from being spectators and consumers of religious goods and services to being contributors and producers of spiritual life and vitality. God puts leaders in the church to help everyone in the church live on mission, and that process comes from people development.

When Jesus followers are living on mission, they become kingdom people, and kingdom people think about the spiritual, relational, and physical well-being of others. In an externally focused church, every person is on mission. The leaders operate like Lowe's: "Let's build something together." The value of the contribution of people is exponentially raised as they serve outside the walls of the church. How do leaders get people serving in the community? Lead Pastor Mike Kessler of Trinity Church in Mount Pleasant, Texas, puts it this way: "We have basically adopted the city calendar, and we've provided volunteers for just about every event that the community has had." It is people that cause a church to be the best church for the community.

High-capacity leaders from other domains pose a special challenge and opportunity for church leaders. When Rick was in his late twenties, he was invited to be part of a turnaround team for Cincinnati Christian University. One of his major responsibilities was increasing the donations that the school received. He explains:

> I won't forget the night I sat in a diner in Philadelphia and asked for a million dollars from a potential donor. I had gotten to know John over the course of ten months, and he had made several smaller gifts to the college. He had invited me to his office to see his work, and then we went to dinner. I knew that I had the relationship, that he liked the school, and that he had the means to give a gift that size (a basic rule of fundraising is that you never offend anyone by asking for a gift bigger than they can give).
>
> After a bit of casual conversation, I did it. I asked John for a million-dollar donation and then followed the second rule of fundraising: I waited. After a moment, John said, "I like the school. I like what you are accomplishing there. I have enjoyed getting to know you and look forward to the relationship continuing. I would like to give you a million dollars, but you haven't given me a million-dollar reason or idea yet."

What a valuable lesson this man gave! Over the years, we have both had the opportunity to meet a lot of high-capacity people like John, and one consistent scenario is how underutilized they are in their local churches. In fact, many of them join boards of national or international ministries or get engaged in some of the larger nonprofit groups in their community. They are looking for something big to do, and we don't have any million-dollar ideas or jobs for them. They don't see the church as a place in which to devote their entrepreneurial energies toward innovation.

We want to share a story about a group Rick started at LifeBridge. It's been a fairly quiet group in our church family—not in terms of the things the group's members have accomplished but rather in the amount of attention they, as leaders, give and get. It is a group of successful businesspeople; most own or did own their companies, and some are the lead people in their organization. A few are retired, but most are still very active in their businesses. They have one common characteristic: they get things done—and usually get them done in a big way. They are high-capacity people. Initially, a few of them were approached and told by Rick, "Here is what I have in mind: I'd like to start a very quiet group of people who are like you to do a couple of things. First, I want this group to spend part of its time looking at how God can use us to make a difference in the world. Second, I'd like to invite in some of our community leaders to discuss the big issues they see in our community and for us to tackle one. Third, I have no idea how we will move things forward." Out of several conversations like that, the Dulos group formed. (*Dulos* is the Greek word for "servant.")

At first, about a dozen people were involved; now it is closer to twenty. They listened to the needs that were significant issues in the community, and the group settled on single mothers (much as Hal and the Pearl Group did, as described in Chapter Eight). The formation of Dulos marked not only the expansion of that area of ministry for LifeBridge but also the beginning of LifeBridge's transition from mercy to justice.

Here is what the high-capacity folks in churches, government agencies, or nonprofits can do that most of us don't do so well: they generally think in terms of sustainable solutions, moving forward, and leveraging opportunities. They are the people who often think up million-dollar ideas or give flight to them. They know that with greater risk can come greater rewards. These five-talent people (Matthew 25:15) are looking for a way to use their gifts, talents, and experience to be a part of what God is up to. How are we helping them do that? How might high-capacity people change what we measure as we seek to be the best church for the community? Table 9.1 indicates a few of the changes deemed necessary by leaders who have been trying to make the shift from an internal to an external focus.

Facilities

How can you raise the value of your facilities from a lower to a greater societal impact? Most church facilities sit empty much of the week. What would it be like to open your facilities to other community organizations? That's what externally focused churches do to extract the maximum value from their facilities. When the music legend Isaac Hayes died in August 2009 and the family was looking for a place to host a memorial tribute, family members approached the leaders of Hope Presbyterian Church in the Memphis area. Craig Strickland, Hope's senior pastor, readily agreed to host the event in the church's five thousand–seat auditorium—whereupon ensued placard-filled protests and outcries from many in the local conservative Christian community because Hayes was a Scientologist.

Table 9.1. People.

Internal Focus	External Focus
Church people	Kingdom people
Clergy and laity	Everyone on mission
Number of people who attend	Number of people who are released to serve, start, or lead ministries
"What do we need?"	"What does the community need?"
Small groups and Sunday school "for us"	Mentoring and tutoring "for them"
People consuming religious goods and services	People equipped to serve others
Trying to bring in more people "like us"	Trying to serve others unlike us
Loving what we do	Loving people and what they do
Growing people through church programs	Growing people through service
People in the pews	People in the streets
People in programs	People development
"How's our church doing?"	"How's our city doing?"

The leaders at Hope nevertheless held their ground. "We're trying to do something good for the community to bring it together," Craig told the media. "That's what the church is for."[10] Clearly, Hope Presbyterian has a firm vision of being the best church for the community. Its director of missions, Eli Morris, adds, "Hayes lived in our neighborhood, and his baby child is in our preschool. This is something we sensed God wanted us to do."[11] Interestingly, as the result of the Isaac Hayes tribute, many people who attended the service have come back to Hope Presbyterian to get closer to God. This approach is not new to Hope, which often makes its facilities available for private and public school events such as graduations and celebrations.

In 2003, when the Vineyard Church of Columbus was engaged in a building campaign to expand its facility, it dedicated 50,000 square feet to a community center that houses medical and dental offices, a gymnasium, a kids' play area, a dance and aerobics studio, and space for after-school tutoring for immigrant children and their parents.

At Northwood Church in Keller, Texas, externally focused leaders have identified an unmet need in the community: parents with special-needs children. These parents are able to drop their kids off at Northwood's facility and enjoy a much needed night out while trained caregivers look after their kids.

In 2008, Christ Community Church in Omaha, Nebraska, hosted an evening of celebration and appreciation for fourteen hundred teachers as part of its Embrace Teachers initiative. A local automobile dealer donated a car that would be given randomly to one of the teachers. Outreach pastor Ian Vickers said, "I don't know how it works, but we were praying that the right teacher would get the car, and when a teacher who took in homeless kids to live with her won the car, all the teachers cheered."[12]

When Hurricane Ike hit the southeastern coast of Texas, University Baptist Church in Houston sent response teams to help the victims. The church also opened its facilities to the public and set up (at no expense to the community) "Camp Ike" to care for children whose schools were shut down for two weeks but whose parents still had to work.

In October 2007, San Diego experienced its worst wildfires in history. Thousands of people evacuated their homes and businesses, but New Song Community Church stayed. New Song opened its facilities as an evacuation shelter. Each night for a week, the church provided beds for more than three hundred people, meeting the collective needs of nearly seven hundred altogether. Good deeds created goodwill, which led to great conversations about faith and life and God, and more than ninety of the evacuees came to Christ. Pastor Hal Seed remarked, "By God's grace, San Diego's worst week in history was New Song's best week in history!"[13]

One of the biggest needs of every community is people to help elementary school students with reading, as learning to read by the third grade is the most determinative and predictive element about a child's future. But who has time during the week to visit a local school? Would it be possible to create a win-win situation by providing two to three hours of free child care each week at the church to every mom who volunteers an hour a week at the school? Moms could help the kids at school and have a little down time for themselves before returning to pick up the kids at church. What mom wouldn't love that?

When founding pastor John Bruce of Creekside Community Church in San Leandro, California, wanted to purchase a former restaurant for his thriving church plant, the city told him that the community already had enough churches and had in fact denied the requests of nine other previous would-be buyers and church planters. So John went back to the drawing board. Could the city use a community center that would serve its people? The answer was a hesitant yes, and Creekside was granted a renovation permit. For the past nine years, the church has opened the facility to schools, community organizations, and the people they serve. In 2008, for example, apart from church programming, the church hosted three Red Cross blood drives; held a Valentine's Day ball for over one hundred developmentally disabled adults; ran a weekly after-school program for at-risk inner-city Oakland students; hosted a Martin Luther King benefit concert for Cox Elementary (an elementary school the church has adopted) with $1,500 in donations raised for the school; hosted Dinner and a Movie night for thirty developmentally disabled adults; ran a martial arts ministry for the community two evenings a week; ran a theater arts program for children in the community, mounting two high-quality productions each year; and hosted a community craft fair that raised $5,000 for the local women's shelter; along with a myriad of other externally focused efforts. John has brilliantly figured out how to leverage the value of the Creekside facility and is discovering what it means to be the best church for the community.

At LifeBridge, one of the ways found to connect with public schools was to offer the use of the facility. Opening doors has provided a venue for teacher training meetings, districtwide administrator sessions, student testing sessions, and parent meetings. The school district has also brought in national speakers to address all of its teachers in one setting. LifeBridge Christian Church has been averaging seven hundred community events annually, organized by seventy-eight organizations of all kinds, including businesses, clubs, seminars, and sports teams. Some sixty thousand people a year attend community events and meetings held there.

One of the most unusual uses was made by the local police department, which used the LifeBridge campus to practice hostage and SWAT training for its officers. Rick offers one piece of advice: make sure you inform the neighbors before a dozen men in black gear holding guns and rappelling from a helicopter are turned loose at night on your campus. It gave local EMTs some practice that night as well.

Rick believes that church facilities exist for the benefit of the community and actively looks for ways to allow groups to use them. Think about your church. How would you use your facilities if you wanted to be the best church for the community? Table 9.2 presents the changes in thinking needed to shift from an internal to an external focus.

Prayer

How can you leverage prayer from a lower level to a higher level of impact? When we pray for people outside of our own congregations, we are taking prayer to a new level. A few years ago, as the pastors of our community in Boulder, Colorado, were trying to figure out how to serve the city, we concluded that the best way to begin was to ask the leaders who served the city—the mayor, the chief of police, the district attorney,

Table 9.2. Facilities.

Internal Focus	External Focus
Facilities are for the church.	Facilities are for church and community.
Counting church people here on Sunday.	Counting people who use the facility during the week.
We need to protect our facilities.	We need to open up our facilities.
Facilities are designed for the congregation.	Facilities are designed for the community.
This is "our house."	This is your house.
Keep the facilities for ourselves.	Market the facilities to the community.

the superintendant of schools, the city planner, and the city manager, among others. During our monthly meetings, we asked these people to share a little bit about their responsibilities, their vision of a healthy community, and three impossible things they wanted to accomplish that no person could do for them. This was our way of asking these leaders for prayer requests, since our God is known for operating in the area of impossibilities. Our customary way to end these gatherings was simply to bless and pray for the "impossible" requests of these leaders. The results were pretty amazing. As we prayed, one leader wiped tears from his eyes and said, "I know people have prayed for me before, but I've never heard anyone pray out loud for me before." Another community leader said, "I came here with apprehension, but I realize I am among friends." Another leader called a couple of months later to ask if she could return and give the pastors three more requests, since all of her "impossibles" had since been answered and resolved. One leader, after being prayed for and blessed, said, "This was one of the greatest days of my life." We often underestimate that fact that everyone wants to be blessed, and it is within the province of Christian leaders to give such blessings.

When Israel was in exile in Babylon and trying to figure out how to follow and serve God in captivity, God sent them this message: "This is what the Lord Almighty, the God of Israel, says to all those I carried into exile from Jerusalem to Babylon . . . : Seek the peace and prosperity of the city to which I have carried you into exile. Pray to the Lord for it, because if it prospers, you too will prosper" (Jeremiah 29:4–7).

The value of prayer is elevated to a new level when we pray for our neighbors, our enemies, and our city. How do we change what we measure on the way to becoming the best church for the community? Table 9.3 provides some answers.

Table 9.3. Prayer.

Internal Focus	External Focus
Prayer inside the church	Prayer on location in the community (schools, places of violence, etc.)
Prayer for our people	Prayer for those outside our church—city officials, human service agency leaders, teachers, etc.
Prayer for our church	Prayer for other churches
Prayer "for" you	Pray "with" you
Prayer for church finances	Prayer for money to be freed up to help others
Prayer for the lost	Prayer for and engagement with three people who don't know Jesus
Prayer gatherings for people in our church	Prayer gatherings with other churches for the community
Prayer for myself (my happiness, security, health, etc.)	Prayer for people in need
Prayer for God to change "them"	Prayer for God to change "me"
Prayer for people to come to church	Prayer for people to be sent out from our church
Prayer for the success of our church	Prayer for expansion of the kingdom
People who pray	People of prayer

Finances

Few things about the church are as internally focused as our use of finances. Look at some recent trends:

- Ninety-seven percent of total income in 2000 was spent on costs benefiting Christians.
- Three percent of total income was spent on costs benefiting non-Christians.
- One hundred six times more money was spent on the salaries of full-time ministers serving Christians than on the salaries of ministers working with non-Christians.
- Virtually all (99.62 percent) of every dollar is spent to benefit the congregation rather than the community.[14]

But if the resources in the pockets of believers could be shifted from a lower return to a higher return, the impact would be incredible. In 2005 "Christians who attend church twice a month or more . . . earned a collective income of . . . more than $2 trillion . . . more than the total GDP of every nation in the world except the six wealthiest."[15] Furthermore, if U.S. church members tithed 10 percent of their income each year, U.S. Christians could evangelize the world, stop the daily deaths of twenty-nine thousand children younger than five worldwide, and provide elementary education across the globe and tackle domestic poverty—and still have $150 billion left over.[16]

But externally focused churches that want to become the best church for the community think and act differently. At the Christmas Eve service in 2008, Pastor Dan Nold of Calvary Baptist Church in State College, Pennsylvania, told his congregation that Christians give only half of 1 percent of their income to the poor, and because Jesus came to bless the world, he wanted the people of Calvary Baptist to double that amount and give 1 percent of their income that evening in an offering for the poor—and the people of Calvary Baptist did it! Dan is increasing the external giving of the church through what he calls "moments of generosity." "I find that people would rather give small amounts to specific projects than just respond to a pledge drive," he explains. This seems to be a trend worth noting as celebrities such as Lance Armstrong and Bono use public events or Web-based applications to motivate large numbers of constituents to give small amounts of money to collectively make a huge impact.

Ohio was particularly hit hard by the recession. On Palm Sunday in 2009, Pastor Rich Nathan gave the opportunity to the congregants of the Vineyard Church of Columbus to help people in the community who were on the verge of losing their homes due to foreclosure, and the people of the Vineyard stepped up and gave $625,000 in cash and checks to help keep people in their homes. (The church's former record for a special collection was about $250,000 contributed for Hurricane Katrina relief.)

Rivertree Christian Church in Massillon, Ohio, is a large, regional multisite church twenty miles south of Akron. The main campus meets in a movie theater, and the usual path is to raise money, buy property, and build. This was Senior Pastor Greg Nettle's dream—an eighty-five-acre farm he had his eyes on and had been praying over for the past twelve years. But as the leaders of Rivertree became more aware of the needs of their neighbors, both locally and globally, spending $40 million to put up a campus didn't seem to make sense anymore. People in the congregation had adopted over a thousand children through Compassion International, and they were increasingly becoming aware of God's big heart for people on the margins. Although for the first time in the church's history they could possibly have raised the money and begun construction, God was leading them in a different direction—a direction that resonated with the hearts of the people. "When we announced that we're not going to put up a $40 million campus, that we're going to be committed to being generous as a church and give money away, people cheered in every service," Greg reports. Finances can be raised from a lower to higher level of return.

In 2008, Christ Community Church in Omaha, Nebraska, employed a Kingdom Assignment (http://www.kingdomassignment.com), a powerful mechanism for multiplying kingdom resources. After telling the story of the master passing out talents to three of his servants, the pastor asked people to come forward if they wanted to take a risk for God. Three hundred fifty people came forward and were given an envelope. Inside the envelope was money. Some people got $20, others received $50; still others opened the envelope to find a $100 bill. In total, $20,000 (donated by a generous member) was given away. The people were told to multiply the money and return what they had to the church at the end of ninety days. The people of Christ Community Church bought and sold on eBay, baked and washed, planted and reaped, invested and gained, held concerts and cleaned houses, and at the end of three months returned $275,000 that was used to help the work of a hospital for women and children in one of the poorest countries in the world, Mali, West Africa.

A few years ago, Eric was in New Zealand talking about externally focused churches to a group of leaders gathered at Spreydon Baptist Church in Christchurch—a church whose DNA winds thick around to poor and marginalized in the local community. The people of Spreydon Baptist are engaged in a number of externally focused efforts and have been for many years. A few years earlier, some folks in the church tried to identify the biggest need of their community. Their answer? Consumer debt. So they started a "bank" in their church called Kingdom Resources (http://kingdomresources.org.nz). Because debt is eating many people for lunch, Kingdom Resources, after screening and debt counseling, lends the money to the debtors to pay off their debt in full, charging them zero interest on their loan. The concept is based on a few key ideas that they linked together. First, many believers have money sitting idle in private banks earning a mere 1 to 2 percent in interest—money that could be used for the kingdom. Many people are trapped in high-interest loans they will never be able to get out from under. The money is pooled from believers who want to put their money to good and godly use. Contributors put in between $100 and $100,000. When Eric was there, Spreydon had already loaned out over $2.6 million to the people of Christchurch and was helping them learn about budgeting, money management, saving programs, and other financial strategies. Over the years, the payback rate has been 98 percent. Kingdom Resources has also trained 130 "budget counselors" to help these folks with budget advice and employment, life, and spiritual counseling. They are setting the captives free. It's really about "little people helping little people," says Spreydon's senior pastor, Murray Robertson.

How does becoming the best church for the community affect the way we understand and deploy our finances? Table 9.4 gives some answers.

Technology

Technology provides the enabling mechanisms that we use to be more efficient or effective in accomplishing our mission and vision. One of the best things about technology is that it is "content-neutral," so it can be quickly repurposed from internal use to external use. Externally focused churches use their technology not just to extend their reach but also to extend their blessing. When two dozen other churches in Orange County, California, wanted to join Rock Harbor Church in Costa Mesa for Serve Day, Rock Harbor's technology team built a Web site that enabled five thousand people to sign up for 275 different projects in the county. When a work project was filled with the required number of volunteers, that project "disappeared" from the site, so it always appeared that every opportunity to serve was still open. Project team leaders had the names

Table 9.4. Finances.

Internal Focus	External Focus
How much we keep	How much we give away
Church is a holding tank	Church is a pipeline
Scarcity mentality	Abundance mentality (loaves and fishes)
Church savings	Microloans
Giving	Empowering
Pledge drives	Jesus-like generosity
Paying for things	Providing seed money
Giving to the church	Giving to the church and other organizations

and contact information for each of their volunteers. The technology was seamless.

In past generations, the local church was a center for both content and community. If you wanted the content of the message, the spiritual stimulus of worship, and the fellowship with believers, you needed to show up at a certain place at a certain time. It worked—then. But with the advent and proliferation of online content and online community, the need to show up at a certain place at a certain time is disappearing, not just for content but also for community, especially among young people. As of June 2009, the Nielsen Company reported that the average teen sends or receives ninety-six text messages on a typical day.[17] The majority of teens have profiles on social media sites. In the past few years, technology has radically enabled not just the one (preacher) broadcasting to the many, via Webcasts or YouTube or the like, but has evolved so that the many can communicate with the many—which allows community to form.

How can you use technology to create community for those outside the walls of your church? How can you use technology to connect people in the church to the needs and dreams outside of the church? Table 9.5 may give you some ideas.

Time

How we spend our time and our money are probably the two most determinative things about us. Some churches build into the job

---

Table 9.5. Technology.

Internal Focus	External Focus
The church campus	The church mission
How to navigate and understand the church	How to navigate and understand the community
Videos of church activities	Videos of missional engagement
Mobilizing the church	Mobilizing the community
Creating opportunities to connect to the church	Creating opportunities to connect to the community
Equipment under lock and key	Equipment shared with the community
Accumulating data	Telling the stories
Expert-built content	Community-built content
Internal church-based links	Links to other churches and community partners
Church Web site	Town square Web site

descriptions of every staff person a half-day of volunteering in a human service agency in their communities. Other churches ask that all staff be involved in one hour of tutoring in the public schools each week. Some churches, such as Perimeter Church in Atlanta, designate full-time and part-time staff to engage, connect, and collaborate in the community.

In the spring of 2009, the elders at Christ Community Church in Saint Charles, Illinois, celebrated the completion of one full year of "Second Saturdays": one Saturday morning each month, an average of 165 people—singles, families, and young people—engaged in serving in the community. Crossroads Church in Cincinnati engages 150 mentors into the school system to make a difference in the lives of students. "Lunch Buddies" is what people from Rolling Hills Community Church in Tualatin, Oregon, call the adult leaders who meet an hour a week with elementary school children who need an adult in their lives. In 2008, volunteers from Hope Presbyterian Church in Memphis logged 312 hours, filed 312 returns and stimulus checks, qualified people for more than $300,000 in refunds and stimulus payments, and saved them more than $21,500 in fees they would normally have paid. At Mariners Church in Irvine, California, 329 volunteers took 283 teens to summer camp, where 45 of the campers made decisions to follow Jesus with their lives. Forty-five volunteers from Mariners regularly serve 120 teen moms in shelters around Orange County. How is the value of time raised when one moves from an internally focused to externally focused church? See Table 9.6.

Table 9.6. Time.

Internal Focus	External Focus
Busyness	Effectiveness
Hours spent in church	Hours spent serving others
Small groups work for the church	Small groups engage the community
Time spent with believers	Time spent with nonbelievers in redemptive relationships
Number of children in Sunday school	Number of children reading at grade level
Staff clocking in	Staff clocking out
Time spent in the church building	Time spent with people anywhere
Structure	Fluidity
Full schedule	Lots of white space
Total number of minutes	Total number of moments

How to Think like an Entrepreneur

Although a certain percentage of people may be exceptionally creative and insightful, we firmly believe that everybody can raise the value of what they have or what they do by applying the same innovative principles that entrepreneurs use to raise the value of the assets they have at their disposal. Peter Drucker tells us, "Innovation is the specific tool of entrepreneurs, the means by which they exploit change as an opportunity for a different business or a different service. It is capable of being presented as a discipline, capable of being learned, capable of being practiced. Entrepreneurs need to search purposefully for the sources of innovation, the changes and their symptoms that indicate opportunities for successful innovation. And they need to know and to apply the principles of successful innovation."[18]

How can we learn to think as entrepreneurs think? We suggest the following three ways of thinking.

1. Look for Areas of Leverage to Make a Difference

In 2009, Chip Sweney from Perimeter Church in Atlanta was visiting relatives in Colorado and came by Eric's house for the evening. As they sat on the back deck, Chip talked about a new ministry Perimeter had started called "Half-Hour Heroes." Half-Hour Heroes are men and women who volunteer at a local public elementary or middle school for thirty minutes, once a week (often during lunchtime), as a tutor or just to be a friend to a student who could benefit from having a positive adult male or female in their life. Chip says, "Our goal is that every child in metro Atlanta public schools in need of a mentor or tutor would have one." Then Chip shared some interesting facts regarding the importance of this new ministry. "Did you know," he began, "that the percentage of students in metro Atlanta who are unable to attain reading proficiency by the third grade—30 percent—is directly proportionate to the number of students that do not graduate from high school?" Not reading by third grade is tied not only to graduation rate but also to teen pregnancy, drug use, and incarceration. In fact, Georgia bases its future prison population on the literacy rates of third graders. As one school administrator explained, "Up until third grade, you learn to read; after third grade, you read to learn." But there was more from Chip. "If a young person graduates high school, waits until age twenty before marrying, and has kids after they are married, the chance of living in poverty is a mere 8 percent. If any of these three factors is compromised, the chance of winding up in poverty are increased tenfold—to 80 percent—so that's why we think what we are doing is important. If every student in need of an adult friend or a tutor had a Half-Hour Hero, we could help more students achieve success in life." Working with children is a leveraged activity that has multiple positive outcomes.

2. Swim in the Blue Oceans

If we want to increase the value of what we do or come up with ideas that help us become the best church for the community, we have to learn to swim in "blue oceans." In 2005, W. Chan Kim and Renée Mauborgne published their best-selling book *Blue Ocean Strategy: How to Create Uncontested Market Space and Make Competition Irrelevant*. The authors talk about two colors of oceans that companies operate in. They write, "Red oceans represent all the industries in existence today. This is the known market space. . . . Here companies try to outperform their rivals to grab a greater share of existing demand. As the market space gets crowded, prospects for profits and growth are reduced. Products become commodities, and cutthroat competition turns the red ocean bloody."

Blue oceans are different. "Blue oceans denote all the industries *not* in existence today. This is the unknown market space. . . . Blue oceans . . . demand creation and the opportunity for highly profitable growth."[19]

Churches, too, can swim in red oceans or blue oceans. Throughout this book, we have tried to distinguish the difference between trying to be the best church *in* the community and trying to be the best church *for* the community. Trying to be the best church in the community puts you in competition with other local churches. You vie for market share in a red ocean. You differentiate by quality or style of worship, preaching, youth programs, and so on. There can only be one best church in the community. But by changing the preposition and striving to be the best church *for* your community, that changes everything. That becomes a blue ocean strategy. There are no competitors; there is no competition. And every church can have this as its goal, and the community is the recipient of their collective efforts.

A few months ago, Eric met with Jay Pathak, lead pastor at Vineyard Church in Arvada, Colorado. Jay came out of Vineyard Church in Columbus, Ohio, a church that is no stranger to innovation. Jay explained one of the church's blue ocean strategies:

> We start by asking, "What are the needs of the city?" not "What should we equip our people to do?" So, for example, about once a

month, we go into a local bar in our community and ask [the owner or manager] to identify its slowest night for business. We then offer to bring a local Indy band into the bar, split the gate with the owner, auction off live art, and sell CDs and T-shirts. We then take the money we raise and give it to local charities. We have raised thousands of dollars for local charities like Habitat for Humanity. It's a win all the way around. The bar makes a bit of money, and the local band gets publicity and often begins associating with the local charity it is helping sponsor. When people ask who we are, we tell them, "We're a group of people that have taken Jesus seriously, and we believe that Jesus cares about things like human trafficking, homeless people, children without clean water, and so on, and we're just trying to make a difference."

This is what it means to be the best church for the community. This is blue ocean strategy.

3. Look for the Unmet Need

To discover unmet needs in your community, the following exercise may be helpful. First, draw a Venn diagram as in Figure 9.2. The three circles represent the needs of your community, your congregation's current engagement and capacity in your community, and what other congregations do well. Then simply start filling in the blanks. An exercise like

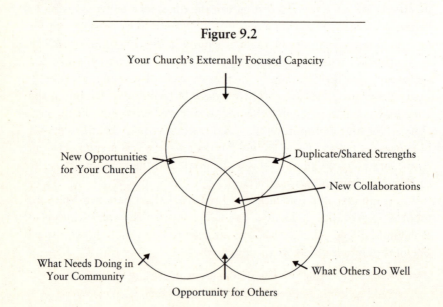

Figure 9.2

Your Church's Externally Focused Capacity

New Opportunities for Your Church

Duplicate/Shared Strengths

New Collaborations

What Needs Doing in Your Community

What Others Do Well

Opportunity for Others

this will help you identify not just opportunities to meet needs as a congregation but also what you can do to partner with other churches and others that love the city as you do.

Pulling It All Together

God's act of creation was really the only original *ex nihilo* creative act. "For he spoke, and it came to be" (Psalm 33:9). Everything else since that time has simply been rearranging the parts. Every color that you see is some combination of only three primary colors (yellow, blue, and red), three shapes (rectangles, circles, and triangles), and three states (solids, liquids, and gases).[20] The diversity of stars, planets, animals, vegetation, processes, and people attest to God's creativity. Since the time of creation, humans have simply rearranged the parts using existing materials. There is nothing new under the sun. Seen in that light, we don't have to be original to be creative. We simply need to bring different parts and pieces to the table and assemble them differently to serve our purpose.

The philosopher William James is said to have observed that "genius is the capacity for seeing relationships where lesser men see none."[21] By his own admission, Thomas Edison had only one completely original invention—the phonograph. Everything else was an adaptation of someone else's idea or discovery. He also purportedly advised, "Make it a practice to keep on the lookout for novel and interesting ideas that others have used successfully. Your idea has to be original only in its adaptation to the problem you are working on."[22] Think of how many solutions or inventions led to other creative solutions—the coin punch and wine press led to the invention of the printing press. How about surfboards and sailboats? Movies and airplanes? The gospel of Luke and movies? Skateboards and skis? How many other good ideas are waiting to be discovered simply by using the known to create usefulness in the arena of the unknown? What new breakthrough strategy is simply awaiting discovery?

A couple of years ago, we were talking with Laurie Beshore from Mariners Church about criteria for beginning a new ministry. She laughed when she told us about the latest ministry her church had launched— Mariners' Dog Ministry. Although Laurie initially wanted to dismiss the idea of a dog ministry, she was willing to try anything once. How can dogs be repurposed for ministry? Laurie went on to describe how dogs will calm crying children in the nursery, bringing peace where there had been chaos. Dogs are particularly good with the elderly and facilitate conversations—ask any single guy with a puppy in the park. Dog owners brought their dogs to the church summer camps, and the kids loved them. Dogs know nothing of social status and love everyone unconditionally. When the dogs show up at after-school programs, the children often prefer to read to a canine friend than to an adult! Each month, Mariners hosts birthday parties for residents in its motel ministry, and the dogs have been an integral part of the church's ministry to foster children. The dog ministry even has a mission: "To put people at ease and begin a process that could lead them to God." How is that for dogma? How do you combine dogs with ministry? Mariners has figured it out.

Looking at the Same Thing and Thinking Something Different

Several years ago, a good friend of Eric's packed up his family and moved to Spain to work on university campuses, winning students over to Christ and helping them become ardent followers of Jesus. As John became more aware of the spiritual attitudes and hungers of Spaniards, he kept searching for ways to embrace the local culture and use what was at hand to begin spiritual conversations. Once a month, during the school year, John and his wife, Carrie, invited students into their home for supper. After supper, John would pass out reproductions of European paintings that depicted one of the many parables that Jesus told. So one night they might look at and discuss Rembrandt's *Return of the Prodigal* or Francesco Bassano's *Parable of the Good Samaritan*. After extracting all the visual clues in the painting, John would take the guests to the New Testament passage, and the discussion would begin anew. Many students who came to embrace Jesus began with dinner at John and Carrie's home.

In 1999, John and Carrie were thinking how they could reach more people with the gospel. They heard of the *Camino de Santiago de Compostela* (The Way of Saint James)—a pilgrimage that has been going on for centuries in which the spiritually committed and spiritually curious trek across northern Spain to the city of Santiago de Compostela, in the northwest. The year 2000 was a special year of celebration, and an estimated one million people were going to walk at least some portion of the trail. Many evangelicals avoided the Camino like the plague. It wasn't part of their faith tradition. But John saw the same thing but thought something different: "Those who walk the trail are probably more spiritually open than those who stay home." Every eight to ten miles along the pilgrim trail were *refugios,* or "pilgrim houses," where pilgrims could stop to rest, drink, eat, and sleep. John raised the money and bought one of these houses, refurbished it, and staffed it with European volunteers. He named the house *Fuente del Perigrino*—the Pilgrim's Fountain. But he did more. He bought five hundred Walkman cassette recorders (remember, this was pre-MP3 technology), and an hour east of *Fuente del Perigrino*, his volunteers handed out the Walkmans with a one-hour audio version of the *Jesus* film in one of several European languages. An hour later, they arrived at the pilgrim house, and many engaged in further conversations, some which led to faith in Christ. Each night during the summer, they fed and housed thirty pilgrims, showed the *Jesus* film during the evening, and followed up with long conversations. When asked how many people he thought his pilgrim house had influenced, he calculated that after six summers of operation, between the cassettes, literature, *Jesus* film, and personal conversations, it was "over a million people." To innovate, we must see the same things as those around us, but we must think about them differently.

The Leadership Challenge

We noted at the beginning of this chapter that all leaders have at their disposal the same missional resources to accomplish their mission. How could you be entrepreneurial by repurposing how you use those resources to become the best church for your community? Think about what you need to do to shift each of the six resources—people, facilities, prayer, finances, technology, and time—to higher productivity and greater yield.

CHAPTER 10

Outcomes: It's About the Game, Not the Pregame Talk

Never doubt that a small group of thoughtful, committed citizens can change the world; indeed, it's the only thing that ever has.

Attributed to Margaret Mead

As THE TEAM FINISHES DRESSING, the head football coach calls them in to have a seat. Some players are looking intently at him with anticipation, while others sit with their elbows on their knees, with fingers interlaced or tented. Many of them are nervously bouncing their heels off the floor. "You all know what day this is," the coach begins. "I don't need to tell you why you are here." He then launches into an inspiring homily on the theme of "courage against the odds." The speech is a barnburner—part William Wallace before his fellow Scotsmen, part Henry V before the Battle of Agincourt. Victory would be tough, but it was not out of their reach—if they would be courageous. As the speech ends, the team members rise to their feet and begin shouting; with helmets held high, they jump and chant in unison, "Win! Win! Win!" The coach revels in the response of the team. He holds both hands up to silence the men, and when he has their full attention, he ends with an admonition to "consider these things and take them to heart and may the Lord add his blessing to what was said today." The team is dismissed, with many players telling the coach on the way out that his pregame speech was one of his very best. And then everyone goes home. Meanwhile, out on the field, where a game was waiting to be played and a battle to be won, the opponent is declared the victor by default.

Oblivious but satisfied with his performance, the coach goes home and starts preparing next week's pregame talk, on the topic "luck favors the prepared." Meanwhile, back in the locker room, a lone player sits and asks himself, "If this was the pregame talk, what happened to the game? Why didn't we play the game?" The pregame talk is needed and appreciated, but the players long to play!

Is the story of the coach and his team really that different from what happens in churches all across our land? We often grade the service by how well the "pregame speech" went rather than the performance of the team on the playing field. We are often long on exposition but come up short on application. Yet it is application that changes lives and changes the world. As the saying goes, "It is better to be ankle-deep in knowledge and neck-deep in application than neck-deep in knowledge and ankle-deep in application!" As learners and gleaners of spiritual insight, we often want to be inspired more than we want to apply anything.

Leaders of externally focused churches think differently about what happens when the team comes together. Like successful coaches, they understand that pregame speeches are good and useful but only as they pertain to what people do once the speech is over and the team leaves the locker room and takes the field.

Everyone Plays

During the 1990s, Eric coached five different Little League teams. They never won a championship, but they had a lot of fun. Eric's goals for each team were very simple; first, he wanted every one of the players to develop and improve on their basic baseball skills, since these skills would come in handy later in life when playing company softball or playing catch with their own kids. Having spent most of the one year of Little League that he played in sixth grade on the bench, Eric realized he didn't know much about baseball, let alone coaching baseball. So he bought a book on coaching Little League and a video titled *Coaching Little League Baseball*. He eventually learned how to play and coach the game.

Eric's second goal was that the players develop a love for the game and want to play the following year. He had met too many kids—really good kids—that didn't want to play because of bad experiences with Little League coaches. He listened to George Will's *Men at Work*, read by Bob Costas, and began to understand the intricacies of the game. Third, he wanted to help the kids learn to win, lose, celebrate, feel good about themselves, and have fun along the way. He instituted what they called "hot dog games": Eric would bring a grill and a cooler filled with hot

dogs and sodas and set everything up right behind the dugout. He'd grill
the hot dogs once the game began, and the players and their families and
friends ate throughout the game. He'd even have one of the players send
a plateful of dressed hot dogs over to the opposing dugout. He told the
team that Babe Ruth used to eat lots of hot dogs during the game, and it
didn't seem to hinder his performance.

Sometimes Eric brought a camera to the game and took action shots of
the kids. After the pictures were developed and printed (remember those
days?), he'd put a stamp on the back of the picture, write an encouraging note, and stick it in the mail. Between grilling hot dogs and taking
pictures, he probably wasn't devoting as much time to coaching, but they
did have a lot of fun. After the games, they'd debrief and celebrate the
little things that went right, even when the team lost. Every year, they'd
take in a Rockies baseball game and a couple of times, thanks to the
generosity of others, they had a catered luxury suite to themselves.

Eric's last goal was that everyone played. What good is practice if
you never get to play? And everyone did play. Some parents were upset
because Eric didn't play their talented child the whole game, but at
the end of each season he had a team of players—not bench sitters. Eric
says he doesn't remember how many games they won or lost or whether
they ever had a winning season, but he knows that his goals were
accomplished—everybody learned, everybody developed skills, everybody
had fun—and everybody played.

Getting Everyone in the Game

Much of what is germane to getting everyone in the game can be found in
Chapter Seven and the structures that are necessary to making service an
integral part of who you are as a church. Once we understand that every
Christ follower is created in Christ Jesus to do good works that God prepared in advance for that person (Ephesians 2:8–10) and that the leader's
role is to prepare and equip those same people for those works of service
(Ephesians 4:11–12), then it is fairly easy to grasp the fact that everyone
needs to get in the game. What else can we do?

Provide Regular Opportunities

The first thing you can do is *provide regular, easy-entry opportunities that
give people the chance to change the world*. In the Leadership Challenge
at the end of Chapter Three, we talked about what success might look
like. What if you measured your effectiveness not by attendance or

budget but by something far greater? What if at the end of the year, everyone in your faith community had a story to tell of how he or she changed the world? For this to happen, the church would need to provide regular opportunities for people to engage the world in such a way that the world would be different because of their action. Wouldn't that be something?

We've already written extensively on one-day service events, but there are many other easy-entry opportunities. In November 2007, in Gwinnett County, Georgia, 12Stone Church initiated "12days12ways"—a creative way to help hurting people in Georgia. The public was able to nominate people and families in need online or at a kiosk in the Georgia Mall. More than two hundred prizes were awarded, including two new Toyotas, a college scholarship, various Christmas gifts, a year's supply of gasoline, and a year's worth of groceries. The project leader and outreach pastor, Norwood Davis, talks about the uniqueness of the 12Stone approach. "Most promotions urge you to enter yourself to win. Our campaign is unique in that we encourage you to think about the needs of others around you. That way everyone wins: the person who nominates is able to give someone a gift well beyond his or her own resources, and the recipient is blessed by the thoughtfulness and the gift itself. Although this campaign lands in the middle of a universal season of giving, we believe it is our mission to give ourselves away to others all year long."[1] Everybody gets to play.

Several Sunday mornings a month, Rick's church invites people to sign up to be "gone for good." (If you're thinking there are some people you'd like to sign up for this, put the thought away; it's not that kind of gone!) Instead of coming into a worship service, people jump into a van and head to a short-term service project. They try to be back (not too sweaty or smelly) for the last service of the morning at 11:00 A.M. It is one of those acts of kindness or "living gracefully" service opportunities. People leave the service and do service. They are "gone for good" (gone to do good). Almost all of the "gone for good" projects are with partners in the community. For example, the local code enforcement agency has often called LifeBridge to assist shut-ins, single moms, or terminally ill residents who face code violations for lawn or snow issues around their homes. Volunteers show up and in a few hours clean up a yard, repair a fence, and remove debris or clear snow. Sometimes people assist a school with a maintenance project or help a single mom with moving issues. Anybody can be on these teams and get in the game.

In the spring of 2009, the Dayton, Ohio, community was one of the hardest-hit areas of the country during the recession. But the people at

Southbrook Christian Church in Miamisburg, Ohio, had ambitious plans. They wanted to finish the construction of an AIDS clinic in Swaziland and help struggling people in their own local community. But how do you accomplish more with less? These innovative leaders came up with what they called the "Southbrook Meltdown": they asked their crowd to donate unworn class rings and broken or unused gold and silver jewelry. Ramping up with teaching from James 5:1–6, an interview with a missionary doctor, a bit of media coverage, and a Brinks armored truck for effect during the weekend "meltdown" offering, they collected jewelry with a scrap value of more than $150,000. This is the entrepreneurial spirit that we wrote about in Chapter Nine. Southbrook literally took something of little value from a jewelry box or sock drawer and raised it to a level that would save lives. Everyone got to play.

In 2007, Pastor (and Illinois State Senator) James Meeks of Salem Baptist Church in Chicago, whose weekend attendance exceeds twenty thousand people, launched Vision 2007, a twenty-six-week initiative to move people from their seats to the streets. Each Saturday for six months, the church closed its doors and all Saturday activities were canceled so that people could get in the game for at least two hours each week. Each week, hundreds of volunteers fanned out over a hundred-block area to serve and bless through clothing, fresh fruit and vegetables, and other foods. The people of Salem Baptist got in the game and on one day gave away more than 750 $10 gas vouchers in a buy-down program designed simply to bless the people of their community. Good deeds create goodwill and establish the platform for sharing the good news. Meeks says that the same week they gave away the gas vouchers, three hundred people were won to Christ.[2] According to an interview with PBS, "Pastor Meeks asks the question he says every congregation should pose to itself: 'If our church were suddenly to disappear, would the community care?' He wants Salem Baptist to be remembered by the answer to that question." And there is a very good chance that is how it will be remembered.

Combine Opportunity with Inclination

"The step from inclination to action is a large one," note Samuel and Pearl Oliner,[3] so a second way to get people involved is to *combine opportunity with inclination.* You've got to strike while the iron is hot. In 2005, at Fellowship Bible Church in Nashville, Tennessee, teaching pastor Lloyd Shadrach told the story of a team of 150 Fellowship members who had traveled to Biloxi, Mississippi, to help victims of Hurricane Katrina.

As they were distributing water, food, and clothing, one of the team members, Dave, met a man without shoes who needed a pair of work boots so he could clean up his home. After Dave learned that they wore the same size shoe, he took off his work boots and gave them to his new friend. The rest of the day, Dave worked in his socks. Like the famed "Shoeless" Joe Jackson, Dave was in the game.

Then Lloyd projected images from a recent team trip to Africa. The pictures were unusual in that they focused on the feet of children wearing their parents' shoes. Lloyd then explained that children in this African village were not allowed to attend school unless they had shoes. So their parents did what parents do: they gave their own shoes to their children so the youngsters could be educated. Lloyd now came to his application:

> There are adults and children in Africa who need a pair of shoes. There are children right here in Nashville that need a pair of shoes. There are adults and children in Peru, Honduras, Sudan, Nigeria, and Biloxi who need a pair of shoes. If I looked at any one of you in the eyes this morning and said, "Do you know there are people who need your shoes?" every one of us would say, "I know that!" Every one of us would say, "I believe that!" Here's the invitation. Let's go beyond that awareness. Let's do something right now—let's give them our shoes—now, in this moment. That's the invitation.[4]

Lloyd was combining inclination to give with the opportunity to give. He then bent down and took his shoes off and laid them on the stage. That morning, twenty-five hundred people got in the game and gave twenty-five hundred pairs of shoes to people who needed them. Imagine the evangelistic opportunities that occurred that week in and around Nashville as hundreds of people told their friends, neighbors, and coworkers, "My pastor asked us to do the craziest thing yesterday. . . ."

In the spring of 2009, Dennis Keating, lead pastor at Emanuel Faith Church in Escondido, California, gave a multiweek series of messages designed to engage congregants in the needs of the world, titled, "God Cares . . . I Care." God cares about the hungry, the thirsty, the prisoners, orphans, the sick, the broken, the prodigal, and so on. Understanding that a person's motivation would not be higher than at the end of the message, each sermon concluded with an opportunity to do something right then and there about the need that was presented. People were asked specifically to give or to go out and help, and hundreds got into the game by responding. Following Dennis's message on God caring for the hungry, families donated more than twenty thousand shopping bags of food to the local food bank.[5]

Rick was preaching a message series on money and finances. In an attempt to illustrate how well-off we are as a society, he told a brief story about children in India:

> I met a man who was doing incredible work there. He was rescuing children from extreme poverty by purchasing them for less than $50 per child so the children could be returned to their families or placed in a caring home. Most of those children were being sold because their families couldn't afford to feed all their children. So they would sell one to feed the others. Most of the children sold in this manner end up in the sex trade industry.
>
> Afterward, I had people stuffing $50 in my hand to give to this man in India to purchase more children out of poverty and save them from a life of misery. One man came up and simply said, "I want to help," and handed me a check for $50,000. Ten minutes later, he returned with his wife and offered an additional $50,000.

That brief but stirring story led to LifeBridge partnering with Central India Christian Mission to rescue children in several communities in India, to provide schools, orphanages, and church planting in those communities. Grace wins again!

Make It Personal

A third essential is to *personally invite people to serve with you*. Don't expect general pleas to work. Although people serve for a number of reasons, including compelling need, surveys show that when somebody they respect asks them personally to serve together, the success rate is 93 percent.[6] The key words are "Do this *with me*." Don Simmons points out that there are three *I's* necessary for attracting and asking volunteers:

1. *Identify.* Identify the specific people who would do a great job serving others in this specific area.
2. *Inform.* Let people know what they are going to be doing if they join you in service. The worst thing you could say to them is "Just pitch in; you'll figure things out when you get there." Keep in mind that this is about equipping, not just recruiting.
3. *Invest.* Give people a chance to try it out before they commit for the long term. An honest no is way better than a dishonest yes.

Your role is to put people in service and to help them discover their unique place and contribution. These people are serving, not just volunteering. Ministering to them is perhaps more important than the ministry of service they are doing. Don refers to this process as "experiential discipleship."

Inviting others personally takes time, effort, and energy, but it can be effective if it is focused on their growth and development. The folks at Vision San Diego believe that modeling is a great approach to developing an external focus. All the Vision San Diego staff take one hour a week to read to students at local schools. What if your staff, elders, or leaders simply modeled an easy-entry point like that and asked one person to go along with them to serve? How many more would get in the game?

Begin with the Willing

In getting people into the game, it is important to recognize that not everybody initially wants to play. That's OK. It is helpful to understand that you don't have to persuade and enlist everyone, or even the majority, before you can begin an externally focused initiative. You can just *work with the willing*—the early enthusiasts—and let them create the working models and tell the stories that will spread to the rest of the folk. The point is that nearly everyone can be persuaded to embrace new ideas, but people need various amounts of information and time before they are comfortable accepting the new and willing to serve. So realistically, creating systems where everyone is enthusiastically engaged will take some time. But be patient. You are in this for the long haul! Remember the words of Thomas Paine: "Time makes more converts than reason"[7]

How to Tell If You Are "Winning"

It is one thing to get everybody playing, but how do we determine the score? How do we measure whether we are winning or not? Measuring begins with mission. Mission is the only solid standard against which you can measure progress. Recently, Eric was a facilitator at a gathering of churches that had come together around the topic of innovation. The first exercise featured a poster board divided into five sectors, as shown in Figure 10.1. The church leaders were instructed to use this model to define the mission of their church and then to evaluate their progress in four specific ways, asking the following questions:

- *What is working?* What are they doing well in relation to the mission? These are strengths they can build on and take into the future.
- *What is stuck?* This identifies a problem or barrier that needs to be overcome in order to make progress toward the mission.
- *What could we start?* What initiatives might they undertake to better fulfill their mission?.
- *What do we need to abandon?* What are they currently doing that does not help accomplish the mission? (Any use of resources that does not further the mission is by definition "waste.")

Note that every evaluative question that reflects how a church is doing makes sense only if it is asked with respect to the mission. Some churches have no idea what their mission is. But leaders who cannot identify their mission cannot evaluate whether they are on the path to success. Every program, every initiative, and every expenditure may be regarded as good simply because there are good intentions behind it. But that is beside the point. Measurement always begins with mission. So if your mission is to be the best church *for* the community, you must measure your efforts against *that* mission.

Figure 10.1

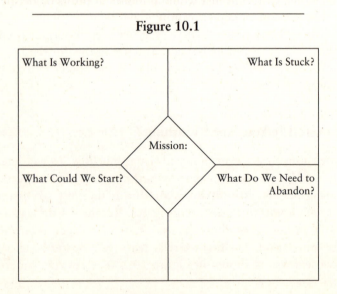

What Exactly Should We Measure?

A few years ago, Jim Collins produced a little thirty-five-page gem titled *Good to Great and the Social Sectors*. Collins writes:

> For a business, financial returns are a perfectly legitimate measure of performance. For a social sector organization, however, performance must be relative to mission, not financial returns. In the social sectors, the critical question is not "How much money do we make per dollar of invested capital?" but "How effectively do we deliver on our mission and make a distinctive impact, relative to our resources? . . ."
>
> It really doesn't matter whether you can quantify your results. What matters is that you rigorously assemble evidence— quantitative or qualitative—to track your progress. If the evidence is primarily qualitative, think like a trial lawyer assembling the combined body of evidence. If the evidence is primarily quantitative, then think of yourself as a laboratory scientist assembling and assessing the data.[8]

The important thing is to decide what you will consistently keep track of to tell you whether you are making progress against the goal and above your baseline. As an example of consistent measurement, Collins cites the example of the Cleveland Orchestra. How does one measure the progress or excellence of an orchestra? Its expressed goal was "artistic excellence," but that was too subjective, so the director, Tom Morris, came up with a scorecard that would provide indicators of artistic excellence. The orchestra would measure six things:[9]

1. Number of standing ovations
2. Number of complex pieces the orchestra can play with excellence
3. Number of invitations from Europe's most prestigious music festivals
4. Number of tickets sold
5. Number of other orchestras that mimic Cleveland Orchestra's style
6. Number of composers who want their work debuted in Cleveland

If your goal is to become the best church *for* the community rather than the best church *in* the community, the scorecard for what you measure must change. This is not to infer that you stop counting the offering or the weekend attendance, but if you really want to be the best church for the community, you need to come up with additional measurements.

In 2008, Dan Nold, senior pastor at Calvary Baptist Church in State College, Pennsylvania, changed the scorecard to reflect the church's missional commitment. It now counts four new things it hadn't counted before:

- Number of community partnerships
- Number of people to whom the church is providing food
- Number of small groups consistently serving in the community
- Number of community-centered God stories

What would you add to Dan's list? Following the lead of our musical counterparts from Cleveland, what might the church creatively measure to gauge its effectiveness in accomplishing its missional goals? Here are a few ideas:

- Number of favorable articles about the church in the local newspaper
- Number of other church leaders that want to see "what you do and how you do it"
- Number of awards that you get from the community
- Number of church-community partnerships listed in the church bulletin

After reading *The Externally Focused Church*, Pastor Jeff Valentine of Missoula Alliance Church (MAC) in Missoula, Montana, went to the principal of a local elementary school and asked if MAC could supply some tutors for the kids. The principal, probably thinking about church and state issues, was cautious. It would be OK if the church sent three tutors. Soon the three tutors became nine tutors as the positive effects on the kids' lives became evident. This particular school has a number of children whose parents are addicted to crack cocaine. Any money coming into the home goes toward crack, and the ones who suffer for it are the kids. So for the Christmas Eve service, Jeff asked the people of MAC to give generously, disclosing that half of the offering would go to the school to spend on children in need.

The following week, the principal received a check for $14,000. He and his team could spend the money on students in distress—money the school just didn't have before. So between shoes, clothing, dental care, and supplies, MAC gave the opportunity for the principal to be a blessing to his students. Unsolicited, the principal put out a press release about what MAC did, and the article made the front page of the local newspaper. Copies of the article were included with every school employee's paycheck.

And there is more to the story. Elementary school kids, simply because they are kids, sometimes "soil themselves" while at school. The ones who did were often terrified to return home because of the humiliation or beatings they would receive from parents. The compassionate teachers began collecting and stocking extra clothing for kids to change into before they went home, and the teachers took turns taking the soiled laundry home to be washed and returned to school. The people of MAC thought they could do more, so they bought a washer and dryer for the school. The principal, initially so hesitant about working with a church, now openly embraces MAC's efforts. Together, MAC and the school are making a tangible difference in the lives of children. MAC's vision is to help Missoula become the healthiest community in the state of Montana. It's not about the church; it's about the city, about the kingdom. MAC's measurement of success looks amazingly different today from how it looked just a few years ago.

Expanding the Church Scorecard

In June 2008, W. David Phillips posted an entry on his blog (http://www .wdavidphillips.com) titled "Measuring Success in Ministry." David reflected on a question Len Sweet had posed in his doctoral class regarding "metaphors that will describe how we measure success in the church in the future." Eschewing the traditional measurements of how many, how often, and how much, here is the list the class (with a few later additions from David) came up with:

1. The number of cigarette butts in the church parking lot
2. The number of adoptions people in the church have made from local foster care
3. The number of pictures on the church wall of unwed mothers holding their newborn babies in their arms for the first time
4. The number of classes for special needs children and adults
5. The number of former convicted felons serving in the church
6. The number of phone calls from community leaders asking the church's advice
7. The number of meetings that take place somewhere besides the church building
8. The number of organizations using the church building
9. The number of days the pastor doesn't spend time in the church office but in the community
10. The number of emergency finance meetings that take place to reroute money to community ministry
11. The amount of dollars saved by the local schools because the church has painted the walls

12. The number of people serving in the community during the church's normal worship hours

13. The number of non-religious-school professors worshiping with you

14. The number of people wearing good, free clothes that used to belong to members of the church

15. The number of times the church band has played family-friendly music in the local coffee shop

16. The number of people who have gotten better because of the free health clinic you operate

17. The number of people in new jobs thanks to the free job training center you opened

18. The number of micro-loans given by members in your church

19. The number of churches your church planted in a 10-mile radius of your own church[10]

Nothing changes until the scorecard changes.

The Externally Focused Scorecard

Five familiar words represent concepts that are important in creating an externally focused scorecard. These words, familiar to nonprofit agencies, are not usually part of the vocabulary of the local church. The causal relationship between the words and their underlying concepts is shown in Figure 10.2.

Inputs are the resources that were dedicated to externally focused ministry—facilities, time, money, materials, and number of people serving.

Activities are the externally focused missional activities and programs of the church, which may include such things as tutoring, mentoring, cleanup projects, school makeovers, and feeding programs.

Outputs include such things as the total hours served outside the church, dollar equivalents of those volunteer hours, and number of peoples served through the activities.

Outcomes are the short- and medium-range changes that occurred in individual lives or families.

Impact is the long-range change in the community, society, or environment.

Outcomes and *Impact* answer the questions "So what?" or "What difference did the inputs, programs, and output make in the lives of others?"

Figure 10.2

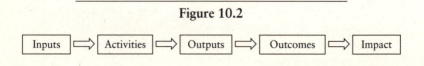

Peter Drucker insists that the bottom line for all nonprofit organizations is always "changed human beings."[11]

Here's an important insight. If you ask a pastor or leader to describe his or her church, the answer will usually be related to inputs, activities, or outputs:

> Inputs: "We have twenty-eight full-time staff and a fifteen-hundred-seat auditorium that sits on twenty-five acres just north of the city."
>
> Activities: "We have four morning services, a Saturday evening service, a full Sunday school program, over a hundred small groups, Men's Fraternity, and . . ."
>
> Outputs: "We attract around thirty-two hundred in weekend worship, seventeen hundred in Sunday school, and over a thousand people in small groups . . ."

And that is where the measurement stops. We must remember, however, that we measure what matters by measuring *outcomes* and *impact*. Inputs, activities, and outputs are always in service to outcomes and impact. Never lose sight of the fact that outcomes and impact answer the questions "So what?" and "What difference did it make?" *Outcomes* specify the changes that occurred in individuals as the result of your activities. *Impact* refers to the long-term changes that are the collective results of the changes of individuals. We define externally focused churches as churches that measure their effectiveness not only by the number of people in the weekend service (output) but also by the transformational effect the church is having on the community (outcomes and impact).

Bethel Church in Richland, Washington, submitted a story that illustrates the relationship between activities and outcomes:

> Through Bethel's car repair ministry, which is called Elijah's Pit Stop (an *activity*), a formerly homeless drug addict has learned to be a mechanic (*outcome*) and is rapidly learning to handle a wide array of administrative functions (*outcome*). Kenny is now working thirty to thirty-five hours per week for Elijah's and five to ten hours per week for the commercial car repair shop that donates repair bay space to Elijah's every other Saturday. Kenny now has a wife, an apartment, and a car (*outcome*). He is also becoming adept at mentoring other homeless people, as well as struggling young men from single-parent homes (*outcome* and *impact*).

What We Can't Measure

There is value in measuring things. After all, if something exists, it exists in some amount, and if it exists in some amount, it can be measured, and if it can be measured, the results can be anticipated. There is an old adage that everyone who earns a living through sales quickly understands: "Get the numbers, or the numbers get you."

Before you start thinking, "I knew it would end up being just about numbers and how to be bigger than the church down the street," bear with us for a moment. You can't deny that the Bible often speaks of numbers. In fact, it seems like every time there was a gathering, someone was counting. It is also true that numbers do give us some idea of what is going on. We think there is good value in us doing what we can to measure *what we can*. We can measure if someone is part of a small group, but we can't measure if there is any change going on in the person's heart. We can measure how many people have gotten involved in a service opportunity, but we can't measure how many of them are serving as committed followers. We can measure attendance, but we can't measure attitude. But the fact that there are things we cannot measure doesn't mean we shouldn't measure.

One of our great mistakes has been measuring success or value simply by attendance numbers. Some of us come to believe we're more effective than perhaps we really are simply because our attendance is growing. Others of us have felt like failures because we aren't as big as the church down the street. This is a tough issue for pastors to navigate, isn't it?

WHAT WE DON'T MEASURE

At LifeBridge, there is one area that Rick has refused to measure. He explains:

> LifeBridge measures how many people (as best we can) are serving through our church, either internally or externally. We also try to keep track of the serving opportunities we have externally. What we don't measure are how many people are coming to LifeBridge Christian Church now or how many have come to Christ as a result of our serving in the community. There is one reason I don't want us to start measuring this—it's me. I know me too well. I might determine the usefulness or need of that service in the wrong way. "Well, we aren't seeing any results *at our church* because of our involvement in the XYZ community agency, so let's just stop doing that."

I want to be committed to our community service with the sim
understanding that there are needs and we have the opportunity
biblical mandate to be engaged in meeting those needs. Make no mistake, I am grateful that it has led to hundreds of people coming to
Christ. We need to make the good deeds, goodwill, and good news
connections. I'm thankful that our community service has changed the
hearts and lives of people in our congregation, and I am grateful that
we have been a small part of meeting some community needs. I just
don't want our service to be somehow about counting scalps; I want
our service to be an opportunity to extend God's goodness and goodwill in our community.

SUCCESS IS NOT ALWAYS UP AND TO THE RIGHT

Sometimes we can measure for the wrong results. Rick was with a church
that talked excitedly about its ministry to the homeless. The director of that
ministry said, "Last year we helped one hundred homeless people, and
next year we are hoping to help two hundred!" Rick understood what
they were saying but couldn't help thinking, "You are going in the wrong
direction. If you were really being effective, you would only help fifty
because fifty were no longer homeless."

In externally focused ministry, if it's messy, you are winning. There
are few, if any, red-carpet events or shiny trophies announcing victory.
It's hard to measure messiness but easy to spot it. The dirt, sweat, and
sometimes tears of externally focused ministry provide glimpses of a winning season. To see people loving and serving in ways and in places they
would have never touched a year ago—that's a measurement of kingdom
success. To see friendships form between the homeless and the formerly
heartless—that's success. To see paint on the preacher and the painter
preach with his life of service—that's success.

Your Scorecard

What is your scorecard? What does "winning" look like? How do
you measure what really counts in your life and in your church? When you
describe your church, do you talk in terms of *inputs* (size of staff,
budget, and facility), *activities* (numbers of Bible studies, ministries,
and programs), and *outputs* (number of people who attended your
events, program, or activities) or in terms of *outcomes* and *impacts*—the
difference you are making in changing lives and changing communities?
As we've said many time, becoming the best church *for* the community
is a different game than wanting to become the best church *in* the

community. You will need new skills, new eyes, and new like-minded companions to help you on this new journey. But we assure you that it will be worth it and you'll have the time of your life.

The Leadership Challenge

We've come to the end of the book but possibly the beginning of a new adventure and direction for your life and ministry. We thoroughly believe that our best years are still ahead of us and ahead of you. We leave you with the following questions to think about and answer.

- What would your community look like if all Christ followers were engaged in meeting the needs and dreams of the community?
- What could you do to get everybody in the game?
- What does your scorecard look like?
- What do you want to measure?
- What can you do to help people discover their Ephesians 2:10 intersection of passion and purpose?
- How could you structure church so that at the end of the year, every person had a story to tell of how, in ways great or small, he or she changed the world?

NOTES

Introduction

1. Martin Luther King Jr., "I've Been to the Mountaintop," speech delivered Apr. 3, 1968, Mason Temple, Memphis, Tenn.
2. John Fitzgerald Kennedy, inaugural address, delivered Jan. 20, 1961, Washington, D.C.

Chapter One: What Kind of Day Is Today?

1. David Smith, *Mission After Christendom* (London: Darton, Longman & Todd, 2003), p. ix.
2. Quoted in W. Chan Kim and Renée Mauborgne, *Blue Ocean Strategy: How to Create Uncontested Market Space and Make the Competition Irrelevant* (Boston: Harvard Business School, 2005), p. 193.
3. Louis Menand, "Everybody's an Expert: Putting Predictions to the Test," *New Yorker*, Dec. 2005, http://www.newyorker.com/archive/2005/12/05/051205crbo_books1
4. *Time*, Dec. 26, 2007, pp. 8, 45.
5. Advent Conspiracy, "Love Wells. Give Wells," 2008, http://www.adventconspiracy.org/water
6. William Knoke, *Bold New World: The Essential Roadmap to the Twenty-First Century* (New York: Kodansha, 1996), p. 13.
7. Fareed Zakaria, *The Post-American World* (New York: Norton, 2008), p. 68, quoting from Niall Ferguson, *Empire: The Rise and Demise of the British World Order and the Lessons for Global Power* (New York: Basic Books, 2004).
8. Knoke, *Bold New World*, p. 8.

9. Google, "Why Google?" 2009, http://www.google.com/enterprise/whygoogle.html

10. Ori Brafman and Rod A. Beckstrom, *The Starfish and the Spider: The Unstoppable Power of Leaderless Organizations* (New York: Penguin Books, 2006), p. 73.

11. Quoted in Don Tapscott and Anthony D. Williams, *Wikinomics: How Mass Collaboration Changes Everything* (New York: Portfolio, 2006), p. 71.

12. Ibid., p. 13.

13. Jason Lymangrover, "Colby Caillat: Biography," Allmusic.com, 2009, http://allmusic.com/cg/amg.dll?p=amg&sql=11:jpfwxq9rldte~T1

14. MSNBC.com, "Democrats Face Off in YouTube Debate," July 23, 2007, http://www.msnbc.msn.com/id/19914962

15. Andrea Bailey, "World Wide Witness: Are People Really Meeting Christ Online? And If So, How?" *Outreach*, Jan.-Feb. 2008, p. 78.

16. Stephen Shields, "Social Networks and Technology," *Rev!* Nov.-Dec. 2007, p. 68.

17. Daniel H. Pink, *A Whole New Mind: Why Right-Brainers Will Rule the Future* (New York: Riverhead Books, 2006), p. 33.

18. Ellen Pearlman, "The *New York Times*'s Thomas Friedman on Globalization," Mar. 25, 2005, http://www.cioinsight.com/article2/0,1397,1777087,00.asp

19. Fareed Zakaria, "How Long Will America Lead the World?" *Newsweek,* June 12, 2006, p. 44.

20. Ted C. Fishman, *China, Inc.: The Relentless Rise of the Next Great Superpower* (New York: Simon &Schuster, 2006), p. 11.

21. Fareed Zakaria, "The Rise of a Fierce yet Fragile Superpower," *Newsweek,* Dec. 31, 2007, p. 38.

22. Ted C. Fishman, "How China Will Change Your Business," *Inc.,* Mar. 1, 2005, http://www.inc.com/magazine/20050301/china.html

23. Fishman, *China, Inc.,* p. 10.

24. Ibid., p. 254.

25. Fareed Zakaria, "India Rising" *Newsweek,* Mar. 6, 2006, p. 34.

26. Ibid.

27. Pink, *Whole New Mind,* p. 37.

28. Fareed Zakaria, *The Post-American World* (New York: Norton, 2008), pp. 41, 321, and 20.

29. Zakaria, *The Post-American World,* p. 98, quoting Josepha Kahn and Jim Yardley, "As China Roars, Pollution Reaches Deadly Extremes," *New York Times,* Aug. 26, 2007.

30. Living Water International, "The Water Crisis," http://www.water.cc/water-crisis

31. Damian Dovarganes, "Evangelical Leaders Join Global Warming Initiative, *New York Times,* Feb. 8, 2006, http://www.nytimes.com/2006/02/08/national/08warm.html?incamp=article_popular

32. Ibid.

33. Ibid.

34. David Biello, "Conservative Climate," *Scientific American,* Apr. 2007, p. 1.

35. Peachtree Baptist Church, "Faith & the Environment," 2009, http://www.peachtreebaptist.net/ministries/faith-environment

36. Pew Research Center for People & the Press, "Religion and the Presidential Vote," Dec. 6, 2004, http://people-press.org/commentary/display.php3?AnalysisID=103

37. Christianity Today Politics Blog, "The Evangelical Electoral Map (Updated)," Nov. 5, 2008, http://blog.christianitytoday.com/ctpolitics/2008/11/the_evangelical.html

38. James Wallace, *God's Politics: Why the Right Gets It Wrong and the Left Doesn't Get It* (New York: HarperCollins, 2005), p. 8.

39. Joseph Gusfield, *Performing Action: Artistry in Human Behavior and Social Research* (Piscataway, N.J.: Transaction, 2000), p. 323.

40. We thank Paul Williams for shaping this idea.

41. Josh McDowell, *Evidence That Demands a Verdict* (Nashville, Tenn.: Nelson, 1979), and subsequent revisions.

42. Philip Jenkins, *The Next Christendom: The Coming of Global Christianity* (New York: Oxford University Press, 2002), p. 163.

43. Scott Thuma, Dave Travis, and Warren Bird, *Megachurches Today, 2005* (Hartford, Conn.: Hartford Institute for Religion Research and Leadership Network, Hartford Seminary, 2006), p. 1.

44. Reggie McNeal, *The Present Future: Six Tough Questions for the Church* (San Francisco: Jossey-Bass, 2003), p. 24.

45. Thuma, Travis, and Bird, *Megachurches Today,* p. 6.

46. Ibid., p. 1.

47. Michael Gerson, "A New Social Gospel," *Newsweek,* Nov. 13, 2006, p. 40.

48. Ibid., pp. 41 and 43.

49. K. Connie Kang, Christianity's Image Taking a Turn for the Worse," *Los Angeles Times,* Oct. 13, 2007, http://www.didihirsch.org/files/u1/LA_Times_10-13-07.pdf

50. Tom Krattenmaker, "A Force for Good," *USA Today,* Nov. 12, 2007, p. 15A.

51. Jerry Adler, "In Search of the Spiritual," *Newsweek,* Aug. 29, 2005, p. 48.

52. Quoted in Vanessa Juarez, "Sexy Woman with the Guitar," *Newsweek,* Sept. 9, 2005, http://www.msnbc.msn.com/id/10387002/site/newsweek

53. Rebecca Barnes and Lindy Lowry, "7 Startling Facts," *Outreach,* May-June 2006, p. 44.

54. McNeal, *The Present Future,* p. 4.

55. George Barna, *Revolution* (Carol Stream, Ill.: Tyndale House, 2005), p. 12.

56. Barnes and Lowry, "7 Startling Facts," p. 44.

57. Quoted in "A Look at the 'Organic' Church: What Pastors Can Learn from the Smallest Churches," *Rev!,* July-Aug. 2008, p. 62.

58. Quoted in Smith, *Mission After Christendom,* p. 33.

59. Ibid., p. 73.

60. Embassy Suites, advertisement, *USA Today,* Feb. 20, 2006, p. 6A.

61. Smith, *Mission After Christendom,* p. 35.

Chapter Two: Focus: They Choose the Window Seat, Not the Aisle Seat

1. John P. Schuster, *Answering Your Call: A Guide for Living Your Deepest Purpose* (San Francisco: Berrett-Koehler, 2003), Kindle locations 235–238.

2. Rodney Stark, *The Rise of Christianity: How the Obscure, Marginal, Jesus Movement Became the Dominant Religious Force in the Western World in a Few Centuries* (San Francisco: HarperOne, 1997), p. 6.

3. David Bosch, *Transforming Mission* (Maryknoll, N.Y.: Orbis, 1991), p. 49. The quotation is from Adolf von Harnack, *The Mission and Expansion of Christianity in the First Three Centuries* (New York: Harper, 1908), vol. 1.

4. Thomas Massaro, *Living Justice: Catholic Social Teaching in Action* (Lanham, Md.: Rowman & Littlefield, 2000), pp. 14–15.

5. Attributed to Vance Havner (1901–1986), the "Dean of American Revival Preachers," a source of numerous *bons mots.*

6. Ram A. Cnaan and others, *The Invisible Caring Hand: American Congregations and the Provision of Welfare* (New York: New York University Press, 2002), p. 10.

7. Thom S. Rainer, "Seven Sins of Dying Churches," *Outreach,* Jan.-Feb. 2006, p. 16.

8. Ellison Research, "Four Out of Ten Pastors Lack Strong Interest in Increasing Community Outreach," Jan. 3, 2007, http://ellisonresearch .com/releases/20070103.htm

9. Eric Swanson, *Ten Paradigm Shifts Toward Community Transformation* (Dallas: Leadership Network, 2003).

10. Swiss Brethren Conference, "The Schleitheim Confession," adopted Feb. 24, 1527 (Crockett, Ky.: Rod & Staff, 1985), http://www.anabaptists.org/ history/schleith.html

11. Bosch, *Transforming Mission,* p. 318.

12. Diana R. Garland, "Church Social Work," in *Christianity and Social Work: Readings on the Integration of Christian Faith and Social Work Practice,* ed. Beryl Hugen (Botsford, Conn.: North American Association of Christians in Social Work, 1998), p. 22.

13. Community Foundation Serving Boulder County, *Quality of Life in Boulder County, 2005: A Community Indicators Report,* (Boulder. Colo.: Community Foundation, 2005).

14. Ram A. Cnaan with Robert J. Wineburg and Stephanie C. Boddie, *The Newer Deal: Social Work and Religion in Partnership* (New York: Columbia University Press, 1999), p. 51.

15. "City Shouldn't Meddle When Religious Groups Perform Good Works," editorial, *Vancouver Sun,* Aug. 23, 2007, http://www.canada.com/vancouversun/news/editorial/story.html?id=4c4081c3-723c-4b34-95a1-1b496621488c

16. Robert D. Lupton, *Theirs Is the Kingdom: Celebrating the Gospel in Urban America,* ed. Barbara R. Thompson (San Francisco: HarperOne, 1989), pp. 60–61.

17. McNeal, *The Present Future,* p. 32.

18. Adam Hochschild, *Bury the Chains: Prophets and Rebels in the Fight to Free an Empire's Slaves* (New York: Houghton Mifflin, 2005), p. 29.

19. Ibid.

20. Ibid., p. 77.

21. Rick Warren, comments, HIV/AIDS Summit, Saddleback, Calif., Nov. 29, 2005.

Chapter Three: Purpose: They Practice Weight Training, Not Bodybuilding

1. Sue Mallory, *The Equipping Church* (Grand Rapids, Mich.: Zondervan, 2001), p. 9.

2. Rick Rusaw and Eric Swanson, *The Externally Focused Church* (Loveland, Colo.: Group Publishing, 2004); Rick Rusaw and Eric Swanson, *The Externally Focused Life* (Loveland, Colo.: Group Publishing, 2009).

3. Alan Roxburgh, comments, Dallas Seminary Missional Church Conference, Dallas, Tex., Apr. 1, 2008.

4. Augustine of Hippo, *Saint Augustine Confessions,* trans. Henry Chadwick (New York: Oxford University Press,1991), p. 60.

5. Abraham H. Maslow, "A Theory of Human Motivation," *Psychological Review* 50 (1943): 370–396.

6. Musana Children's Home, "The World as Our Oyster," Nov. 27, 2008, http://musanachildrenshome.weebly.com/the-story--video.html

7. Ibid.

8. Elie Wiesel, *Night* (New York: Hill & Wang, 2006), p. 120.

9. Bob Roberts Jr., "Power of the 'Glocal' Church," *Rev!*, Sept.-Oct. 2008, p. 138.

10. Center for Family & Community Ministries, "The Role of Faith in the Service of Christian Volunteers," 2006, http://www.baylor.edu/content/services/document.php/22974.pdf

11. Kevin G. Ford, *Transforming Church: Bringing Out the Good to Get to Great* (Colorado Springs, Colo.: Cook, 2008), p. 32.

12. Michael E. Sherr, Diana R. Garland, Dennis R. Meyers, and Terry A. Wolfer, "Community Ministry Powerful Factor in Maturing Teens' Faith," Jan. 22, 2007, http://www.baylor.edu/pr/news.php?action=story&story=43671

13. Thom S. Rainer and Sam S. Rainer III, *Essential Church? Reclaiming a Generation of Dropouts* (Nashville, Tenn.: B&H Books, 2008), p. 155.

14. Greg L. Hawkins and Cally Parkinson, *Reveal: Where Are You?* (Chicago: Willow Creek, 2008), p. 13.

15. Ibid., p. 36.

16. Ian Bradley, *The Celtic Way* (London: Darton, Longman & Todd, 2003), p. 44.

17. We owe this insight to a conversation between Eric and Geoffrey Hsu, formerly with Campus Crusade for Christ, who was struggling to come up with a replacement watchword for Campus Crusade's "Win, Build, Send" approach to college students. Geoffrey argues that today's students are more attracted to the idea of "believe, belong, and bless." He currently serves with Church Resource Ministries in San Diego, California.

18. George Barna, "A Faith Revolution Is Redefining 'Church,' According to New Study," Oct. 10, 2005, http://www.barna.org/barna-update/article/5-barna-update/170-a-faith-revolution-is-redefining-qchurchq-according-to-new-study

19. Ronald Rolheiser, *The Holy Longing: The Search for Christian Spirituality* (New York: Doubleday, 1999), p. 69.

20. Bill Bright, *Have You Heard of the Four Spiritual Laws?* (Orlando, Fla.: NewLife, 1964).

21. Richard Laliberte, "4 Ways to Live Longer," *Good Housekeeping,* Mar. 2009, p. 52.

22. Ibid.

23. Ibid.

24. Martha Manning, *A Place to Land* (New York: Ballantine Books, 2003), as excerpted in *Reader's Digest,* Sept. 2003, p. 128.

25. Omar Reyes, Leadership Network podcast, 2009.

Chapter Four: Story: They Live in the Kingdom Story, Not a Church Story

1. Tim Keller, "What Is Jesus' Mission?" Gospel Christianity, course 1, unit 7 (New York: Redeemer Presbyterian Church, 2003), p. 4.
2. Based on Pink, *Whole New Mind,* p. 102.
3. Cain's answer to God, "Am I my brother's keeper?" (Genesis 4:9), demonstrates the devastating consequences of sin. In many ways, the rest of the Bible is God's answer to this question.
4. Michael Frost and Alan Hirsh, *The Shaping of Things to Come: Innovation and Mission for the 21st-Century Church* (Peabody, Mass.: Hendrickson, 2003), p. 33.
5. E. Stanley Jones, *The Unshakable Kingdom and the Unchanging Person* (Nashville, Tenn.: Abington Press, 1972), p. 30.
6. Howard Snyder, *Liberating the Church* (Downers Grove, Ill.: InterVarsity Press, 1983), p. 11.
7. N. T. Wright, *Simply Christian: Why Christianity Makes Sense,* 9th ed. (San Francisco: HarperOne, 2006).
8. Pink, *Whole New Mind,* p. 102.
9. James Montgomery Boyce, *Two Cities, Two Loves: Christian Responsibility in a Crumbling Culture* (Downers Grove, Ill.: InterVarsity Press, 1996), p. 152.
10. Krista Petty, "Going Glocal, Leadership Network, http://www.leadnet.org; also available at http://www.externallyfocusednetwork.com/cp/uploads/Externally_Focused_Small_Groups.pdf
11. Bob Moffitt, *If Jesus Were Mayor* (Phoenix, Ariz.: Harvest, 2004), p. 10.
12. Roberts, "Power of the 'Glocal' Church," p. 138.

Chapter Five: Missions: The Few Send the Many, Not the Many Send the Few

1. Smith, *Mission After Christendom,* p. 78.
2. David Neff, "Global Is the New Local," *Christianity Today,* June 2009, p. 39.
3. Ibid.
4. Rob Wegner, personal interview, Mar, 10, 2009.
5. Philip Jenkins, *The Next Christendom: The Coming of Global Christianity* (New York: Oxford University Press, 2002), p. 1.
6. Ibid., p. 2.
7. David A. Livermore, *Serving with Eyes Wide Open: Doing Short-Term Missions with Cultural Intelligence* (Grand Rapids, Mich.: Baker Books, 2006), p. 33.

8. Jenkins, *Next Christendom*, p. 71.

9. Ibid.

10. Rob Moll, "Missions Incredible," *Christianity Today*, Mar. 2006, p. 28.

11. Livermore, *Serving with Eyes Wide Open*, p. 40.

12. William Gibson, quoted in "Books of the Year," *Economist*, Dec. 4, 2003.

13. Attributed to Bishop Desmond Tutu, https://www.pcusa.org/missionconnections/letters/jonesk/jonesk_0512.htm

14. Matt Olthoff, personal interview, Mar. 17, 2009.

15. Stacey Campbell, personal interview, May 6, 2009.

16. Scott White, personal interview, May 5, 2009.

17. Tim Senff, personal interview, Mar. 10, 2009.

18. Tom Mullis, personal interview, Mar. 17, 2009.

19. Mike Kenyon, personal interview, Mar. 24, 2009.

20. Matt Olthoff, personal interview, Mar. 17, 2009.

21. Steve Hanson, personal interview, June 25, 2009.

22. Bob Roberts Jr., *Glocalization: How Followers of Jesus Engage a Flat World* (Grand Rapids, Mich.: Zondervan, 2007), p. 137.

23. Keith West, personal interview, June 16, 2009.

24. Durwood Snead, personal interview, May 6, 2009.

25. Eric Hanson, personal interview, Apr. 8, 2009.

26. Steve Hanson, personal interview, June 25, 2009.

27. Matt Olthoff, Leadership Network I-3 Conference, Dallas, Texas, Jan. 28, 2009.

28. Ian Stevenson, personal interview, Mar. 10, 2009.

29. Keith West, personal interview, June 16, 2009.

30. Quoted in Timothy C. Morgan, "Purpose Driven in Rwanda," *Christianity Today*, Sept. 23, 2005, http://www.christianitytoday.com/ct/2005/october/17.32.html?start=2

31. Saddleback Church, "The PEACE Plan," http://www.saddleback.com/aboutsaddleback/signatureministries/thepeaceplan/index.html

32. Rick Warren, "After the Aloha Shirts," *Christianity Today*, Oct. 2008, p. 44.

33. Steve Hanson, personal interview, June 25, 2009.

34. Mark Connelly, personal interview, May 7, 2009.

35. Branded PHX, "Modern Day Slavery," 2009, http://www.brandedphx.com/learn-more/modern-day-slavery

36. StreetLight PHX, "About Us," 2009, http://streetlightphx.com/#

37. David Thoresen, personal interview, May 5, 2009.

38. Jonathan Martin, personal interview, June 15, 2009.

39. Neff, "Global Is the New Local," p. 39.

40. Mike Robinson, personal interview, Mar. 17, 2009.

41. See Jonathan Martin, *Giving Wisely: Killing with Kindness or Empowering Lasting Transformation?* (Redmond, Ore.: Last Chapter Publishing, 2008).

42. Kirk DeWitt, personal interview, Apr. 2, 2009.

43. John Chung, personal interview, May 7, 2009.

44. Dave Hall, personal interview, May 7, 2009.

45. Durwood Snead, personal interview, May 6, 2009.

46. Dave Hall, personal interview, May 7, 2009.

47. Joey Shaw, personal interview, Mar. 24, 2009.

48. Scott White, personal interview, May 6, 2009.

49. Neil Hendershot, personal interview, June 17, 2009.

50. Brian Petak, personal interview, May 15, 2009.

51. Ian Stevenson, personal interview, Mar. 10, 2009.

52. David Thoresen, personal interview, May 5, 2009.

53. Tim Senff, personal interview, Mar. 10, 2009.

Chapter Six: Partnering: They Build Wells, Not Walls

1. Rusaw and Swanson, *Externally Focused Church*, p. 97.

2. Attributed to Rupertus Meldenius (1627).

3. Michael Frost and Alan Hirsch, *The Shaping of Things to Come* (Peabody, Mass.: Hendrickson, 2004), p. 47.

4. Step Out and Serve 2009, "About Us: Mission," 2009, http://www.stepoutomaha.com/index.php?option=com_content&view=article&id=47:about-us&catid=38:about&Itemid=53

5. Ian Vickers, e-mail, Sept. 8, 2008.

6. Quoted in Krista Petty, "Church-to-Church Collaboration on the Rise," Leadership Network, 2009, http://www.leadnet.org/resources.asp

7. Crossroads, "GO Cincinnati," video clip, 2009, http://www.gocincinnati.net; Tim Senff, personal interview, Mar. 10, 2009.

8. Leadership Network, *Kingdom Impact Report* (Dallas, Tex.: Leadership Network, 2008).

9. Petty, "Church-to-Church Collaboration on the Rise."

10. Helen Lee, "Missional Shift or Drift?" *Christianity Today,* Nov. 7, 2008, http://www.christianitytoday.com/le/2008/fall/7.23.html

11. Petty, "Church-to-Church Collaboration on the Rise."

12. Bosch, *Transforming Mission,* p. 249.

13. Dave1988, "How Many Protestant Denominations Are There?" Apr. 12, 2005, http://www.bringyou.to/apologetics/a120.htm

14. Rusaw and Swanson, *Externally Focused Church,* p. 187.

15. John R. W. Stott, *Christian Mission in the Modern World* (Downers Grove, Ill.: InterVarsity Press, 1975), p. 30.

16. Christopher Quinn, "Sex-Trafficking Fight Goes Beyond Streets," *Atlanta Journal-Constitution,* June 14, 2009, http://www.ajc.com/metro/content/metro/atlanta/stories/2009/06/14/atlanta_sex_trafficking.html

17. Chip Sweney, personal interview, July 14, 2009.

18. StreetLight, "About StreetLight," 2009, http://streetlightphx.com/about-us-2/about-streetlight

19. Leadership Network, *Kingdom Impact Report.*

20. Omar Reyes, personal interview, Mar. 11, 2009.

21. Luis Palau Association, "Church and School Partnerships: 'Enormous Mutual Benefit,'" 2009, http://www.palau.org/festivals/season_of_service/past/stories/churches_and_schools.

22. Modus360, "Season of Service, Mar. 11, 2009, http://www.themodus360.com/season-of-service

23. Phill Butler, *Well Connected: Releasing Power, Restoring Hope Through Kingdom Partnerships* (Waynesboro, Ga.: Authentic Media, 2005), pp. 34–35.

Chapter Seven: Systems: They Create Paradigms, Not Programs

1. Jim Collins, "Turning Goals into Results: The Power of Catalytic Mechanisms," *Harvard Business Review,* July-Aug. 1999, http://harvardbusiness.org/product/turning-goals-into-results-the-power-of-catalytic-mechanisms/an/99401-PDF-ENG

2. Jim Collins, "The Most Creative Product Ever," *Inc.,* May 1997, http://www.jimcollins.com/article_topics/articles/the-most-creative.html

3. D. Michael Henderson, *A Model for Making Disciples: John Wesley's Class Meeting* (Nappanee, Ind.: Evangel, 1997), p. 19.

4. Ibid., p. 23.

5. Ibid., p. 28.

6. Ibid., p. 30.

7. Wallace, *God's Politics,* p. 212.

8. Mariners Outreach, "History of Local Ministries," http://www.marinerslighthouse.org/index.php?option=com_content&view=article&id=398:history-of-local-ministries&catid=288:mariners-outreach

9. Rudy Heintzelman, personal interview, Nov. 16, 2005.

10. Henderson, *Model for Making Disciples,* pp. 48–49.

11. Glen Brechner, Next Big Idea conference, Baylor University, Feb. 10, 2009.

12. Don Simmons, speech, Leadership Community gathering, Dallas, Tex., Sept. 18, 2008.

13. Leadership Network, *The Show,* May 19, 2009, http://learnings.leadnet .org/2009/05/learning-about-missional-small-groups-with-matt-carter.html

14. Eric Hoffer, *The True Believer: Thoughts on the Nature of Mass Movements* (New York: HarperCollins, 1989), p. 120. (Originally published 1951.)

15. Robert Moffitt, "Transformation: Dream or Reality?" *Evangelical Mission Quarterly,* Oct. 2005, http://www.disciplenations.org/uploads/jF/f4/ jFf4sCDLx_07SLS94sTKXQ/Transformation-Dream-or-Reality.pdf

Chapter Eight: Evangelism: They Deploy Kingdom Laborers, Not Just Community Volunteers

1. George Barna, *The State of the Church, 2005* (Ventura, Calif.: Barna Group, 2005), p. 14.

2. Thom S. Rainer, "Seven Sins of Dying Churches," *Outreach Magazine,* Jan.-Feb. 2006, p. 16.

3. Todd Rhoades, e-mail to Eric Swanson, July 30, 2008.

4. Lupton, *Theirs Is the Kingdom,* p. 50.

5. Stott, *Christian Mission,* p. 30.

6. Dave Gibbons, Leadership Network's Camp Improv, Dallas, Tex., Oct. 1, 2003.

7. Ben Ecklu, Global City Movement meeting, Montserrat, Spain, June 29, 2008.

8. See "Fresh Coat Cleveland Channel 23 Newscast," July 17, 2007, http:// www.youtube.com/watch?v=lGX9b4A6jEc

9. As reported by Ian Vicker in Leadership Network, *Kingdom Impact Report.*

10. The Annie B. Casey Foundation Web site is an excellent resource for data on children's health and well-being in your community. This specific data on Boulder County, Colorado, comes from http://datacenter.kidscount.org/data/ bystate/stateprofile.aspx?state=CO&cat=276&group=Category&loc=1220 &dt=1%2c3%2c2%2c4

11. Doug Pollock, personal interview, Nov. 3, 2005.

12. Steve Sjogren, David Ping, and Doug Pollock, *Irresistible Evangelism* (Loveland, Colo.: Group Publishing., 2004).

13. David Kinnaman and Gabe Lyons, *UnChristian: What a New Generation Really Thinks About Christianity . . . and Why It Matters* (Grand Rapids, Mich.: Baker Books, 2007), p. 25.

14. *Golf Digest,* Nov. 2007.

15. Sjogren, Ping, and Pollock, *Irresistible Evangelism,* p. 5, with minor modifications.

16. Rick Rusaw and Eric Swanson, *The Externally Focused Life* (Loveland, Colo.: Group Pub., 2009).

17. Hal Seed, e-mail to Eric Swanson, Sept. 23, 2004.

18. Reid Carpenter, City Impact Roundtable, San Antonio, Tex., Apr. 18, 2007.

19. Guy Kawasaki, "The Art of Evangelism," Jan. 12, 2006, http://blog.guy kawasaki.com/2006/01/the_art_of_evan.html

Chapter Nine: Creativity: They Innovate, Not Replicate

1. "Watch This Video: Innovative Churches Are Different," Learnings @ Leadership Network, Aug. 4, 2009, http://learnings.leadnet.org/2009/08/ watch-this-video-innovative-churches-are-different.html

2. Tom Kelley with Jonathan Littman, *The Ten Faces of Innovation: Ideos's Strategies for Beating the Devil's Advocate and Driving Creativity Throughout Your Organization* (New York: Doubleday, 2005), p. 6.

3. Quoted in Kermitt Pattison, "How to Kill an Idea: An Interview with Ram Charan," *Fast Company,* May 30, 2008, http://www.fastcompany.com/ articles/2008/05/interview-ram-charan.html

4. Elaine Dundon, *The Seeds of Innovation: Cultivating the Synergy That Fosters New Ideas* (New York: AMACOM, 2002), p. 6.

5. Peter F. Drucker, *Innovation and Entrepreneurship* (New York: HarperCollins, 1985), p. 21.

6. Ibid., p. 34.

7. Tom Baldwin, "How Do You Build a Paper Clip into a House? First, Swap It for a Fish Pen . . . ," London Times, July 12, 2006, http://www .timesonline.co.uk/tol/news/world/us_and_americas/article686129.ece

8. Quoted in Stephen Shields, *Churches in Missional Renaissance: Facilitating the Transition to a Missional Mind-Set* (unpublished Leadership Network paper), Aug. 12, 2008.

9. See Reggie McNeal, *Missional Renaissance: Changing the Scorecard for the Church* (San Francisco: Jossey-Bass, 2009).

10. Lindsay Melvin, "Isaac Hayes Service Prompts Outcry," *Memphis Commercial Appeal,* Aug. 14, 2008, http://www.commercialappeal.com/ news/2008/aug/14/hope-presbyterian-catches-flak-hosting-isaac-hayes

11. Eli Morris, e-mail to Eric Swanson, Mar. 26, 2009.

12. Ian Vickers, Leadership Network I-3 Conference, Dallas, Tex., Jan. 27, 2009.

13. Hal Seed, personal interview, Nov. 19, 2007.

14. Christian Smith, Michael O Emerson, and Patricia Snell, *Passing the Plate: Why American Christians Don't Give Away More Money* (New York:

Oxford University Press, 2008), p. 52; Matt Van de Bunte, "Study Says Church Giving Lacks External Focus," *Presbyterian News Service*, http://www.pcusa.org/pcnews/2007/07019.htm

15. Smith, Emerson, and Snell, *Passing the Plate*, p. 52.

16. Van de Bunte, "Study Says."

17. Rob Wilkins, "Finding and Keeping the Next Generation," *Outreach Magazine*, Sept.-Oct. 2009, p. 52.

18. Drucker, *Innovation and Entrepreneurship*, p. 19.

19. Kim and Mauborgne, *Blue Ocean Strategy*, p. 4.

20. This idea stems from a conversation with Erwin McManus at Mosaic in July 2003.

21. William James, http://www.allthingswilliam.com/genius.html

22. Quoted in Tricia Armstrong, *The Whole-Brain Solution: Thinking Tools to Help Students Observe, Make Connections and Solve Problems* (Portland, Md.: Stenhouse, 2003), p. 80.

Chapter Ten: Outcomes: It's About the Game, Not the Pregame Talk

1. 12Stone Church, "12Stone Church Unveils Holiday Giving Campaign," press release, Nov. 12, 2007, http://downloads.12stone.com/news/12days12waysCampaignRelease.pdf

2. "Faith Chicago—Rev. Senator Meeks—Salem Baptist Church," YouTube.com, video, http://www.youtube.com/watch?v=6ATkEIo1MhA

3. Samuel Oliner and Pearl Oliner, *The Altruistic Personality: Rescuers of Jews in Nazi Europe* (New York: Free Press, 1988), p. 187.

4. Fellowship Bible Church, "The Only Life Worth Living: Shoe Sunday," video, Sept. 18, 2005, http://www.fellowshipnashville.org/content/media/messages.aspx

5. Dennis Keating, personal communication, Aug. 21, 2009.

6. Don Simmons, speech, Leadership Network Leadership Community gathering, Dallas, Tex., Sept. 18, 2008. Statistics from http://www.independentsector.org/programs/research/charts/table3.html

7. Thomas Paine, "Introduction," *Common Sense* (1776).

8. Jim Collins, *Good to Great and the Social Sectors* (New York: HarperCollins, 2005), pp. 5 and 7.

9. Ibid., p. 7.

10. W. David Phillips, "Re-Imagining Success," blog posting, June 6, 2008, http://www.backyardmissionary.com/2008/06/re-imagining-success.html

11. Peter F. Drucker, *Managing the Nonprofit Organization* (New York: HarperCollins, 1998), p. xiv.

Eric Swanson has a passion for engaging churches worldwide in the needs and dreams of their communities toward the end of spiritual and societal transformation. He served with Campus Crusade for Christ for twenty-five years before joining the staff of Leadership Network, where he currently works as a missional specialist, serving as leadership community director for externally focused churches, missional renaissance, and global connection, working with scores of missional churches throughout North America. He has also led numerous transformational community initiatives around the world, helping churches connect service and evangelism for kingdom. He holds a D.Min. degree in transformational leadership in the global city from Bakke Graduate University and is coauthor (with Rick Rusaw) of *The Externally Focused Church* and *The Externally Focused Life*. He has written articles on churches that are transforming their communities and is a sought-after speaker and church and ministry consultant. Eric has been married to Liz for more than thirty years, has three married children and three grandchildren, and resides near Boulder, Colorado. He can be contacted at http://www .ericjswanson.com.

Rick Rusaw is passionate about people discovering the Ephesians 2:10 things in their life and for helping the local church discover how people can make a difference in their community. He has been the lead pastor at LifeBridge Christian Church in Longmont, Colorado, since 1991 and has helped lead the church's growth in both attendance and community impact. He is the coauthor of several books, including *60 Simple Secrets Every Pastor Should Know,* and (with Eric Swanson)

The Externally Focused Church and *The Externally Focused Life*, and is a sought-after church and business consultant and an on-air host for the Worship Network. Rick has been married to Diane for more than twenty-five years, and they have three children and one grand-daughter. They reside in Longmont, Colorado.

Old Testament

Genesis 1:26	72
Genesis 2:15	72
Genesis 2:19	72
Genesis 12:3	40
Exodus 18	78, 178
Exodus 22	138
Leviticus 25:23–24	15
Deuteronomy 1	78, 178
1 Kings 10:7	30
1 Chronicles 12:32	6
Psalm 24:1	75
Psalm 68:5	159
Psalm 72	61
Ecclesiastes 7:18	179
Isaiah 10:12–19, 45:1–6	77
Isaiah 61	139–140
Jeremiah 29:4–7	187
Ezekiel 34:17–18	15

New Testament

Matthew 3:2, 4:17	75
Matthew 4:23, 9:35	30
Matthew 5:13	36
Matthew 5:14	36
Matthew 6:10	75
Matthew 6:33	75
Matthew 7:21–23	78
Matthew 8:4	168
Matthew 8:14–15	157
Matthew 9:38	155
Matthew 10:7	75
Matthew 11:20	160
Matthew 12:33	159
Matthew 15:32	156
Matthew 22:2–5	28
Matthew 22:9	29
Matthew 22:37–39	48
Matthew 24:14	35
Matthew 25:15	183
Matthew 25:31–46	158
Matthew 25:40	140
Mark 1:38	140
Luke 4:18, 19	139–140
Luke 6:31–35	48
Luke 6:36	30
Luke 6:43	133
Luke 10	37
Luke 10:25–27	140
Luke 10:25–37	157
Luke 10:29–37	30
Luke 12:54–56	6
Luke 13:4	73
Luke 14:18–20	28
Luke 14:21, 23	29
Luke 15	37, 39
Luke 15:4	140
Luke 15:20	39
Luke 17:11–17	160
Luke 17:21	75
Luke 19:10	74

John 2	78
John 3:3–5	78
John 3:16	169
John 3:17	169
John 5	4
John 13:1	140
John 13:34, 35	30
John 17:23	114
Acts 2:14	75, 166
Acts 2	166
Acts 3:10	167
Acts 3:12	167
Acts 6:1–7	140
Acts 9:43	40
Acts 10:36–38	156
Acts 11:18	40
Acts 17:6–7	74
Acts 19:30–32	78
Romans 8:22	73
Romans 10:17	161, 167
Romans 15:4	114
Romans 16:3	131
1 Corinthians 6:17	34
1 Corinthians 12:28	114
Galatians 2:10	140
Ephesians 2:8–9	45, 46, 181
Ephesians 2:8–10	45, 202
Ephesians 2:10	45, 46, 146, 181
Ephesians 3:4–10	40
Ephesians 4:3–6	114
Ephesians 4:11	181
Ephesians 4:11–12	202
Ephesians 4:11–13	90
Ephesians 5:11–12	46
Colossians 1:19–20	73–74
Colossians 4:2–6	172
1 Timothy 6:17–18	47
2 Timothy 3:17	46
Hebrews 10:24	46
James 2:1–13	140
James 5:1–6	204
1 Peter 1:12	161
1 Peter 4:10	47

Page references followed by *fig* indicate an illustrated figure; followed by *t* indicate a table.

A

Adam and Eve, 73
Adaptation (film), 70
Addams, Jane, 30
Africa: genocide in, 19; missionaries from countries of, 93; Musana Children's Home (Uganda) service in, 48–49; social crises in, 41
Africa Inland Mission, 92
Agape (love of the unconditional), 65
AIDS epidemic, 7, 19, 77, 81
AIDS hospice (South Africa), 96
Aisle-seat churches: blindness and nearsightedness of, 40–41; description of, 26–28; internal program focus of, 38–39; leadership challenge of changing from, 43; missional factors encouraging, 31–34; personal factors encouraging, 36; secular factors encouraging, 35–36; theological factors encouraging, 34–35
Alpha movement, 60
Amazing Grace (hymn), 40
Amillennialists, 35
Andrew, 157
Ankerberg, William, 81
Answering Your Call (Schuster), 26
Apologetics, 168–169
Aristotle, 71
Armstrong, Lance, 189
Art Source International, 92
Asiarchs, 78
"Attractional church," 28–29
Austin Stone Community Church (Texas), 106, 148

B

Baby boomers, 9
Back Door Ministry, 84
Bacon, Francis, 17
Bagley, Hal, 164
Ball Aerospace, 110
"Bar evangelism," 165
Barna, George, 21, 57, 155
Barna Group, 169
Baylor University School of Social Work study (2006), 50–51
Behavior: creating structures based on valued, 134; creating systems that influence, 137–154; impact of small groups on, 143–150; John Wesley's example of structure affecting, 135–137, 143–144
Believing, belonging, and blessing, 57*fig*–59
Berlin Wall, 7
Beshore, Laurie, 197–198
Bethel Church (Washington), 213
Big Brothers Big Sisters of Central Ohio, 83
Blake, Bishop Charles E., Sr., 14
Blindness and nearsightedness, 40–41
Blue Ocean Strategy: (Kim and Mauborgne), 195
Blue oceans strategy, 195–196
Bodybuilding, 44, 45
Bold New World (Knoke), 7–8
Bono, 20, 24, 41, 78, 81, 189
Booth, William, 30
Borel, Calvin, 98

Bosch, David, 30, 35, 118
"Both-and" thinking, 178–179
Boulder County Department of Human
    Services, 130
Boulder County Social Services, 130
Bounded set, 111–112*fig*
Boyce, James, 78
Bradley, Ian, 55
Branson, Richard, 14, 78
Brechner, Glen, 144, 145, 146
The Bridge, 165
"Bridges out of Poverty" seminar
    (Crossroads Christian Church), 153
British Museum, 135–136
Bruce, John, 185, 186
"Bubbly" (Caillat song), 9
Buffett, Warren, 78
Bush, George W., 16
Business as mission trend, 105–108
Bussey, Todd, 152, 153
Butler, Phill, 125

C
Cage, Nicolas, 70
Caillat, Colbie, 9
Caldwell, Kirbyjon, 45
Calvary Baptist Church (Pennsylvania),
    189, 210
Calvary Bible Evangelical Free Church
    (Boulder), 62–63, 124, 162
Calvary Community Church (California),
    62, 104
"Cambridge Seven," 92
Camino de Santiago de Compostela
    (The Way of Saint James) pilgrimage,
    198–199
Campbell, Stacey, 95–96
Campus Crusade, 161, 162
Campus Crusade's Athletes in Action, 165
Carmichael, Amy, 92
Carpenter, Reid, 168
Carroll, Danny, 44, 167
Carter, Matt, 148–149
Catholic Church: Reformation and
    separation from, 34, 118; social
    practices of the, 31
"Cell group" model, 149
Celtic Christianity: Celtic knot symbol
    of, 55–56*fig*, 58, 59; "The Celtic Trail"
    class study of, 20, 55; early history of,
    55–56*fig*
"The Celtic Trail" class, 55
The Celtic Way (Bradley), 55

Centered set, 112–114
Central American Mission (CAM), 92
Central Christian Church (Arizona), 107
Central India Christian Mission, 206
Chapman, Helen, 92
Charity and Faith Mission Church (South
    Africa), 96–97
Chase Oaks Church (Texas), 144–146*fig*
Chestnut, Randy, 163
Child prostitution, 101–102
China: environmental problems faced by,
    13; growing economy of, 11, 12; quasi-
    free-market economy embraced by, 15
China, Inc. (Fishman), 12
Christ Church (Illinois), 193
Christ Community Church (Colorado), 95
Christ Community Church (Illinois), 99,
    172
Christ Community Church (Omaha), 58,
    163, 185, 190
Christ Fellowship Church (West Palm
    Beach), 11
Christianity: Celtic, 20, 55–59; changing
    centers of, 91–93; new face of
    evangelical, 19–20; stairstep approach
    to, 53–55; worldview of, 71–72
Christianity and Social Work
    (Garland), 35
Christianity Today, 93
Christians: danger of link between faith
    and politics for, 16–17; environmental
    activism by, 14–15; global percentage of,
    1–2; good works of early church, 30–31;
    reasons for community disengagement
    of, 31–36
Christians of Stark County, 116
Christology, 138
Chung, John, 105
"Church in the city" concept, 114
Church leaders: aisle-seat mentality of,
    26–28; "both-and" thinking of, 178–
    179; changing focus of their questions,
    5; entrepreneurial mission, 93–94;
    Facts & Trends survey (2007) of, 32;
    implications of understanding purpose
    for, 45–47; influence of megachurch, 19;
    as innovative church resource, 181–183,
    184*t*; interviewed on global outreach,
    94; investing in strong mission, 98–100;
    quest of, 2; shift from internal to
    external by, 19; understanding the
    liminal state of today, 22–24. *See also*
    Leadership challenges; Paradigms

Church of the Open Door (Minnesota), 98, 99, 101

Church scorecards: expanding the, 211–212; externally focused, 212*fig*–213; measuring for the wrong results, 215; measuring your own, 215–216; questions to ask for measuring, 207–208*fig*; what should be measured for, 209–211; what we can't measure, 214; what we don't measure, 214–215

Church of Scotland, 20

Church of the Sea Captains, 60

Churches: aisle-seat, 26–41, 43; attractional and missional, 28–29; blue oceans strategy of, 195–196; comparing kingdom of God and, 76; downward trend of public reliance on, 18; the early, 30–31; getting it into the community, 30; innovative, 174–199; Internet, 10–11; kingdom experiment by, 79–80; kingdom of God work as work of, 77–78; looking for unmet needs, 196*fig*–197; paradigms created by, 133–154; perception of good deeds by, 162*fig*; "pretty good church" concept of, 84–86; question on community and, 2, 3; reasons for withdrawal from community by, 31–36; Reformation splitting, 34, 118–119; rise of the megachurch form of, 18–19, 93; shift from internal to external, 19; spiritual "revolutionaries" leaving the, 21, 57; Vineyard Church's example of engagement by, 82–83; weight-training versus bodybuilding, 44–45; window-seat, 26–43. *See also* Externally focused church; Partnering; Protestant Churches; Religion

Churchwide projects: believing, belonging, and blessing elements of, 57*fig*–59; engaging in regular, 150–152; LifeBridge's approach to, 52–53, 129–131, 141, 142

Cincinnati Christian University, 182

Clean drinking water, 7, 13

Cleveland Orchestra, 209

The Closet (clothing center), 52, 164

Cnaan, Ram, 31–32, 35, 36

Coaching Little League Baseball (video), 201

Cole, Neil, 21

Collins, Jim, 134–135, 137, 209

Colorado Community Church, 159

Columbine school tragedy, 53

Communication: church use of digital, 10–11; innovative church approach to, 191–192*t*; missionary work using technological, 108–109; technology impact on, 9–10

Communism, 15, 16

Community: "dots" organization of isolated, 8; factors influencing church withdrawal from, 31–36; finding other entities vested in the, 119–120; getting the church into the, 30; looking for unmet needs of, 196*fig*–197; question on church and, 2, 3; relational capital building in, 129, 144–146*fig*. *See also* Society

Community development: built through work, 144; global ministry focus on, 102–103; need-based and asset-based, 102

Community Health Evangelism (CHE), 102–103

Community service: believing, belonging, and blessing elements of, 57*fig*–59; building capacity in young people for, 51–52; depth and frequency of engagement in, 62–67*fig*; getting everyone in the game for, 202–207; greater impact over marketing of, 168, 171–172; health and longevity benefits of, 59; how to tell if you are "winning" at, 207–216; "in" and "out" triangle representing, 60*fig*–61; leadership challenge to facilitate, 69; marketing kept separate from, 127–128; Musana Children's Home (Uganda) example of, 48–49; partnering for days of, 115; purpose of strength and capacity for, 61–62; relational capital building through, 129, 144–146*fig*; research on faith, spiritual growth, and, 50–51; role of prayer in, 67–69; by small groups, 143–150; small groups for moving from organized to organic, 146, 147*fig*; stairstep approach to, 53–55; Willow Creek Community Church study (2004) on, 53. *See also* Volunteers

Community service engagement: frequency of, 64*fig*–67*fig*; money and things level of, 62; people level of, 63–64; projects level of, 62–63; role of prayer in, 67–69

Community Service Impact (CSI) Ministry [Chas Oaks Church], 145–146*fig*

Community transformation: church focus on, 38–39; church resources expended on, 39–40; creating something better through, 78–79; Hope Presbyterian Church's work for, 41–42; opening our eyes to need for, 40–41; partnering for rural, 116; a story that changes the world through, 86–88; Vineyard Church's efforts at, 82–83. *See also* Missional activities; Social action

Confluence Ministries (Denver), 117

Connelly, Mark, 101–102

Costas, Bob, 201

Council on Foreign Relations, 19

Cox Elementary (San Leandro), 186

Craigslist, 178

Creation: God's act of, 197; taking innovative approach to, 197–198

Creekside Community Church (San Leandro), 185–186

Crossroad Community Church (Cincinnati), 96–97, 108, 115, 163, 193

Crossroads Christian Church (Evansville), 152–154

Culture: comparing church's perception of good deeds to, 162*fig*; perception of good deeds by, 161–162

Cummings, Eric, 153

D

David, King, 24, 61

Davis, Stephanie, 122

Deen, Paula, 29

Delta's Gold Medallion status, 26–27

Denver Broncos, 169–170

Descartes, René, 17

DeWitt, Kirk, 104–105

Discover grace, 68, 140

Disney, Walt, 135

The Distribution of Christian Religions Throughout the World (1886 atlas), 92

Do you want to get well? question, 4

Dog Ministry (Mariner's Church), 197–198

Drucker, Peter, 177, 194, 213

Duke University, 59

Dulos group (LifeBridge), 182–183

Dundon, Elaine, 175

E

Early church, 30–31

Ecclesiology, 138

Economics: current state of U.S., 11; current U.S. role in global, 13; outsourcing trend and impact on, 11–12

Edison, Thomas, 135, 175, 197

"Either-or" thinking, 178

Emanuel Faith Church (Escondido), 205–206

Embassy Suites Hotels ad, 22

Embrace Teachers initiative (Christ Community Church), 185

Emmanuel Faith Church (California), 105

Empowerment: evangelism connection to, 161–162; LifeBridge's ministry of, 164–165; ministry of, 159–160

Engagement. *See* Community service engagement

Engineers Without Borders, 110

Entrepreneurs: innovation as tool of, 194; learning to think like an, 194–197; looking for areas of leverage to make difference, 194–195; looking for the unmet need, 196*fig*–197; swimming in "blue oceans," 195–196

Entrepreneurship: definition of, 177; examples of, 197–199; how to think like an entrepreneur for, 194–197; innovation relationship to, 177–179; leadership challenge related to, 199; trading from paper clip to house example of, 178. *See also* Innovative churches

Environment: Christian activism related to the, 14–15; clean drinking water issue of, 7, 13; as social and political issue, 13–14

Evangelicals: authenticity over apologetics, 168–169; ministry of empowerment by, 159–160; ministry of evangelism by, 161–162*fig*; ministry of mercy by, 156–159; the new face of, 19–20; two questions asked of, 163

Evangelism: "bar," 165; early history of, 92–93; golf metaphor for, 165–166; good deeds/good news trend of, 100–103; goodwill created through good deeds of, 162, 166–167; Great Commission of, 91; greater impact of service over marketing of, 168, 171–172; as intentional, 163; leadership challenge related to good deeds of, 172; LifeBridge's ministry of, 164–165; mercy and empowerment connection to, 161–162; as ministry of empowerment,

159–160; as ministry of mercy, 156–159; ministry of, 161–162*fig*; Prodigal Son parable call to, 37; role of expectancy in, 169–170; ten fundamental principles of, 170–171. *See also* Missional activities

Every Child a Reader, 121

Evidence That Demands a Verdict (McDowell), 17

Expectancy, 169–170

The Externally Focused Church (Rusaw and Swanson), 1, 2, 5, 45, 111, 119, 210

Externally focused churches: building systems that influence behavior, 137–154; comparing internal focus of facilities versus, 187*t*; comparing internal focus of finances versus, 191*t*; comparing internal focus of people versus, 184*t*; comparing internal focus of prayer versus, 188*t*; comparing internal focus of technology versus, 192*t*; comparing internal focus of time versus, 193*t*; creating structures for what we value, 134; getting everyone in the ministry "game," 202–207; "go to" or missional, 29–30; how to tell if you are "winning," 207–216; systems elevated above strategy by, 134–135; window-seat mentality of, 26–28, 30–36. *See also* Churches; Window-seat churches

Externally Focused Churches Leadership Communities, 116

The Externally Focused Life (Rusaw and Swanson), 45, 166

Externally focused scorecard, 212*fig*–213

Externally focused small groups, 149–150

Extreme Community Makeover initiative, 117

F

Facebook, 9, 108

Facilitation Space of Leadership Network (Dallas), 37

Facts & Trends study (2007), 32

Faculty Commons ministry (Campus Crusade), 161

Faith: as coming from hearing the message, 161; danger of linking politics and, 16–17; entering kingdom of God by, 78; research on service, spiritual growth, and, 50–51. *See also* Spirituality

Faith in Action, 120

Faith and Environment Ministry (Peachtree Baptist Church), 15

Falk, David, 50

The Fall, 73, 74

Fellow worker concept, 131

Fellowship Bible Church (Little Rock), 103

Fellowship Bible Church (Nashville), 107, 204–205

Ferguson, Niall, 8

"Field preaching," 137

"The 50 Fastest-Growing Churches," 2

"The 50 Most Innovative Churches," 2

Finances: accountability related to, 103–105; innovative churches and, 188–191*t*; Kingdom Resources "bank" to help with, 190–191

First Baptist Church (Huntsville), 87

"First-dimension" technology, 8

Fish, Nick, 124

Fishman, Ted, 12

Flake, Floyd, 14

Flay, Bobby, 29

Focus of mission trend, 106–108

Food Finders (Long Beach), 179

Ford, Kevin, 51

Forster, E. M., 72

Fortune 500 companies, 12

The Four Spiritual Laws, 165

Four Spiritual Laws booklet, 58

Franklin, Benjamin, 137

Franklin, Shirley, 122

Franz, Dan, 83

Frazier Memorial United Methodist Church, 143

Frequency of engagement, 64*fig*–67*fig*

Fresh Coat Cleveland, 163

Friedman, Thomas, 11–12

Frost, Michael, 113–114

Fuente del Perigrino (Pilgrim's Fountain), 199

Full Gospel Central Church (Seoul), 93

Fuller Theological Seminary, 111

Future studies, 5–6

Futurists: on economics, 11–13; on the environment, 13–15; on politics, 15–17; on religion, 17–18; on society, 7; STEEPR constructs used by, 6–18, 174; on technology, 7–11

G

Gabriel, Charles, 92

Gallup Organization, 18

Garland, Diana, 35, 51

Gates, Bill, 78

Gates, Melinda, 78

Gelinas, Robert, 159
Gerson, Michael, 19–20
Gibbons, Dave, 108, 162
Gibson, William, 94
Gin Lane (Hogarth engraving), 136*fig*
Giving money engagement, 62
Global Media Outreach, 10
Global warming, 14
Global X (North Point Church), 99
Globalization: economics and, 11–13; U.S. role in economic, 13
GO Cincinnati event, 50, 115
GO Grub, 50
Go Ministries at The Crossing (Costa Mesa), 97
"Go to" churches, 29–30
God: act of creation by, 197; the Fall and man's relationship with, 73, 74; story defining man's relationship with, 72. *See also* Jesus Christ; Kingdom of God
God channel, 17–18
"God in the gaps," 17
God's Word, creating structure around, 134
Goforth, Jonathan, 92
Goldman Sachs, 12
Golf metaphor for evangelism, 165–166
"Gone for good" program (LifeBridge), 203
Good deeds: culture's and churches's perception of, 161–162*fig*; God preparing us for, 45; good news verified through, 167; goodwill created through, 162, 166–167; greater impact over marketing of, 168, 171–172; leadership challenge related to, 172; ministry of empowerment as, 159–160; ministry of evangelism as, 161–162; ministry of mercy as, 156–159; as new evangelism trend, 100–103; ten fundamental principles of evangelism on doing, 170–171; understanding purpose of, 45–47. *See also* Kingdom of God work
Good news: as evangelism trend, 100–103; good deeds clarified by, 167; leadership challenge related to, 172. *See also* Missional activities
Good Samaritan parable, 2–3, 37, 71, 157
Good Shepherd Community Church (Oregon), 103–104
Good to Great and the Social Sectors (Collins), 209
Good works. *See* Good deeds

Goodwill, 162, 166–167
Google, 9
Gore, Al, 14
Grace Brethren (Long Beach), 115
Granger Community Church, 91
Great Commandment, 48
Great Commission, 91
"Great reversal," 35
Grow in Grace, 68, 140
Guder, Darrel, 21–22

H

Habitat for Humanity, 62
"Half-Hour Heroes" (Perimeter Church), 194–195
Hall, Dave, 105, 106
Hanson, Eric, 99
Hanson, Steve, 98, 99, 101
Hartford Institute for Religion Research, 19, 174
Harvard Business Review, 134
Harvard University study, 59
Harvest field workers. *See* Kingdom workers
Harvest Foundation, 81
Harvest Ministries, 150
Healing Place Church (HPC) [Baton Rouge], 158
Healthy agnosticism, 168
Heintzelman, Rudy, 143
Helbig, Dave, 11
Hendershot, Neil, 107
Herring, Dick, 110
Hiebert, Paul, 111–112, 113
Hierarchy of needs, 47
Hirsch, Alan, 113–114
HIV/AIDS epidemic, 7, 19, 77, 81
Hoffer, Eric, 149
Hogarth, William, 136
Holy Spirit, 166
Homeless ministry, 36
Homes of Hope, 102
Hope Presbyterian Church (Memphis), 41–42, 62, 183–184, 193
Hunter, Joel, 14
Huntsville Prison, 87
Hurricane Ike, 185
Hurricane Katrina, 13, 139, 145, 189, 204–205
Hurricane Rita, 13, 139
Hus, Jan, 118
Hybels, Bill, 41
Hybels, Lynne, 41

I

If Jesus Were Mayor (Moffitt), 81

Imago Dei (Portland), 123–124

Inc. magazine, 135

An Inconvenient Truth (documentary film), 14

India: Central India Christian Mission rescuing children in, 206; growing economy of, 12

Information: accessing news, 10; technology and access to, 9

Innovation: condition required for, 178–179; definitions of, 175–176; entrepreneurship relationship to, 177–179; as entreprenurial tool, 194; results and effort components of, 176*fig*–177

Innovative church resources: facilities, 183–186; finances, 188–191*t*; learning to shift, 180–181; people (leaders and others), 181–183, 184*t*; prayer, 186–188*t*; technology, 191–192*t*; time, 192–193*t*

Innovative churches: decided what they want to accomplish, 179–180; defining characteristics of, 175–177; examples of activities by, 197–199; leadership challenge related to, 199; self-description by, 174–175; shifting resources practice of, 180–193. *See also* Entrepreneurship

Institute for International Economics, 12

Intergovernmental Panel on Climate Change (IPCC), 14

Internet churches, 10–11

iPhone, 10

Iranian election (2009), 10

Irresistible Evangelism (Sjogren, Ping, and Pollock), 165

J

James, William, 197

Japan Bible Society, 92

Jenkins, Phillip, 18, 93

Jesus Christ: amillennialists teaching on reign of, 35; believing as our connection to, 57*fig*–58; continued popularity of, 21; imaging him as mayor, 81–82; invalid at pool of Bethesda and, 4–5; as King, 74; on laborers for the harvest field, 155–156; ministry of mercy by, 156–157; premillennialism teaching on the return of, 34–35; questions asked by, 2, 4; restoration by, 73–74; storytelling

practice by, 71; "What Would Jesus Do?" question on, 79. *See also* God; Parables

Jesus (film), 2, 199

Jethro, 178

Jezreel, Jack, 65, 159

Jolie, Angelina, 78

Jones, E. Stanley, 75

Joseph of Egypt, 180

JustFaith Ministries, 65

K

Kawasaki, Guy, 170–171

Keating, Dennis, 205

Keller, Tim, 71

Kelley, Tom, 175

Kenyon, Mike, 97

Kessler, Mike, 123, 181–183

Kids Café, 123

Kim, W. Chan, 195

King, Martin Luther, Jr., 2–3

Kingdom of God: becoming part of the, 78; comparing the church and the, 76; parable on, 28–30; Scriptures on importance of, 75–76. *See also* God

Kingdom of God work: creating something better through, 78–79; defining, 77; Rick's church's experiment with, 79–80; as story that changes the world, 86–88; Vineyard Dayton as "pretty good church" doing, 84–86; Vintage Vineyard doing, 82–83. *See also* Good deeds

Kingdom parable, 28–30

Kingdom Resources, 190–191

"Kingdom" thinking: paradigm and system building using, 152–153; questions to stimulate, 152

Kingdom workers: community volunteers becoming, 156; Jesus Christ on harvest field and, 155–156; ministry of empowerment by, 159–160; ministry of evangelism by, 161–162*fig*; ministry of mercy by, 156–159; two questions asked of, 163. *See also* Volunteers

Kinnaman, David, 169

Knoke, William, 7–8

Korea Mission Association, 93

Kuilan, Pastor, 149

L

Lagasse, Emeril, 29

Lake Avenue Church (Pasadena), 96

Lake Pointe Church (Texas), 99, 100

Leadership challenges: changing from aisle to the window seat, 43; to encourage community service, 69; innovation and entrepreneurship, 199; ministry outcomes, 216; missional activities, 109–110; moving from good deeds to good news, 172; paradigms and systems, 154; partnering, 131–132; storytelling, 88; understanding changes impacting the world, 25. *See also* Church leaders
Leadership Community for Externally Focused Churches, 53
Leadership Journal, 117
Leadership Network, 82, 89, 116, 117, 174
Leadership Network's 1-3 conference (2009), 148
Life Group (Chase Oaks Church), 145–146*fig*
Life Mission (Granger Community Church), 91
LifeBridge Christian Church: Central India Christian Mission partnering with, 206; The Closet project of, 52, 164; discover grace, grow in grace, and live gracefully approach by, 68, 140; Dulos group formed by, 182–183; engagement with schools by, 63, 186; "gone for good" program of, 203; keeping marketing and service separate at, 127–128; lessons learned about partnering by, 126–129; mercy, empowerment, and evangelism ministry of, 164–165; partnership between Boulder County and, 129–131; service provided by student ministry of, 52–53; "Summer of Love" series of, 141; SWAT training on campus of, 186; what is deliberately not measured at, 214–215; "A Year with Jesus" series of, 142
LifeChurch.tv, 11
Lilly Foundation study (2002), 18
Liminality: coping with changing times and, 23; description of, 22–23; understanding positive aspects of, 24
Literary Digest, 6
Little League coaching, 201–202
Live gracefully, 68, 141
Lorenzen, Jay, 161
Los Angeles Times, 20
Love our neighbor commandment, 48
Love (*phileo* to *agape*), 65
Luis Palau Association, 123

"Lunch Buddies" program (Rolling Hills Community Church), 193
Lupton, Robert, 38, 159–160
Luther, Martin, 117–118

M
MacArthur Study of Successful Aging, 59
McCartney, Bill, 113
Mcdonald, Kyle, 178
McDonald's, 22
McKee, Robert, 70–71, 73, 74, 88
McKinley, Rick, 20, 123, 124
McManus, Erwin, 24
McNeal, Reggie, 21, 38–39, 82, 180–181
Malawi Children's Hospital, 81
Manning, Martha, 62
Mariners Church (Irvine), 97, 138–139, 193, 197
Mariners' Dog Ministry, 197–198
Mariners Outreach, 138–139
Marketing: greater impact of service over, 168, 171–172; keeping service separate from, 127–128
Marsh, Eric, 115, 179
Martin, Jonathan, 103–104
Marx, Karl, 15
Marxist worldview, 71
Maslow, Abraham, 47
Masarro, Thomas, 30–31
Mauborgne, Renée, 195
Mavis, Brian, 129–131
Mavis, Julie, 129
Mbiti, John, 93
Mead, Margaret, 200
Meals on Wheels, 58
Measures. *See* Church scorecards; Ministry success measures
"Measuring Success in Ministry" (Phillips blog), 211
Meeks, James, 204
Megachurch, 18–19, 93
Megachurches Today, 2005 study, 19
Megan, 61
Men at Work (Will), 201
Mercer, Arlene, 179
Mercy: evangelism connection to, 161–162; Good Samaritan's deeds as, 157; LifeBridge's ministry of, 164–165; as making a difference for "that one," 158
Message Trust (England), 169
Methodists, 137
Ministry of empowerment: description of, 159–160; LifeBridge's, 164–165

Ministry of evangelism: description of, 161–162*fig*; LifeBridge's, 164–165

Ministry of mercy: examples of, 157–159; Good Samaritan's, 157; Jesus Christ's example of, 156–157; LifeBridge's, 164–165

Ministry outcomes: getting everyone in the game, 202–207; how to tell if you are "winning," 207–216; leadership challenge related to, 216; relationship between activities and, 213. *See also* Social action

Ministry success factors: begin with the willing, 207; combining opportunity with inclination, 204–206; making it personal, 206–207; providing regular opportunities, 202–204

Ministry success measures: deciding exactly what to measure, 209–211; expanding the church scorecard for, 211–212; the externally focused scorecard, 212*fig*–213; questions to ask for, 207–208*fig*; what cannot be measured, 214; what is your scorecard?, 215–216; what we don't measure, 214–215; for the wrong results, 215

Miranda, Jesse, 14

Missiology, 138

Mission After Christendom (Smith), 4, 22, 89

Mission at Park Street Church (Boston), 105

Mission Community Church (Arizona), 101, 102

Mission funding: business as mission approach to, 105–108; financial accountability issue of, 103–105

Missional activities: of the Celtic church, 56; current trend of decreasing, 32–34; distinguishing between local and global, 89–91; eight trends shaping future of, 94–109; four domains of, 90–91*fig*; Great Commission of, 91; history of, 31–32; Hope Presbyterian Church's focus on, 41–42; interviews with church leaders on, 94; leadership challenge related to, 109–110; from other countries, 93; recent shift in, 93–94; small groups helping people with, 146–148. *See also* Community transformation; Evangelism; Good news

Missional churches, 29–30

Missional Renaissance Leadership Community, 82, 180–181

Missional trends: business as mission, 105–106; combining good deeds and good news as, 100–103; communication technology use as, 108–109; greater financial accountability as, 103–105; investing in leaders as, 98–100; mutuality as, 95–97; new focus as, 106–110; partnering as, 97–98

Missoula Alliance Church (MAC) [Montana], 210–211

Moffitt, Robert, 81, 82, 150

Moody, D. L., 92

Morin, Peter, 53

Morris, Eli, 62, 184

Morse, Joni, 110

Moses, 20, 178

"The Most Creative Product Ever" (Collins), 135

Mott, John R., 92

Mullins, Tom, 11

Mullis, Tom, 97

Musana Children's Home (Uganda), 48–49

Mutuality of missions, 95–97

MySpace, 9

N

Nathan, Rich, 37, 83, 180, 189

National Election Pool exit poll (2004), 16

National Outreach Convention (San Diego), 59

Nearsightedness and blindness, 40–41

Needs: to believe, bless, and belong, 57*fig*–58; looking for the unmet, 196*fig*–197; physical, 47–48; for prayer, 67–68; spiritual growth related to, 47–48*fig*

Nehemiah, 180

Neilson, Peter, 20

Nettle, Greg, 189

Nevius, John Livingston, 92

New Song Church, 162

New Song Community Church (Oceanside), 167, 185

New York Times, 11, 14, 19

News communication, 10

Newsong Church (Irvine), 108

Newsweek International, 12

Newsweek magazine, 21

Newsweek poll (2005), 20

Newton, John, 40

The Next Christendom (Jenkins), 18, 93

Nicodem, Jim, 172

Nicodemus, 78, 161
Nielsen Company, 192
Night (Wiesel), 49
Ninety-Five Theses (1517), 118
Nold, Dan, 189, 210
North Point Church (Atlanta), 99
Northwood Church for the Community, 98
Northwood Church (Texas), 50, 64, 123, 184
Nupedia, 9

O

Oliner, Pearl, 204
Oliner, Samuel, 204
Olthoff, Matt, 95, 97–98, 99
One hundred sheep parable, 39
"The 100 Largest Churches," 2
Organic Church (Cole), 21
Organic service: moving from organized to, 146; process of program-driven to passion-driven, 147*fig*
Ortberg, John, 59
Out of the Cold program (Tenth Avenue Alliance Church), 36
Outcomes. *See* Ministry outcomes
Outreach Inc., 120

P

Paine, Thomas, 207
Pantano Christian Church (Tucson), 102, 107, 151
Parables: Good Samaritan, 2–3, 37, 71, 157; Kingdom, 28–30; one hundred sheep, 39; Prodigal Son, 37, 39; surprise endings of, 71; ten coins, 39; window-seat, 39–40. *See also* Jesus Christ; Storytelling
Paradigms: creating structures for what we value through, 134; creating systems that influence behavior, 137–154; description of, 133; elevated above strategy, 134–135; John Wesley's system and, 135–137, 143–144; leadership challenge related to, 154. *See also* Church leaders; Systems
Partnering: avoiding past barriers to, 117–119; bounded set vs. centered set of beliefs for, 111–112*fig*, 113; for catalytic days of service and unity, 115; centered set of shared interests for, 112–114; Central India Christian Mission and LifeBridge's, 206; "church in the city" concept of, 114; definition of, 125;

fellow workers concept of, 131; finding other entities vested in community for, 119–120; formed around common love and commitment, 119; leadership challenge related to, 131–132; lessons learned from, 126–129; as mission trend, 97–98; relational capital and care built through, 129; rural transformation through, 116; suggestions for effective, 116–117; sustaining, 125–126; when it doesn't work out, 128–129. *See also* Churches
Partnering examples: Central India Christian Mission and LifeBridge, 206; Imago Dei's Portland service, 123–124; Sharefest (Little Rock), 63, 124–125*t*, 162; Street GRACE (Atlanta), 121–122; StreetLight Phoenix, 122; Titus County Cares, 122–123; Vision San Diego, 120–121
Pastors.com, 100
Pathak, Jay, 195–196
Patrick, St., 55
Paul, 75, 78, 114, 131
PEACE Plan, 101
Peachtree Baptist Church (Atlanta), 15
Pearl Group, 164–165
People engagement level, 63–64
Perimeter Church (Atlanta), 97, 193, 194–195
Personal invitations to serve, 206–207
Peter, 40, 157, 161
Phileo (love of preferential), 65
Phillips, W. David, 211
Ping, David, 165
Pink, Daniel, 12, 77
"Placeless" society, 8–9
Pledge of Allegiance, 16
Political boundaries: current global forces shaping, 15–16; danger of linking religion to, 16–17; division along religious lines, 18
Politics: current global forces shaping, 15–16; danger of linking faith and, 16–17; of environmental issues, 14; failures to accurately forecast, 6; secular and spiritual issues related to, 16–17; September 11, 2001, impact on world, 16
Pollock, Doug, 165
Pothiphar's wife, 180
Prayer: as innovative church resource, 186–188; internal versus external focus

of, 188*t*; learning to write a, 67–68; to service, 172

Preaching: "field," 137; LifeBridge's "Summer of Love" series, 141; Life-Bridge's "A Year with Jesus" series, 142; system building through regular, 139–141

Pregame talk: by football coach, 200–201; putting too much focus on, 201

Premillennialism, 34–35

The Present Future (McNeal), 38–39

Presidential election debate (2007), 10

"Pretty good church," 84–86

Princeton Pledge, 92

Procter & Gamble, 9

Prodigal Son parable, 37, 39

Program for Religion and Social Policy Research (University of Pennsylvania), 31

Project 1.27 (Colorado Community Church), 159

Project engagement level, 62–63

Project Mentor (Ohio), 83

Promise Keepers, 169

Promise Keepers conference (1990s), 113

Protestant Churches: number of U.S., 18; social practices pioneered by, 31. *See also* Churches; *specific churches*

Proust, Marcel, 174

Purpose: of strength, 61–62; understanding, 45–47; weight-training versus bodybuilding, 45–46

Purpose Driven Seminar, 100

Q

Quality of Life in Boulder County, 2005: A Community Indicators Report, 35

Questions: asked of kingdom workers, 163; changing focus of church leaders', 5; do you want to get well?, 4; Good Samaritan's, 2–3; "kingdom," 152; measuring ministry success, 207–208*fig*; setting church leaders on their quest, 2; "What Would Jesus Do?," 79

R

Rainer, Sam, 51–52

Rainer, Thom S., 32, 51–52, 155

RAISE, 104

Raitt, Bonnie, 20

Ray, Rachel, 29

ReachOut (Crossroads Church), 108, 115

Red oceans concept, 195

Redeemer Presbyterian Church, 71

Reformation, 34, 118

Refuge Church (North Carolina), 10

Relational capital: Chase Oaks Church's approach to building, 144–146*fig*; partnering to build, 129

Religion: cultural shift related to, 17–18; current global trends related to, 18–22; danger of linking politics with, 16–17; lose of spirituality in construct of, 20; political issues related to, 15–17. *See also* Churches

Religious right, 16–17, 20

Religious trends: changing meaning of "evangelical," 19–20; division of the world along religious lines, 18; rise of the megachurch, 18–19; rising interest in spirituality/movement away from organized church, 20–22; shift from internal to external movements, 19

de Renty, Gaston-Jean-Baptiste, 144

Revelation 11:15, 76

Revolution (Barna), 57

"Revolutionaries," 21, 57

Reyes, Omar, 64, 123

RiverTree Christian Church (Ohio), 116, 189–190

Roberts, Bob, 50, 86, 89, 98

Robertson, Murray, 70, 191

Robinson, Mike, 103

Rock Harbor Church (Orange County), 97, 108, 115, 179, 191–192

Roe, Doug, 84–85

Rolheiser, Ronald, 57–58

Rolling Hills Community Church (Oregon), 31, 173, 193

Roman Road, 165

Rotary Club, 58

Roxburgh, Alan, 24, 46

Rural transformation, 116

Rusaw, Brittany, 80

Rusaw, Chelsea, 52, 53

Rusaw, David, 80

Rusaw, Rick: Cincinnati Christian University experience of, 182; on discovering grace, grow in grace, and live gracefully, 68; *The Externally Focused Church* by Swanson and, 1, 2, 5, 45, 111, 119, 210; on kingdom experiment by church, 79–80; Little League coaching by, 201–202; on need for prayer, 67–68; on service provided by LifeBridge youth, 52–53; on what is deliberately not measured at LifeBridge, 214–215

S

Saddleback Church, 100
Saddleback Web site, 101
Saint Paul's Church (East London), 60
Salem Baptist Church (Chicago), 204
"Salt and Light" Award, 88
Schleiermacher, Frederick, 57–58
Schleitheim Confession (1527), 34
Schmidt, Monte, 31, 173
Schuster, John P., 26
Science, 17
Scofield, C. I., 92
Scofield Reference Bible, 92
Scott, Peter Cameron, 92
Scriptural foundation, 138–139
"Scrubs Team" (Hope Presbyterian
  Church), 41–42
"Second dimension" technology, 8
Secular factors: church withdrawal from
  addressing social problems, 35–36;
  legal cases over spiritual versus, 16–17;
  professionalism of social services, 35
Seed, Hal, 167, 185
Senff, Tim, 96–97, 108, 115
"Separation from the Abomination"
  (Schleitheim Confession), 34
September 11, 2001, 16
Serve Day (Orange County), 115, 179
Service Learning International (ELI), 48
Service. See Community service
"Seven Sins of Dying Churches"
  (Rainer), 155
Sex trafficking, 101–102
Shadrach, Lloyd, 204–205
Shared Hope International, 102
Sharefest (Little Rock), 63, 124–125t, 162
Shaw, Joey, 106
Shearer, Will, 82
Shirk, Tom, 63
Shutterfly, 9
Sichuan earthquake (2008), 10
Simmons, Don, 147, 206–207
Simply Christian (Wright), 77
Sjogren, Steve, 165
Skinner, Gary, 150
Slave trade, 40
Sliver, Scott, 84
Small groups: Chase Oaks Church (Texas)
  use of, 144–146fig; creating community
  through, 148–149; externally focused,
  149–150; helping people live missionally,
  146–148; infusing service into,
  143–146fig; moving from organized

to organic service, 146, 147fig; people
  helped through externally focused,
  149–150
Smith, David, 4, 22, 89
Smith, Linda, 102
Snead, Durwood, 99, 105, 108–109
Snyder, Howard, 76
Social action: as bringing people
  together, 149; church withdrawal
  from, 35–36; Good Samaritan parable
  on, 2–3, 37, 71, 157; as kingdom of
  God work, 77; ministry to homeless,
  36; professionalism of social services
  approach to, 35; relationship between
  outcomes and, 213; to stop sex
  trafficking, 101–102; tongue in cheek
  criteria for, 38; Vineyard Church's efforts
  toward, 82–83. See also Community
  transformation; Ministry outcomes
Society: changes in the past 20 years, 7;
  "dots" organization of, 8; technological
  role in placeless, 8–9. See also
  Community
Sojourners (publication), 16
Solomon, 61, 179
Southbrook Christian Church (Ohio), 204
"Southbrook Meltdown" program, 204
Speeches on Religion for Those
  Among the Cultured Who Despise It
  (Schleiermacher), 58
Spiritual growth: depth and frequency of
  engagement for, 62–67fig; examples of
  "weight training" for, 48–50; research
  on service, faith, and, 50–51; stairstep
  approach to, 53–55; tipping point of,
  47–48fig
Spiritual "revolutionaries," 21, 57
Spirituality: lost in construct of religion,
  20; moving away from organized church
  but rising interest in, 20–22. See also
  Faith
Sprydon Baptist Church in Christchurch
  (New Zealand), 190
Stairstep approach, 53–55
Stanley, Andy, 109
Starbuck's, 16, 22
STEEPR approach: on economics, 11–13;
  on the environment, 13–15; on politics,
  15–17; on religion, 17–18; on society, 7;
  on technology, 7–11; writing categories
  and timeline exercise on, 174
Step Out and Serve (Omaha), 115
Stetzer, Ed, 21

Stevenson, Ian, 97, 99–100, 107

"Story" (seminar), 70

Storytelling: compelling nature of kingdom story, 80–81; creating something better through, 78–79; the Fall as "inciting incident" of, 73, 74; by Jesus Christ, 71; leadership challenge related to, 88; "mandatory scene" on restoration by Jesus, 73–74; a story that changes the world, 86–88; the "thicker" version of, 72; unexpected ending of Jesus as King, 74; worldview represented by, 71–72. *See also* Parables

Stott, John, 119, 160

Street GRACE (Atlanta), 121–122

StreetLight Phoenix, 102, 122

Strickland, Craig, 183–184

Student Volunteer Movement, 92

"Summer of Love" series (LifeBridge), 141

"Summer of Service" (2009), 63

Sunday morning concept, 24

Swanson, Andy, 61, 69

Swanson, Eric: on changing the world through church, 69; *The Externally Focused Church* by Rusaw and, 1, 2, 5, 45, 111, 119, 210; on journey of Christianity, 54; Missional Renaissance Leadership Community founded by, 82; on purpose of strength, 61; visit to British Museum, 135–136

Sweet, Len, 211

Sweney, Chip, 122, 194–195

Swenson, Bob, 169–170

Swiss Brethren Anabaptists, 34

Synergos (synergy), 131

Synod of Whitby (mid-600s), 55

System building: engage in regular churchwide projects, 150–152; infuse service into small groups, 143–150; "kingdom" thinking for, 152–153; leadership challenge related to, 154; LifeBridge's "Summer of Love" series for, 141; LifeBridge's "A Year with Jesus" series for, 142; make it part of your plans, 142–143; preach about it regularly, 139–142; small groups used for, 143–150; strong scriptural foundation for, 138–139; think "kingdom" not "church" for, 152–153

Systems: created around paradigms and values, 134; created to influence behavior, 137–154; elevated above strategy, 134–135; John Wesley's, 135–137, 143–144. *See also* Paradigms

T

TAG Consulting, 51

Technology: advances in the past 20 years in, 7–11; entertainment access and customization using, 9; first, second, and third dimension, 8; as innovative church resource, 191–192t; missionary work use of communication, 108–109; placeless society and role of, 8–9

Ten coins parable, 39

Ten Commandments legal cases, 16, 19

Tenth Avenue Alliance Church, 36

Tetlock, Phillip, 6

Texas Department of Criminal Justice, 87–88

Theirs Is the Kingdom (Lupton), 38

Theological factors: behavior shaped by theological trends, 34–35; Reformation and following separations, 34

"Third dimension" technology, 8

Thoresen, David, 102, 107

Thorpe, Ric, 60

3M, 135

Time magazine, 21

Time resources: innovative churches and, 192–193; internal versus external focus of, 193t

Titus County Cares, 122–123

TOMA study, 127

"Toward the Common Good" (Nathan), 83

Transforming Church Index survey (TAG Consulting), 51

The Trinity, 55, 56fig

Trinity Baptist Church (Alor Star), 149

Trinity Baptist Church (Texas), 123, 181

The True Believer (Hoffer), 149

Truth: cultural shifts in perception of, 17; liminal state of, 22–24

"Turning Goals into Results: The Power of Catalytic Mechanisms" (Collins), 135

Tutu, Bishop Desmond, 95

12Stone Church (Georgia), 203

Twitter, 9, 10

U

U2 concert (2005), 24

UnChristian (Kinnaman and Lyons), 169

Unconditional love (*agape*), 65

Unite!, 122

United States: annual church donations from the, 103; current economic status of the, 11; current global economic role of, 13; number of Protestant churches and attendance in the, 18; September 11, 2001, impact on foreign by, 16; societal changes in the past 20 years in the, 7

United Way, 82

University Baptist Church (Houston), 5, 185

University of Colorado, 63

University of Texas, 59

Unmet needs, 196fig–197

The Unshakable Kingdom and the Unchanging Person (Jones), 75

USA Today, 22

V

Valentine, David, 87, 210

Vancouver Sun (newspaper), 36

Vickers, Ian, 36, 58–59

Vineyard Church (Colorado), 195–196

Vineyard Church (Columbus), 37, 82–83, 180, 184, 189, 195

Vineyard Community Center, 83

Vineyard Dayton, 84–86

Virgin Group, 14

Vision 2007 initiative, 204

Vision Abolition, 102

Vision San Diego, 120–121, 207

Volunteers: becoming kingdom workers, 156; begin with the willing, 207; combining opportunity with inclination, 204–206; making it personal, 206–207; providing regular opportunities for, 202–204. *See also* Community service; Kingdom workers

W

Waldo, Jeff, 5–6

Wales, Jimmy, 9

Wallace, Jim, 16

Wallace, William, 200

Warren, Rick, 14, 40–41, 100–101, 140

Water of Life Community Church (California), 167

Webcasts, 192

Wegner, Rob, 91

Weight training: bodybuilding versus, 44; examples of spiritual, 48–50

Well Connected (Butler), 125

Wesley, John, 135, 137, 143–144

West, Keith, 99, 100

"What Would Jesus Do?," 79

White, Scott, 96, 106

Whitefield, George, 135, 137

Whittier Area Church, 80–81

A Whole New Mind (Pink), 77

Wiesel, Elie, 49

Wikipedia, 9

Will, George, 201

Willow Creek Community Church study (2004), 53

Willow Creek Leadership Summit, 81

Wilson, Matt, 169

Wilson, Walt, 10

"Win, Build, Send" ministry training, 54

Window-seat churches: aisle-seat mentality versus, 26–28; the early church as, 30–31; Hope Presbyterian Church (Tennessee) example of, 41–42; leadership challenge of changing into, 43; missional barrier to, 31–34; personal barrier to, 36; secular barrier to, 35–36; theological barrier to, 34–35. *See also* Externally focused churches

Windsor Village United Methodist Church (Houston), 45

Woods, Tiger, 44, 165

Woodstock (1969), 141

Work with the willing, 207

World Vision, 120

World Water Council, 7

WOW JAM festival, 167

Wright, Louie, 170

Wright, N. T., 77

Wycliffe, John, 118

X

"X factor," 13

Y

"A Year with Jesus" series (LifeBridge), 142

YouTube, 10, 192

Z

Zacchaeus, 74, 161

Zakaria, Fareed, 12

Zwemer, Samuel, 92

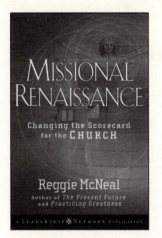

Missional Renaissance

Changing the Scorecard for the Church

Reggie McNeal

ISBN 978-0-470-24344-2
Cloth | 224 pp.

"There are spheres of human activity in which gold medalists rule the Olympian heights. In the sphere of church renewal, Reggie rules. Missional Renaissance is a must-have resource in helping every church keep its "eyes on the prize" of God's high missional calling."

— **Leonard Sweet**, Drew University, George Fox University,
www.sermons.com

The book is filled with in-depth discussions of what it means to make the transition to a missional congregation. With an understanding of the nature of the missional church and the practical suggestions outlined in this book, church leaders and members will be equipped to move into what McNeal sees as the most viable future for Christianity.

As a follow-on to his best-selling book, *The Present Future, Missional Renaissance* offers a clear path for any leader or congregation that wants to breathe new life into the church and to become revitalized as true followers of Jesus.

REGGIE MCNEAL serves as the Missional Leadership Specialist for Leadership Network of Dallas, Texas. McNeal is the author of *A Work of Heart: Understanding How God Shapes Spiritual Leaders*, the best-selling *The Present Future: Six Tough Questions for the Church*, and *Practicing Greatness: 7 Disciplines of Extraordinary Spiritual Leaders* from Jossey-Bass.

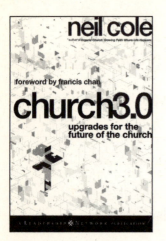

Church 3.0

Upgrades for the Future of the Church

Neil Cole

ISBN 978-0-470-52945-4
Cloth │ 304 pp.

"In this comprehensive labor of love, Neil brings his wonderfully unique, home-grown, and organic insights to bear on what it means to reawaken a movement ethos in the twenty-first century church. Nothing less than the spontaneous expansion of the church is being considered here. This is perhaps the book that Neil was born to write."

—**Alan Hirsch**, author, *The Forgotten Ways*, and coauthor, *Untamed*, *The Shaping of Things to Come*, *reJesus*, and *The Forgotten Ways Handbook*

In *Church 3.0,* Cole makes the argument that Christianity needs more than new programs, buildings, or worship formats. It needs a complete upgrade to a new "operating system." Organic churches experience a shift from a program-driven and clergy-led institutionalized approach to one that is relational, simple, intimate, and viral in the way it spreads.

Church 3.0 offers insight and information about how to make this shift to a more organic form of church that is based on Cole's extensive experience in starting, nurturing, and mentoring hundreds of churches. Practical issues are discussed such as how to deal with heresy, how to handle finances, ways to involve children, how to train leaders, how to form disciples, and what to do with worship, rituals, and ordinances.

NEIL COLE is an experienced and innovative church planter and pastor. He is the founder of the Awakening Chapels, which are reaching young postmodern people in urban settings, and a founder and executive director of Church Multiplication Associates. He is the author of *Organic Church* as well as *Search and Rescue*, *Organic Leadership*, and *Cultivating a Life for God.*

Other Books of Interest

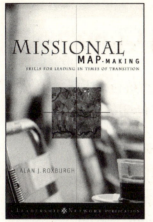

Missional Map-Making

Skills for Leading in Times of Transition

Alan J. Roxburgh

ISBN 978-0-470-48672-6
Cloth | 240 pp.

"This important book provides insightful historical perspective toward clarifying the contours of our present landscape, while also being deeply instructive for helping reflective and courageous Christians develop skills for creating new maps toward participating more faithfully in God's mission."

— **Craig Van Gelder**, Ph.D., Professor of Congregational Mission, Luther Seminary

In the burgeoning missional church movement, churches are seeking to become less focused on programs for members and more oriented toward outreach to people who are not already in church. This fundamental shift in what a congregation is, does, and thinks is challenging for leaders and congregants. Using the metaphor of map-making, this book explains the perspective and skills needed to lead congregations and denominations in a time of radical change over unfamiliar terrain as churches change their focus from internal to external.

ALAN ROXBURGH is President of Missional Leadership Institute (MLI) and has pastored congregations in small towns, urban centers and the suburbs. He has served in denominational leadership as well as on the faculty of a seminary where he was responsible for teaching in the areas of leadership and domestic missional church leadership. Alan teaches in numerous seminaries as well as lecturing (including at the emergent church conventions) and consulting all over North America, Australia, and Europe in the areas of leadership, transition, systems change, and missional theology.

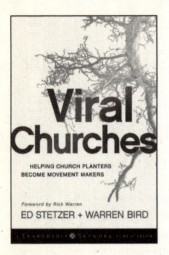

Viral Churches

Helping Church Planters Become Movement Makers

Ed Stetzer | Warren Bird
Foreword by Rick Warren

ISBN 978-0-470-55045-8
Cloth | 256 pp.

"This book by...my dear friends and partners in ministry...is pure gold....There is simply no better way to reach, teach, train, and send out disciples than through churches that are planted with the intentionality of planting others."

— **Rick Warren**, Saddleback Church

This book reveals the best practices in church planting and uncovers the common threads among them. A much-needed resource, this book will inform, guide, and even catalyze today's many church planting leaders. The authors clearly show leaders how to plant churches that create a multiplication movement and offer inspiration for them to do so. The book addresses their questions about what to do next in their church planting strategies, in light of research on what's actually working best.

ED STETZER has been a church planter, as well as a trainer of pastors and church planters worldwide. He is a columnist for *Outreach Magazine* and *Catalyst Monthly*. He has extensive experience teaching at colleges and seminaries and is the president of LifeWay Research.

WARREN BIRD is well-versed personally and professionally in church planting. He has coauthored 19 books, including *Starting a New Church*, *Emotionally Healthy Church*, *Culture Shift*, and *Multi-Site Church Revolution*. He has taught at Alliance Theological Seminary, and currently directs the research division at Leadership Network.